The Other Side of Sin

THE OTHER SIDE OF SIN

*Woundedness from the
Perspective of the Sinned-Against*

Edited by

ANDREW SUNG PARK

and

SUSAN L. NELSON

STATE UNIVERSITY OF NEW YORK PRESS

Published by
STATE UNIVERSITY OF NEW YORK PRESS
ALBANY

For information, address
State University of New York Press,
90 State Street, Suite 700, Albany, NY 12207

Production, Laurie Searl
Marketing, Fran Keneston

Library of Congress Cataloging-in-Publication Data

The other side of sin : woundedness from the perspective of the sinned-against / edited
by Andrew Sung Park and Susan L. Nelson.
    p. cm.
Includes bibliographical references and index.
ISBN 0-7914-5041-4 (hardcover : alk. paper) — ISBN 0-7914-5042-2 (pbk. : alk. paper)
    1. Sin. 2.Victims—Religious life. I. Park, Andrew Sung. II. Nelson, Susan L. (Susan
Louise)

BT715 .O84 2001
241'.3—dc21

                                                                        2001020007

10 9 8 7 6 5 4 3 2 1

CONTENTS

ACKNOWLEDGMENT

We would like to express our deep appreciation to our contributors, for they had to complete their writings with no map to guide them as they explored new territory. In addition, they have graciously waited for the publication of this book for a long time. We applaud their patience and cooperation. Particularly to Walter Brueggemann, who completed his chapter long before the others and shared it with the other contributors, all the contributors owe very much. His chapter was, however, first published in *Horizons of Biblical Literature* and is published here with their permission. We thank Jacquelyn Grant who was willing but could not be part of this project due to schedule complications. To our editor Nancy Ellegate of the State University of New York Press, we are indebted for her support and kindheartedness. Betty Stutler, faculty secretary of United Theological Seminary, who read, edited, and formatted chapters into the final version, Becky Schram, who did indexing, and Sheryl Gilliland at Pittsburgh Theological Seminary, who coordinated the earlier steps in our process, we cannot thank enough. Without their help, this book could not be what it is. Their efficient work and technical editing skills were superb.

During the time of working on this project, S. Jane Myong, Andrew Sung Park's spouse, and David Lutz, Susan L. Nelson's spouse, have invisibly supported our project. How sympathetically they understood our work and pressure to complete our project deserves more than our words of gratitude. Indeed, they have been our coeditors, too.

Why Do We Need Another Book
on the Subject of Sin?

A patient comes to see a doctor. The doctor diagnoses his or her symptoms and prescribes medicine. If the diagnosis is wrong, a medicine prescribed according to that diagnosis will not be effective and the patient's health can be in jeopardy. We cannot emphasize the importance of a proper diagnosis too much for the healing of a patient.

Every Sunday Christians come to church to worship and hear a minister proclaim the good news of salvation. Before preaching, the minister needs to know the needs of the people who should be helped. Without diagnosing their problems accurately, the good news of salvation would not be good news; perhaps it would even be wrong news. If the minister understands the problems of people well, she or he can deliver an appropriate and strong message.

In the pews, we find all kinds of people from various walks of life. There are sinners (liars, adulterers, molesters, abusers, rapists, and murderers), victims (the deceived, molested, abused, raped, and bereft), and victims' family members sitting and waiting for a healing message.

In Christian theology, there is only one category used to diagnose the wrong of the world: sin. Sin, its guilt, and death are the primary categories from which we can be saved. In this mode of thinking, freedom from sin will resolve all the problems of the world, since sin is the major culprit of wrongs in the world. But what about the healing of the sinned-against? Naming a problem is the beginning of its solution. It is necessary for us to specify the pain of the sinned-against.

The good news of Jesus Christ should be real good news to everybody. Demanding repentance of sin from the abused, the hungry, and the humiliated is not good news, but absurd news. To be reasonable to these wounded Christians, we need to present a more comprehensive picture of Christian analysis of wrongs than the simple formula of sin-repentance.

For the past two thousand years, we have inadequately treated the victims of sin by neglecting to formulate doctrines for them while they walked through the valley of the shadow of death. Based on the doctrine of sin, the church has developed a map of the salvific doctrines for sinners or offenders: the doctrines of regeneration, justification by faith, sanctification by faith, and glorification or Christian perfection. It is time for the church to think about a salvific path for the sinned-against. To do so, we need to understand the pain of the wounded, listening to their agonies and studying biblical, historical, and theological messages for their salvation. *The other side of sin* is our common endeavor to start a new journey of faith for the sinned-against.

THE OTHER SIDE OF SIN

Of course, to suggest that the category of victims of sin is underdeveloped in Christian thought is not to suggest that the *experience* of being victimized by sin is unknown. In reality, suffering from the sin of others is as old as evil and lamentation. The children of Israel cried out for liberation from oppression; the psalmist knew enemies who threatened his life and well-being; second Isaiah spoke of a suffering servant whose suffering was on account of others' sins; Jesus was asked whether the man born blind was bearing the price of his parents' sin; the cross resonates through history of the symbol of an innocent man crucified for the sins of others. Sin, suffering, and evil are as old as the hills.

To focus on the victims of sin is to push Christian theology to locate the doctrine of sin within the context of the experience of evil. Classical theology has placed evil within the context of sin. Human beings, created for freedom, have misused that freedom out of a desire to be like God. The result is fall, bondage to sin, inherited guilt, suffering, and death. The central problem in this classical theological paradigm is sin. Evil is the fruit of human sinfulness. But, when the situations of oppression, victimization, and radical suffering (suffering that is undeserved and that cannot be justified) are the theological starting points, the paradigm threatens to shift. What if there is undeserved suffering that cannot be redeemed? What if the suffering of victims calls forth revenge that is a central piece in the cycle of violation? What if sin is born of experiences of violation that cry out for justice when no justice is to be found? What if suffering and evil are the paradigmatic center of our theology, and sin is a *symptom* of human vulnerability and the extreme to which human beings are willing to go to protect ourselves from the threat of damage?

To focus on victims of sin, is to place the doctrine of sin in the context of evil from which it probably emerged. "It's not the way it's supposed to be," quickly migrates into "we're not the way we're supposed to be."[1] The question of theodicy that asks what kind of a world this is where such evil can happen and what kind of God would create and govern such a world, is classically answered by the doctrine of sin. God in God's goodness and power creates free creatures who have the possibility to know and worship God but who chose to use that freedom to make themselves the center of the world.

Sin is the cause of much of the world's suffering and evil. Theologians from "the other side of sin" do not dispute this reality. And so the classical theological paradigm has answered the question of evil with the answer of sin: actual and original. Actual sin refers to sin committed in deliberate violation of God's will; original sin (linked with original guilt) to the state of guilt and bondage to sin that human beings inherited from our ancestors. With original sin and guilt as the answer, evil still persists, but the problem of theodicy disappears. There is no innocent suffering. God's good providence remains unchallenged.

Although universal sinfulness was espoused by patristic theologians such as Justin Martyr, Irenaeus, Tertullian, and Origen, Augustine was the one who shaped universal sinfulness into the doctrine of original sin. In Adam's Fall, all humanity sinned. Adam's sin of *pride* results in death, guilt, and the inability not to sin for himself and his descendants. Eve is blamed with luring Adam to his Fall, and women have been branded "Eve, the devil's gateway."

But the Augustinian resolution has not enjoyed universal affirmation. Contemporaries argued with him that the death of infants cries out to God for vindication.[2] What kind of a God would punish a whole race for the sin of two people? Can people be justly held accountable for sin when they were born without the possibility to do otherwise? Theologians questioned how the plague of sin and guilt was passed on from generation to generation. Is it in the seed? In the act of conception? And wondered about the serpent, since Adam and Eve did not sin apart from temptation. Where did the serpent come from? Is the creator God ultimately responsible for the reality of temptation? Augustine found his answer in a cosmic dimension. Angels fell and lured humanity to their death. But the problem persisted; why, after all, did Lucifer fall?

But, is original sin really the best answer to Augustine's dilemma?[3] Was Augustine accurate in seeing the root of evil in sinful pride? And, was Augustine correctly interpreting his own experience when he came to this conclusion of original sin and guilt?

THE CONTEXT OF SIN

One way to resolve the dilemma of original sin and guilt has been to reconsider the garden, the context of sin. Perhaps all really was not perfect in the garden (after all, the dis-ease of temptation preceded the primal couple's act of disobedience). Perhaps the human condition is more precarious than the story of the perfect garden would suggest.

The initial proponent of this shift in perspective was Søren Kierkegaard. While retaining the traditional insight that sin is the result of human failure to trust in God and that sin is universal to the human race, Kierkegaard argued that the human condition as created by God is itself the context of human sin, the crucible in which our sin is formed. Human beings, he said, are created finite and free. Caught in the tension between limit and possibility, the consciousness of that tension, the awareness of our finitude, death, and our possibility for failure, human consciousness is plagued by anxiety. Sin is born in that anxiety. While optimally we could resolve this anxiety by trusting in God, human beings instead turn from God and find some other way to protect ourselves from the ravages of angst. This is idolatry.

Kierkegaard's insight, echoed and amplified in the writings of Reinhold Niebuhr, is a neat modern solution to the problem of original sin. Sin and Fall are original to each human being. We are no longer born without the possibility not to sin (as Augustine would have it). But, because the condition into which we are born is one of anxiety, and because the world is already contaminated by sin that amplifies evil, suffering, and anxiety, we inevitably do sin. Yet, because the choice to sin is our own, each of us is culpable for our own sin. The doctrine of sin becomes understandable.

But, in making the human condition the context for human sin, Kierkegaard subtly shifts the axes of suffering and evil. While evil is still understood as the result of human sin, sin is born of a prior condition of anxiety, and salvation lies not only in delivery from sin, but also from resolution of the anxiety in the possibility of trust and faith. If the core problem in the classical tradition is that of sin, Kierkegaard exposes a core within a core. Technically, because creation is good, and thus our anxiety is good (it is after all the ground of great creativity), it is not a problem from which we are to be saved. Trust in God is the possibility of living faithfully within the same human condition. Thus, it would seem, nothing is really changed after all. But, perhaps not.

SIN AND DAMAGE

Kierkegaard's insight has borne much fruit in the twentieth century. Niebuhr became his most stalwart interpreter, expanding the concept of sin to meet the tragic dimensions of evil in the mid-century. Feminist theologians cut their theological teeth on Niebuhr's centrality of the sin of pride and argued that sin could also be a choice to hide, the loss of self, echoing Kierkegaard's initial insight into the dilemma of despair over ever being a self. Paul Tillich turned the fall into estrangement as an inevitable fact of birth, expanded the tensions of the human condition to include sociality and pressures that follow being social creatures, and placed redemption in the "courage to be," the risk of nonbeing where one discovers "Being itself," a concept that echoed Kierkegaard's leap of faith. Most recently, Edward Farley has added the dimension of the interhuman (the realm of face-to-face relation) to the description of the human condition.[4] The human tension between finitude and freedom still remains, but now it is found within three spheres: the agential, the social, and the interhuman. With this addition of the interhuman, the individualism of Kierkegard's schema is transcended and the core context of human anxiety is revealed. The human condition is now not only anxiety laden, it is threatened with vulnerability. This was evident in Kierkegaard's schema in the inevitably of death and in the possibility of failure. But in a world where human beings are inherently relational, vulnerability is the possibility of ruptured relation and ruptured relation can become the context of human sin. There is no longer only the problem of sin from which human beings need redemption, there is also the damage that results from another's sin. (And, damage need not only be from sin, damage can result from the conflict that is inevitable in a free and diverse world.) In fact, for some, damage may have become the core problem, and, unhealed, it can fester into more damage: a cycle of violence and evil.[5]

In the light of the various form of "victim defense" that have been used in courts of law in the United States, sin and damage may seem to be diametrically opposed categories. If one is a victim, then the argument goes, the evil we do is understandable and we are not responsible. Perhaps it is just this either/or thinking that tempts theologians into arguing that sin is the universal problem for all humanity. Once we allow that humans may be vulnerable to damage, then it would seem that lines of clear accountability for sin are eroded.

But why think in either/or categories? Rita Nakashima Brock in *Journeys by Heart*[6] argues persuasively that sin (by which she means both actual and original sin) is the *symptom* of our vulnerability. If Kierkegaard argued that sin is born of anxiety, Brock argues that sin—both our sense of being sinful and our proclivity to secure ourselves in damaging ways—reveals both our vulnerability to, and the actuality of, our damage. *Brokenheartedness*—to use her word for this damage that disrupts the "erotic power" of creation—is not an excuse for sin. It is at the core of our sin—and both call out for healing. Sin as symptom then changes our perception of the problem. Sin language is not just about guilt and responsibility, it is also a danger sign that calls for attention lest more damage be accomplished. If our wills are in bondage to sin, then our souls are also deeply wounded and, as long as they remained unhealed, in bondage to the evil that caused the damage—an evil that cries out for restitution and more damage. If the doctrine of original sin has traditionally meant that humanity is in bondage to evil, then brokenheartedness and the sin that grows out of it bear testimony to that truth.

SIN AND EVIL: THE QUESTION OF THEODICY

> *Why do bad things happen to good people?*
> *Do bad things happen to good people?*
> *Are there any good people?*

The Fall of humanity has been a traditional answer to the problem of evil. Where does evil come from? It is the result of human sin. Is God responsible for evil? God is responsible only in creating humans with the possibility to sin. God risked evil; we are responsible for it. Created with the possibility not to sin, humanity chose to sin, and evil and the bondage to original sin are its fruits.

And for the most part, that is an adequate answer. Much of the misery in the world is the result of human action or failure to take action. Holocausts of every type point the finger at human perpetrators. We are hard-hearted; we do rationalize others' sufferings; we do fail to see the face of our neighbor (let alone our enemy). Evil is the fruit of human sin.

However, the category of sin can also be used to disguise and obfuscate human evil. In this postmodern world, we have learned that the power to name is the power to create—and the power to name "sin" is the power to name who is sinful and what is evil. The power to name sin can be used not only to strip perpetrators of their deceptions (the traditional prophetic role), but also to shackle and maim those who would resist those in power. It can turn those out of power against themselves, teaching them to shackle themselves in the name of righteousness. In the naming of sin, great evils can be done.

Yet when we listen to the voices of theologians of relation and of the tragic,[7] we realize that the world is so interconnected that we are all implicated in evil. If Augustine said it is not possible for humans not to sin, then relational theologians echo, it is not possible for us not to be complicit in the suffering of the world. Innocence is not a possibility. In this sense, guilt and accountability are universal to the human condition and we are all implicated in the evil that results. Evil and sin do go together.

But, when we ask the question of evil—why it is, where is its source—from the perspective of the one violated, sinned-against, the question of evil shifts. The answer that evil is caused by sin feels skewed when the one who asks the question is one who has done nothing to deserve their suffering. In her book, *Tragic Vision and Divine Compassion,* Wendy Farley asks the question directly to those who would use a moral worldview (that evil is ultimately justified as the result of sin) to explain evil without responding compassionately to it. The fact of *radical suffering*—suffering that is not deserved and that is beyond the possibility of redemption—Farley says thrusts us into a world where "even the death of a savior cannot atone" for the suffering of such evil. If atonement heals sin—saves sinners, then what could possibly heal the evil of radical suffering? Evil may be caused by sin, but the fact that the innocent do suffer raises the question of the ultimate morality of the world and the goodness of God: "The evil I suffer is not caused by my sin. What kind of a world is it when the innocent suffer for the sin of others?" Our neat justification of a moral trajectory from sin to evil is disrupted. Sin and evil sit side-by-side as twin alienations crying out for redemption. And we ask, can the shadow of the cross fall in two directions at once?

ALIENATION, WOUNDEDNESS, AND THEOLOGIES OF SIN

Within and without the Christian theological tradition, there have been efforts to portray the effects of sin on sinners and victims. By examining some of these efforts, we will get some clues as to what should be done to develop doctrines that speak to the experience of woundedness caused by another's sin. Sin causes suffering or pain on the part of victims. Using the notions of *alienation* and *woundedness,* we will seek in this section to describe the other side of sin as it has been embedded in Western tradition. In the history of the Western thought, we come across the evidence that people were aware of this situation—particularly as the addressed situations of evil. In this discussion, we will include Christian and non-Christian approaches to the subject.

In the history of Western Christian theology, no one has been as influential as Augustine (354–430 C.E.). He did discuss the other side of sin, as we shall see. But, he did not form any doctrinal insight out of that discussion. For example, in the *City of God*, Augustine discusses the noble Roman matron Lucretia. As a youth, she was subdued and raped by the son of King Tarquin. Later, she revealed the crime that had been perpetrated against her to her husband Collatinus and to her kinsman Brutus and bound them to take revenge. Overwhelmed by the pain of shame of her situation, she then committed suicide. Augustine's telling of this story reveals his awareness of situations of the other side of sin. But Augustine focused his treatment of the story on the question of virtue rather than on the violation of rape. Arguing that chastity was not a matter of bodily integrity but a virtue of the soul, he could term her *chaste* despite her rape (thus recognizing her virtue). But, if she had not lost her chastity, then there was no reason thus for her to kill herself. On the other hand, if she was not chaste but an adulteress (we would assume, inviting the rape), she would be full of shame unworthy of people's admiration. By extrapolating from the given fact of her death and the assumption that the rape would only have been shameful if she had actually been an adulteress, Augustine deemed her to be an adulteress who killed herself out of "her sense of shame."[8] Thus, blaming the victim.

Preoccupied with the category of sin, Augustine apparently could not see the pain of the victim. Most rape victims undergo depression, isolation, despondence, and self-worthlessness. Augustine understood little of Lucretia in terms of her victimhood, perhaps confusing the shame of the victim (and the victim's tendency to blame herself) with the guilt of a willing participant. Lucretia suffered not from the guilt of sin, but from the intense shame of the other side of sin. Unable to suffer its pain any longer, she ended her life. Augustine, focusing on the idea of sin, particularly pride and concupiscence as original sin, missed seeing the woundedness of the victim. Augustine could talk about the wounds of sinners quite often, but showed little awareness of the wounds of victims.[9]

St. Thomas (1227–1274) appears to have been more aware of the other side of sin than Augustine was. For Thomas the contagion of original sin is actually a wound: our first parents' sin inflicts *the wound of ignorance, the wound of malice, the wound of concupiscence,* and *the wound of weakness* on their descendents. These wounds, he stressed, were the *wounds* resulting from others' sins.[10]

The wounds of original sin afflict human nature, and our actual sins aggravate them. This wounding of our nature, Thomas thought, makes a person sick and unable to perform at the level he or she is expected to perform. This sick person must be healed by God's grace first in order to do good.[11] This wound caused by sin could, however, be perfectly healed by the satisfaction achieved by the cross. In Christ, human beings could be made whole. Thomas thus acknowledged the effects of sin as wounding and rightly envisaged the healing of the wounds as a necessary step to the solution of human predicament.

In a similar fashion, John Calvin (1509–1564) understood that sin distorts the whole person. Because of this distortion (depravity) everything a human being does is sinful.[12] To him, sin is more than moral actions. It is the deranged structure of our existence. Sin is not human nature, but abides in it as a resident and ruins it. Calvin called this a "deadly wound" that clings to human nature.[13] Sin results in wounds and afflicts us. But we are so caught in our wounded nature, that the true sinfulness of human nature distorted by the Fall is only exposed through the life of Christ.[14]

Immanuel Kant (1724–1804) in his *Religion within the Limits of Reason Alone* discusses the problem of human sinfulness as *radical evil*. Kant struggled between the two views of human nature that prevailed: the optimistic view of the Enlightenment that espoused human freedom from any evil bondage or proclivity and the more pessimistic view of the total corruption of human nature. Kant rejected both views as well as the view of the inheritance of the proclivity for evil, and located the source of our sin in human free will (*willkür*). Human nature is essentially good, but perversion came into human nature with its finitude: "but with us sin is represented as resulting from an already innate wickedness in our nature."[15] Against the spirit of the Enlightenment, then, he asserted that something radically wrong with humanity preceded our actions. Thus, our maxim or principle of action by which we act is warped. Yet, despite his belief that radical evil is rooted in the structure of human existence, Kant believed that the moral evil in us has no conceivable ground in origin.[16] Although he was not specific regarding a victim's perspective, he pointed out the tragic character of human finitude in the cosmic drama of sin and evil.

To Georg Wilhelm Friedrich Hegel (1770–1831), evil is a structural dimension of the universe. Since human nature is characterized by a tension between finitude and the potential to become spirit (through the exercise of human freedom), Hegel thought the Fall (our original sin is to affirm the particular, including the self, as different from the universal) was unavoidable. It is the source of evil, leading humanity to the knowledge of good and evil. Evil, thus, takes an ontological seat in history (it is inevitable due to human finitude); the world proceeds from the reaction to it; and humans are tangled in evil by growing to be something other than the union of self and God. This *otherness* gives birth to self-consciousness which, though to be valued, educes alienation. Alienation is not evil itself, but gives rise both to evil and to the need for reconciliation. "It is in this disunion that independent Being or Being-for-self originates, and it is in it that evil has its seat; here is the source of the evil, but here also the point which is the ultimate source of reconciliation."[17] Hegel saw this alienation appear in the unhappiness of Greco-Roman culture and in the anguish of Jewish religion. His category of unhappiness and anguish is the other side of sin.

Friedrich Schleiermacher (1768–1834) distinguished social/moral evil from natural evil: social/moral evil is due to human action, natural evil is independent of human action.[18] Within the category of social evil, one person's sin becomes another's evil: "It is true that social evils too presuppose sin; what in one person issues from sin becomes an evil for another, and probably for himself as well."[19]

Schleiermacher rejected the traditional belief of original sin. While sin and evil are interrelated to each other as cause and effect, he proposed the following: First, if there were no sin, there would be nothing in the world that could properly be considered evil. Second, the human race is the proper sphere of sin and sin the corporate act of the race, and the whole world in its relation to humans is the proper sphere of evil, and evil is the corporate suffering of the race. Third, without such evil, there can be no other consequence of sin that bears upon the relationship of the world to humans, and that our religious consciousness makes no claim to substantiate the magical effect of original sin.[20]

He denied that evil was the origin and sin the derivative. For all evil is the punishment of sin: social evil is direct punishment, and natural evil indirect punishment. When we reverse the order of the connection between sin and evil, then we might fall into heathenism.[21] Schleiermacher's concept of evil as the effect of sin reflects an awareness of the other side of sin. However, because he sees all evil as punishment for sin and views the human race collectively, there is no room in his system for the undeserved suffering of victims of sin.

For Karl Marx (1818–1883), alienation (which is his major category and not sin) arises from the miserable structure of bourgeois society. It results in dehumanization. Thus, while theologians talked about original sin, Marx addressed people in their actual situation of alienation.[22] Alienation in society has at least three dimensions. First, alienation from self is laborers' separation from the products of their labor: "The worker puts his life into the object and his life then belongs no longer to himself but to the object. The greater his activity, therefore, the less he possesses.[23] Second, alienation from the process of production points to imposed and forced labor for the workers: "The worker therefore feels himself at home only during his leisure time, whereas at work he feels homeless. His work is not voluntary but imposed, forced labor."[24] The workers become ever cheaper commodities as they produce more goods. Third, alienation from fellow human beings means that we exploit others and are exploited by them. This is dehumanization. The naming of all three types of alienation complements the missing points of the Christian doctrine of sin by focusing on the situations of victims—those who are dehumanized by the sins of others.

In line with the social visions of his predecessors, a prominent leader of the Social Gospel movement, Walter Rauschenbusch (1861-1918), highlighted the social dimension of sin. To him, the significance of the doctrine of original sin lies in its focus on the solidary nature of the sin of the human race, which has been entrenched in social customs and institutions: "These hereditary social evils are forced on the individual embedded in the womb of society and drawing his ideas; moral standards, and spiritual ideals from the general life of the social body."[25] The idea of the biological transmission of evil does harm to the religious mind by diverting its energy from the power of social transmission to the nonessential.

Rauschenbusch discovered the solidaristic vision of the Old Testament. The prophets treated the nation as a gigantic personality in the matters of sin, suffering, and repentance. He was convinced that individualistic thinking is insufficient in our vision for the establishment of the kingdom of God on earth. The church, he felt, had trained its people in the individualistic concept of sin and salvation. Thus they do not recognize the super-personal structure of reality or composite personalities. Because Rauschenbusch recognized that the super-personal forces of evil systematically corrupt and exhaust human resources, he called the church to organize itself to redeem the world as well as the individual. Christianizing social institutions along with individuals was required for the arrival of the kingdom of God on earth. Behind alcoholism, militarism, and capitalism, he discerned the power of the super-personal evil forces driven by the profitableness of the evil.[26] These structures of super-personal forces are transmittable through the channel of social tradition. Without understanding the reality of the social idealizations of evil, the concepts of individualistic sin, salvation, and ethics are not only fragmentary but also distorted.[27] Through "the kingdom of evil"—the "solidarity and organic concept of the power of evil in the world"[28]—the evil of one generation is harvested in the following one and thus increases its strength as evil keeps reproducing itself. The kingdom of evil is the universal radical sin of humanity and each generation is wounded by the evil it inherits.

In the twentieth century, Reinhold Niebuhr (1892–1971) focused on the human being as sinner. Like Kierkegaard, Niebuhr recognized that human beings are free. But freedom creates anxiety because in it we have to choose "either/or." Before the insecurity of freedom, human beings vacillate, deny the anxious state of our finitude, and fall into the sin of pride. Or, we give up on exercising our cumbersome freedom by forgetting ourselves in intoxication or bodily pleasures and fall into the sin of sensuality. For Niebuhr, this is what is meant by original (universal) sin. Sin is thus inevitable; but it is not necessary.

As a Protestant theologian, Niebuhr focused on the universality of sin: everyone is a sinner. But Niebuhr was aware of the issue of the sinned-against. If sinners and the sinned-against are equally sinful, would there be any difference between their sinfulness? His answer was that the oppressor and the oppressed are all sinners before God (sin is universal), but the oppressor suffers from deeper guilt (there is an equality of sin, but inequality of guilt). Niebuhr stopped short of any further theological reflection on this inequality. However, he did realize the problem. Mover, we could argue that the fact that in Niebuhr's system pride and sensuality are inevitable, human beings are depicted as victims in the universal tragedy of history.

Affirming Niebuhr's tragic nature of sin, Paul Ricoeur held that sin has three dimensions. First, sin is the human being's true situation before God, apart from human consciousness of it.[29] Second, from the outset, the sinful condition has a communal dimension. The transbiological and transhistorical solidarity of sin constitutes the metaphysical unity of the human race. Third, sin is not only a state, a situation in which humans are caught, but also a power that binds them captive. It is the gap between "I want" and "I can." It is "misery."

Ricoeur articulated the inevitability of sin for humans before the Fall and Fall as the symbol of evil. (The doctrine of original sin is a theological reflection on the symbol of evil.) According to Ricoeur, human experience of the fault in the world (it's not the way it's supposed to be) initially leads to an awareness of the reality of evil. Human beings then seek an explanation of the existence of evil through using a confessional language such as symbols and myths, not a rational language.[30] The result is the story of the fall. Human will is servile to evil. But human beings are paradoxically responsible for the inevitable fault of original sin despite its unavoidability. In this scheme, humans are victims of evil as well as its perpetrators.

Feminist theology, along with black theology and liberation theology has awakened a whole new consciousness in the slumbering church and in its theologians. Valerie Saiving's essay, "The Human Situation: A Feminine View" (1960), set a milestone for the new consciousness of women's theological perspectives on the concept of sin. In this pivotal article, Saiving lifted up the one-sidedness of Reinhold Niebuhr's and Anders Nygren's theologies of sin and love respectively. She rejected the universalization of their own definitions of sin and love by suggesting that women's experience of those notions is different from men's. Men's sin might be pride and men's love is selfishness, but women's sin is lack of pride and women's love is the inclusion of self in the circle of love: " [the feminine forms of sin] are better suggested by such items as triviality, distractibility, and diffuseness; lack of an organizing center or focus; dependence on others for one's own self-definition; tolerance at the expense of standards of excellence; inability to respect to the boundaries of privacy; sentimentality, gossipy sociability, and mistrust of reason—in short, underdevelopment or negation of the self."[31] Pinpointing women's dilemma as the opposite of men's, she drew two different maps for the sin and salvation of men and women. If men emphasize salvation as selfless love, Saiving realized that such a drive might result in no self-identity for women.[32] Thus, she suggested the redefinition of the categories of sin and redemption.

Saiving's understanding of sin has radically challenged and changed the traditional male-centered concept of sin. While affirming that women are capable of sinning, Saiving's insight into the different contexts of men and women in a patriarchal society revealed that women's sin of negation of self reflects not only their agency, but their status as "other" in that society. The sins of women are both sins and a reflection of the wounding of the systemic sins of patriarchal society: both sin and its other side.[33]

In the late 1960s, Latin American liberation theologians, particularly Gustavo Gutiérrez, treated sin as socioeconomic oppression. There are three aspects of sin in Gutiérrez's system. First, sin is social, economic, and political oppression that exploits the poor. Second, sin is historical determinism that deters the oppressed from becoming the subject of their own destiny. Third, sin is a breach of communion with God and neighbors that harms the human spirit. (He calls this "spiritual sin.")[34] His first and second concepts of sin are not really sins from the perspective of the oppressed. They are the unmistakable marks of the other side of sin. He used these aspects of sin to portray victims' pain under oppression and their helpless resignation. The third type of sin is the sin of the oppressor as well as of the oppressed. Spiritual sin calls our attention to the fact that even the oppressed are "sinners."

Since the late 1960s, James Cone has raised his voice for liberation for African Americans with his stress on the combination of "black power" and black theology. In *A Black Theology of Liberation*, Cone discussed the sin of black and white communities. Cone describes sin in a communal sense. He rejects the universal definition of sin—both the white fundamentalist view of sin as moral purity and liberal and neo-orthodox understanding of sin as broken relationship with God. For Cone, the sin of white communities is to define their existence in terms of their whiteness. This, he argues, has led to Native American reservations, black concentration camps, and the Vietnam War. Sin is whiteness—the desire to play God in the world.[35] For blacks, sin is "a desire to be white," the "loss of identity," accepting the oppressive condition as it is,[36] a statement of their estrangement from self and God. Whites cannot talk about the sin of black communities. Only blacks can define their own existence.

Cone's black sin is not the sin of the first cause. It is the consequence of white sin. White sin is a sin of commission; black sin is submission to it. His definition of black sin is his effort to describe the other side of sin, the estranged condition of black communities.

In the 1980s, womanist theologians began to speak to the experience of African American women. Jacquelyn Grant and Delores Williams have spearheaded this movement. They have pointed out the failures of white feminist theologians, who assumed that they had spoken for African American women as well as for themselves. It is unacceptable for womanists, they argued, that Euramerican feminists speak for them again, although both feminist and womanist theologians share the common resistance against patriarchy. To womanist theologians, even African American male theologians have failed to include African American women's issues for their theological construction, although the women affirm their struggle against racism. Unlike feminist and African American male theologians, womanist theologians take account of the issues of gender (sexism), race (racism), and class (classism). This means that they see the problem of sin not only as diffuseness, distractability, and lack of an organizing center (which definition can sound more individualistic and less like a critique of a social system), but also discrimination, poverty, and dehumanization. Their cry is the voice of the victim's victim. This movement is important in exposing the reality that even victims can victimize the weaker and that no one is free from the potential of oppressing others. Furthermore, the threefold nature of African American women's problems opens a door to the liberation of the oppressed from the multidimensional oppression of life.

Another feminist theologian, Mary Potter Engel, has heightened the importance of viewing sin from "the other side" in her description of sin in the context of the evil and violence suffered by the vulnerable in situations of domestic and sexual violence. For her, sin is individualistic, while evil is systemic. Individuals' sins, however, reinforce the structural dimension of evil. In this sense, sin and evil buttress each other. Potter Engel speaks of sin as the condition of the perpetrator and evil as that of both victims and perpetrators. Our language of sin and evil must be appropriate to the context in which it is spoken, otherwise when we stress sinfulness to victims, we invite the development of self-blame. For victims, evil is about lament and the accepting/assigning of appropriate blame. For perpetrators in these situations, sin is lack of moral sensitivity, betrayal of trust, distortion of boundaries, and lack of consent to vulnerability.[37]

These scholars have tried to transcend a one-dimensional understanding of human sin and have delved into the deeper dimension of sin, alienation, and evil when viewed from both sides. All of these thinkers have written from an awareness of the other side of sin and of the importance of that awareness for Christian churches and for the healing of the world. Our intention in this book is to continue in this project to make theology more relevant to the sinned-against, voicing their pain and their predicament and incorporating their issues into theological discourse. The wounds and alienation of the sinned-against require us to deepen our theological reflection. The category of sin by itself is insufficient to tackle the wounds and alienation of the sinned-against. Evil is not just about sin. It is interwoven with woundedness and alienation, what Ted Peters names "the effect of sin such as loss, pain, suffering, and destruction."[38]

To several of the theologians we have reviewed, Schleiermacher and Peters for example, sin is the cause, evil the effect. In fact, we would argue that wounds and alienation that are not attended or healed generate evil. In this sense, we realize that the doctrine of sin can itself perpetrate evil from victims' perspective.

THE CONTENTS

We start this task from the Old Testament. In his chapter "The Shrill Voice of the Wounded Party," Walter Brueggemann challenges the prevalent proclivity to diminish the theology of the Old Testament to a simple formula of sin and punishment. He does not deny the strong presence of a retribution theology in the Old Testament, but would not merely reduce Old Testament theologies to it either.

First, Brueggemann finds three players in the community that generated the Hebrew Bible. In the Exodus narrative, he finds Yahweh, Pharaoh, and Israel. Yahweh plays the third role—advocating Israel as the sinned-against. In the prophetic traditions, he becomes aware of Yahweh, the urban elite of the Jerusalem establishment, and the marginalized as the three players. Yahweh as the third player always shows the divine solidarity with the marginalized. Second, Brueggemann sees the witness of the Old Testament strike at the foundations of the ethical structures of deeds-consequences. In the story of the garden (Gen 2–3), like Milton and Ricoeur, he highlights the fact that before our involvement, something already happened. Beyond a mere "sin-punishment" theology, the narrative addresses the misery that binds human beings. Third, Brueggemann sees the psalms of complaint also deabsolutizing the oversimplified formula of "sin-punishment" and "deeds-consequences." They are the voices of the wounded and weak within the three parties of speakers, God, and the enemy. The poets of these Psalms call for God's attention to intervening against abuses and threats. Fourth, the great poem of Job that culminates in the Old Testament moves against simplistic and absolutizing ethical schemes of deeds—consequences. Job declares that God is morally unreliable, and therefore the entire theory of a moral order to reality is absurd. God approved Job's theology, not that of his friends. Brueggemann's God is the God who embraces Job's accusation of Godself, siding with Job—the sinned-against.

Beyond the formula of sin and punishment God's love is abundant for sinners. How much more compassionate and gracious God would be for the innocently sinned-against! Brueggemann implies that humanity is, after all, a victim of the cosmic drama of creation and of the Fall. This fact that the God of the Hebrew Bible is a God of mercy and grace is the foundation of the Old Testament theology. In contrast with the popular mechanistic image of God in the theology of retribution, Brueggemann has cogently brought out the *compassionate* and *generous* image of God who allows a hermeneutics of suspicion of God's own justice and goodness.

His understanding of the merciful God, however, raises a question about God's justice and anger. For him, the fact that God sides with the wounded party is God's judgment upon sinners. While not neglecting the side of God's justice, Brueggemann articulates God's mercy, the expression of justice, for all in this cosmic drama. He thinks that the oppressor and the oppressed are the victims of this cosmic drama. We should not, however, attenuate the difference between the oppressors and the oppressed under the rubric of the universal tragedy. For him, on account of God's mercy, the universal drama does not end as a zero-sum game, but as a win-win story.

While Brueggemann cares for the wounded party in the Old Testament, Andrew Sung Park is concerned about the experience of the wounded in the Bible, including the New Testament. In his chapter "The Bible and Han," he notices that the Bible revolves around the sinned-against rather than around sinners (oppressors). God works for the deliverance of victims from their plight. The Bible cares about the suffering of victims more than about the well-being of their oppressors. Consequently the pain of victims, not the sin of oppressors, is a key to understanding the redemptive deliverance of God. It is difficult to find a term that describes victims' deep pain in the West, thus with his Asian-American (Korean) background, Park introduces a term from the East that expresses the victims' pain: han. Han is a victim's deep wound that festers from within. It is the hopelessness and helplessness of the powerless, the marginalized, and the voiceless in the world. In Brueggemann's term, it is "the shrill voice" of the victim. Han is also the silence of the wounded. Sinners can repent of their sin. Victims cannot repent of their han. Han needs to be healed. Job's episode shows that God judges Job's friends who demanded repentance from

Job, a han-ridden victim, not understanding the han of a victim. Even God cannot bear such a unilateral theology of sin. Why do we?

In the New Testament, Jesus mainly contacted the so-called sinners—the downtrodden and he ministered to their physical and spiritual wound, han. When Jesus said that he came to call the sick, not the righteous, he made his mission of caring for the wounded clear. Park analyzes the Lord's Prayer as a good example of showing to whom that teaching was mainly given. Jesus' ministry was built around resolving the han of the sinned-against, challenging the oppression of the sinners. Park acknowledges that Jesus was for both sinners and the sinned-against. However, he holds that since Jesus primarily taught and healed the sinned-against in his ministry, the Bible should be primarily interpreted for their sake in light of han in addition to the doctrine of sin. In such an interpretation of the Bible, the notion of han may be a great asset. Wherever sin is named, han should be taken into account together. No more sin-talk alone.

Park's notion of han concurs with Justo L. González's idea of *alienation*. In his chapter "The Alienation of Alienation," González treats the other side of sin, *alienation*. Questioning the denotation of the term *alienation*, González is critical of its exclusively psychological usage in church history. Such a psychologized term enhances the internalization and individualization of sin. Using Pelagius and Augustine, he explains the individualization of sin in terms of the atomization of reality and the privatization of sin. Drawing upon Abelard's and Anselm's theology, he further explores the meaning of the internalization of sin.

On the one hand, using Anselm's concept of sin, González points out that sin should be seen not only from the will and intention of the sinner, but also from the perspective of the sinned-against. On the other hand, against Anselm's idea of hierarchical authority and its consequential assumption of sin, González points to the subversive principle of the gospel concerning the concept of sin. Without denying the necessity of some measure of order, he rejects any authoritarian and hierarchical suppression in the process of the internalization of sin.

In opposition to the effort to fix the sin of internalization through psychotherapy, he suggests "the alienation of alienation." For him, the term *alienation* means not only becoming psychologically dysfunctional, but also turning into something alien from God and from ourselves. With his ample knowledge of Christian history, he discloses the abuse of the doctrine of sin for two thousand years. The church, he argues, has internalized and individualized the significance and breadth of its notion. He brilliantly suggests that we alienate the alienation of the doctrine of sin for the sake of the alienated. Unlike Hegel who believed in reconciliation with alienation, he negates or alienates the alienation of the doctrine of sin. He directly contradicts Freudian psychoanalytic diagnosis of social wrongs. His idea of *alienation* as widespread among Christians matches Marx's concept of *alienation* prevalent among laborers. Contrasting with Marx who wanted to remove religion altogether, his notion of theological alienation can redeem Christianity by alienating the alienation of the traditional doctrine of sin.

González's "alienation sin " is compatible with Susan L. Nelson's "shame brokenheartedness." In her chapter "For Shame, for Shame, the Shame of it All: Postures of Refusal and the Broken Heart," Nelson explores the way in which for victims of sin, sin and the experience of brokenheartedness can blend together. Thus, she muddies a too simplistic polarity between categories of sinners and victims of sin. If sin is the refusal of the vulnerability and possibility of the human condition (Nelson's description of Kierkegaard's critical insight), then Nelson argues, many "postures of refusal" are rooted in the experience of being refused—sinned-against. Using shame as an example of refusals that wound and relating how the spiral of shame can spin one into deep self-alienation and defensive and aggressive postures of refusal, Nelson argues that much sin may well be born of a broken heart. If her analysis is correct, then reconciliation from sin cannot be only repentance and forgiveness—but also must include a "balm"—for the broken heart, a healing of interhuman relations, and a resistance against systems that perpetuate refusals.

Her system exposes the full vicious cycle of evil. She treats it at a deep root level. The ambiguity of the line between sinners and the sinned-against speaks to the people in the age of postmodernity. Her notable contribution is interpreting the present world of brokenness more accurately. The *brokenheartedness* of sinners and the sinned-against in Nelson's analysis and in González's *alienation* converge in describing the experience of the victims of sin.

Ched Myers discusses González's *alienation* and Nelson's notion of *shame* and *brokenheartedness* at a societal level. In his chapter "Beyond 'The Addict's Excuse': Sin, Public Addiction and Ecclesial Recovery," Myers stresses the structural side of sin. He insightfully analyzes sin as addiction: as sin in the two-thirds world is *oppression*, the inability to affirm life due to injustice, so sin in the first world is *addiction,* the inability to refuse greed due to pathological wants. He regards alienation as the primary metaphor of addiction. The major focus in his exploration is not individualistic addiction, but public addiction: consumerism, colonialism, militarism, and sexism.

To Myers, the church should be involved in the public recovery movement through the traditions of *repentance, resistance,* and the *evangelical disciplines.* To the addicted society, he recommends *conversion* or *repentance* as recovery. He believes that the Twelve-Step recovery of Alcoholics Anonymous provides three important insights for a theology of recovery. The first insight is to acknowledge that the addictive system controls and destroys us. The second is to begin with our own experience of pain, oppression, culpability, and responsibility. The third is to support a sustained resistance to the addictive system. He raises a unique voice in the world of epidemic addictions. When an individual is drunk, it is rather easy to confront and bring him or her to sobriety. When a society is drunk, it is even more difficult to challenge and wake it up from within. His attempt is unique in applying a hermeneutics of suspicion to the public, not to a text.

As the community of *resistance, recovery,* and *disciplines,* Myers believes, the church needs to name our sinful condition clearly and to identify itself as a community committed to recovering addicts. If the church is addicted, however, who will wake it up? Marx accused Christianity of being the opium of the people. It is undeniable that many churches are addicted to their own numerical growth (expansionism), sexism, and racism. It is necessary for the church to apply a hermeneutics of suspicion to itself. For Myers, rather than dissolve itself, the church should learn from its own traditions of *repentance, resistance,* and the *evangelical disciplines* that includes the monastic Rule of St. Benedict: poverty (e.g., the "simple living" movement), chastity (e.g., giving up private control), and obedience (e.g., civil disobedience). These are new categories for the church that enables it to practice its own new hermeneutics of suspicion.

Myers's *societal addiction* mutually reinforces Theodore Jennings's *ecclesial idea of sin.* Calling our attention to the inadequacy of the traditional doctrine of sin, Jennings revamps the idea of sin. In "Reconstructing the Doctrine of Sin," he undertakes the task of rebuilding the doctrine of sin by overcoming the seven ideas of sin manipulated by structures of domination. They are the verticalizing of sin, individualizing of sin, criminalizing of sin, interiorizing of sin, pride, eroticizing of sin, and sin as irremediable.

Instead of upholding these unilateral sins, he recasts the notions of sin by suggesting the following: (1) the violation of the fellow creature (horizontal sin) is inseparable from that of the divine (vertical sin); (2) the recovery of the essentially social significance of sin is necessary for a reconstruction of the doctrine of sin; (3) the violation of justice (sin) should be differentiated from the violation of laws (crime) and the issue of justice to draw attention to public, historical, and social dimensions in the category of sin; (4) sin as the violation of the other person should not be overshadowed by interiorizing of sin; (5) sin as the arrogance of elites who humiliated the vulnerable needs to be checked in light of the aspiration of the marginalized; (6) sin as class exploitation and neocolonial exploitation should be highlighted in place of the association of sin with sexuality; and (7) the notion of sin as remediable should replace the pessimistic idea of sin as irremediable.

For Jennings, the reconstruction of the doctrine of sin starts with an awareness of the fact that cultural elites have often defined doctrinal perimeters to serve the interests of a religious institution in association with the dominant social forces of the world. His major concern is to know for whom doctrinal formulations are structured and what formulations adequately represent the freeing intention of the gospel.

Jennings carefully analyzes each subject with deconstructive and reconstructive insights. His proposal is not to keep a harmonious balance between the idea of sin for the dominant and the reality of sin for the dominated, but to restructure the present notion of sin. It is deeply disturbing for him to maintain the present form of the doctrine of sin, which is an ecclesial *addiction,* to use Myers's term. He boldly suggests an innovation of the doctrine of sin, implementing the liberative intention of the gospel into the theological idea. Like Paul Ricoeur, Jennings presents the negative side and the positive side of *suspicion* of the doctrine of sin, emphasizing the latter.

While Jennings undertakes the mission of reconstructing the concept of sin in the church, Marie M. Fortune focuses on the social dimension of sin in the context of abuse and violence. In "The Conundrum of Sin, Sex, Violence, and Theodicy," Fortune articulates the inadequacy of the dominant framework of defining sin as our social reality: sin as disobedience to social values. She reviews the biblical, historical, contemporary treatments of victims, considering the whole matter from the view of the sinned-against, particularly of sexual victims—the sexually molested and homosexuals.

With her experience in the work of the Center for the Prevention of Sexual and Domestic Violence, Fortune convincingly articulates how sin, sex, violence, and evil are cyclically interlocked in our life. She points to the inadequacy of the dominant moral framework toward the victims of sexual, domestic violence, and gender discrimination in ministry. In the Bible, sin is basically defined as *disobedience* and *harm-done-to-others*. To her, sin as disobedience apparently serves the interests of the privileged while sin as harm-done-to-others concerns the marginalized. In Brueggeman's "sin-as-harm-done-to-others," she finds a moral category that speaks to margainalized woman, children, gays, and lesbians. Jesus was much concerned about those who were regarded "sinners" by the dominant group. She adamantly advocates the rights of victims, and freely uses the term *victim*, for victims are those who have no choice about being victims. Thus she argues, avoiding the term *victim* would not be helpful in alleviating the reality of the condition of victimization. For Fortune, moral values are extremely important in the analyses of sin and violence. Concerned for the process of healing, she rebuffs the traditional understanding that healing should rely on a victim's efforts. To her, the actions of the perpetrator and the community should concur with those of the victim.

Facing the culture of resistance to a victim-friendly moral order, Fortune suggests that we choose a moral order that treats sin as harm-done-to-others. This is compatible with Jennings's "degrading of others." From an ethical aspect, she further asks us to side with the victim who beckons bystanders to action, engagement, and remembering, rather than with the perpetrator who asks them to do nothing. Only when pushed into a corner does the perpetrator ask for forgiveness. Her perspective here is Niebuhrian in espousing a realistic approach to the dark side of human nature and balancing power dynamics.

Without a new theological framework, it is difficult for pastoral counselors to work for healing and a new beginning for victims. Along with Brueggemann's categories, Jennings's new categories of sin—socializing of injustice, violating of justice, degrading of others, and humiliating of the humiliated—will also provide Fortune and other counselors with the tools for naming some problems in counseling the abused. Although Freud criticized religion as an illusion, Fortune's efforts for the victims deconstruct Freud's suspicion on religion.

Fortune's care for the victims of abuse and violence finds its partner in Mary Elizabeth Mullins Moore's *fear*. Her chapter "Teaching Justice and Reconciliation in a Wounding World" speaks to the need of radical change in the world of suffering and terrorist violence. From her perspective as a Christian educator, Moore starts her theme, not with dry discourse, but with poignant stories. From her retelling of the Oklahoma City bombing, Moore explores the way of teaching reconciliation through four points.

First, *the fear of knowing* or fear of being in relationship is the fear of knowing violence, the fear of not finding answers, and the fear of knowing what we do not know. The fear of knowing violence tempts us to bury our wounds and the scars of violent experience. Second, *the yearning to know* is yearning to find life beyond violence, to face questions without answers, and to know what we do not know. The yearning to find life beyond violence is the quest for the life and hope for wisdom. The yearning to face questions without answers means engaging serious questions without the certainty of finding answers. Third, *education as searching* is the practice of truth-telling, of living with questions, and of searching for what we do not know. True education takes place when educators engage people in experiencing, exploring, deconstructing, and reconstructing symbols. Fourth, *education as reconciliation* is the practice of posing alternatives, the practice of repentance, the practice of remembering and covenantal eating, and the practice of meeting in ordinariness. Being a reconciling community is an alternative in the world of violence. This practice of posing alternatives is to stir our creative imagination of diverse, yet harmonious life in the midst of hostile human relations.

Moore articulates the problem of our society—fear. Like Kierkegaard's *anxiety,* Moore's *fear* is not sin, but can be a precondition to sin. How to resolve fear without falling into sin is Moore's chief task. Emerging from the context of abuse and violence, fear alienates the alienated. People, Christians or non-Christians, grapple with fear in this raging world. She cogently reasons that fear will come to an end only through educating people. The content of education is to teach people how to practice God's gifts of reconciliation: questing, truth-telling, questioning without answers, and acknowledging our unawareness. In this sense, we do not educate people, but participate in God's teaching of the peace that passes our understanding.

While educating people of fear within the community is Moore's concern, reorientating church liturgy for victims is Ruth C. Duck's. In her chapter "Hospitality to Victims: A Challenge for Christian Worship," Duck challenges the church to be more hospitable to victims in its worship. Understanding sin from a victim's perspective, she proposes innovating Christian liturgy from the perspective of the violated. For the violator, the Eucharist means the forgiveness of sin. For the violated, the Eucharist is the medium of welcoming into the community of faith or celebrating joy, life, abundance, and community. Turning to Psalms, she differentiates confession from lament; confession is understood as the cry of the violator, while lament as the cry of the violated. A number of worship settings may include several stragegies to heal the violated. There can be liturgies of lament for healing the wounded. Liturgies can "name and condemn the actions of violators in the name of love and justice, for the sake of their victims," "pray for the enemy and ask for God's transforming grace for the violator," or include " a touch of humor or satire."

For healing liturgies, we can use healing prayer, anointing the violated, a prayer of thanksgiving for healing, and a new understanding of sin. From a hospitable viewpoint toward the violated, she reinterprets forgiveness, confession, absolution, and reconciliation in liturgy and preaching. Above all, worship should be hospitable to victims by embodying justice. That means calling people to live in love, interceding on behalf of the violated, reorienting liturgy to be a foretaste, and rehearsing justice and reconciliation on earth.

Duck is suggesting a revolution in liturgy. While we have had liturgies for sinners, we have not had any liturgies for the sinned-against. Her vision will make the Eucharist the medium of God's grace for healing the wounded as well as the act of confession for sinners. When the sinned-against are healed and sinners are forgiven, our worship will be truly alive, empowering, and a celebration of God's grace. As we pray for the healing of our wounds as well as confess our sins in the Eucharist, worship will turn into an occasion of true thanksgiving, celebration, and peace.

In such a worship, the shrill voice of the wounded will turn into praise, their han will begin to melt, their alienation will be alienated, their shame and broken heart will be healed, the addicted society will be challenged, the oppressed will hear the liberative proclamation of the gospel, the abused will naturally cry without shame, and the people of fear will feel no evil in the community of God. If Nietzsche were to attend such a worship service, he would realize that Christianity is not a religion of weakness, but is about the empowerment of the wounded and the repentant.

Prospect

By publishing this volume, we hope that the sinned-against in the church and society are directly helped. This shared project is not a merely academic exercise. It is a concrete proposal for helping people and for reformulating theological and ecclesial concepts. By acknowledging, delineating, and taking on the issue of the other side of sin, the church can change its practices for the sinned-against in the areas of Bible study, historical teaching, doctrinal teaching, ethical implementation, pastoral counseling, church education, and Christian liturgy. Outside the church, people have developed various kinds of helpful steps for different victims through psychotherapy, sociological analyses, ethical rules, legal procedures, and medical treatments. Inside the church, we have not taken the issue of victims' rights and their restoration processes as seriously as the society has. Our common task is to stimulate theological (in a broad sense) dialogue so that more people may be engaged in transforming the reality of alienation and woundedness from the perspective of the sinned-against. In this matter, theological renovations are long overdue.

Furthermore, we would like to see more theological ideas for the sinned-against developed from diverse theological fields. Beginning with the theme of the other side of sin, we should take on the issue of the deliverance of the sinned-against from their pain and suffering. Salvation for sinners is one thing; the liberation of their victims is another. When we consider numerous victims sitting in the church, it is urgent for us to make a new set of guidelines available for their liberation. We hope that such approaches come into sight in the near future.

Moreover, we need to develop some processes to insure the well-being of the sinned-against. In addition to the efforts of pastoral counseling and psychotherapy, we need theological reflections on the procedures of their healing at a doctrinal level. We hope that more people respond to this need. In this new century and millennium, it might be one of the most important tasks for the church.

NOTES

*All Bible quotes are from NRSV unless otherwise stated.

1. See Cornelius Plantinga Jr.'s *Not the Way It's Supposed to Be: A Breviary of Sin* (Grand Rapids: Eerdmans, 1995) for a discussion of sin that starts with this awareness.

2. See Elizabeth Clark, "From Originism to Pelagianism: Elusive Issues in an Ancient Debate," *Princeton Seminary Bulletin* 12, no. 3 (1991) 283–303, for an exploration of early dialogues on the doctrine of original sin as it relates to infant baptism.

3. See Elaine Pagels's *Adam, Eve, and the Serpent* (New York: Random, 1988) for a discussion of the development of the doctrine of original sin and its place within the experience of evil.

4. See Edward Farley, *Good and Evil: Interpreting a Human Condition* (Minneapolis: Fortress, 1990).

5. While the Kierkegaardian strain of Christian theology has reinterpreted the Augustinian intuition of the sinfulness of human beings through the lens of existentialist philosophies, another approach to the Augustinian doctrine has been to reexamine Augustine himself. What if Augustine's story belies his conclusions? What if Augustine was himself the victim of sin? And is original sin a rationalization of unjustifiable experiences of suffering and evil? See *The Hunger of the Heart: Reflections on the Confessions of Augustine,* ed. by Donald Capps and James E. Dittes (West Lafayette, Ind.: Society for the Scientific Study of Religion, 1990).

6. Rita Nakashima Brock, *Journeys by Heart: A Christology of Erotic Power* (New York: Crossroads, 1988).

7. Here we are referring to feminist theologians, process thinkers, and some liberation theologians. See in particular Marjorie Hewitt Suchocki, *The Fall to Violence* (New York: Continuum, 1994); and Wendy Farley, *Tragic Vision and Divine Compassion* (Louisville: Westminster/John Knox, 1990).

8. Augustine, *City of God,* trans. by Gerald G. Walsh et al. abridged (New York: Doubleday, 1958) 53–55.

9. Of course, it is also possible to argue that Augustine was himself a victim of sin who chose to interpret his suffering from a moral perspective (punishment for his sin) rather than admit that the world is one in which the innocent can suffer—with all of the theological implications suggested in such a view. For an extended dialogue on Augustine's own woundedness see *Hunger of the Heart.*

10. St. Thomas Aquinas, *The Summa Theologica*, I–II Q85, A3.

11. Ibid., I–II Q109, A2.

12. Jean Calvin, *Corpus Reformatorum* (Calvin's Works), ed. by G. Baum, E. Cunitz, and E. Reuss (Brusvigae: C. A. Schwetschte, 1869) 29:338.

13. John Calvin, *Institutes of the Christian Religion*, trans. by Henry Beveridge (Grand Rapid: Eerdmans, 1957) II:1, 10.

14. Ibid., II:3, 4.

15. Immanuel Kant, *Religion within the Limits of Reason Alone* (New York: Harper and Row, 1960) 38.

16. Ibid.

17. G. W. F. Hegel, *Lectures on the Philosophy of Religion: Together with a Work on the Proofs of the Existence of God*, trans. from the second German ed. by E. B. Speirs and J. Burdon Sanderson, ed. by J. B. Speirs (London: K. Paul, Trench, Truner, 1895) III:48.

18. Friedrich Schleiermacher, *Christian Faith*, 2 vols. ed. by H. R. Mackintosh and J. S. Stewart (New York: Harper and Row, 1963) I:316.

19. Ibid.

20. Ibid., 317.

21. Ibid., 317–319.

22. Paul Tillich, *A History of Christian Thought*, ed. by Carl Braaten (New York: Simon and Schuster, 1967) 476–480.

23. Karl Marx, *Marx's Economic and Philosophical Manuscripts*, trans. by T. B. Bottomore, in *Marx's Concept of Man,* by Erik Fromm (New York: Ungar, 1961) 95–96.

24. Ibid., 98–99.

25. Walter Rauschenbusch, *Christianizing the Social Order* (New York: Macmillan, 1916) 392.

26. Bauschenbusch, *Theology for Social Gospel* (Nashville: Abingdon Press, 1945) 66–67.

27. Ibid., 78.

28. Ibid., 87.

29. Paul Ricoeur, *The Conflict of Interpretations: Essays in Hermeneutics*, ed. by Don Ihde (Evanston, Ill.: Northwestern University Press, 1974).

30. Ricoeur, *Fallible Man*, revised trans. by Charles A. Kelbley, intro. by Walter J. Lowe (New York: Fordham University Press, 1986).

31. Valerie Saiving, "The Human Situation: A Feminine View," in *Womanspirit Rising*, ed. by Carol P. Christ and Judith Plaskow (San Francisco: Harper and Row, 1979) 37.

32. Ibid., 41.

33. This insight that women are both complicit of their sin, and victims in a society that terms women *others* was an initial insight of Simone de Beauvoir in *The Second Sex*, trans. by H. M. Parshley (London: Jonathan Cape, 1953; New York: Knopf, 1953). See also Plaskow, *Sex, Sin and Grace: Women's Experience and the Theologies of Reinhold*

Niebuhr and Paul Tillich (Washington, D.C.: University Press of America, 1980); Susan (Dunfee) Nelson, *Beyond Servanthood* (Lanham, Md.: University Press of America, 1985); and Nelson, *Healing the Broken Heart* (St. Louis: Chalice Press, 1997).

34. Gustavo Gutiérrez, *A Theology of Liberation: History, Politics, and Salvation*, trans. and ed. by Sister Caridad Inda and John Eagleson (Maryknoll: Orbis, 1973) 25–37.

35. James Cone, *A Black Theology of Liberation* (Maryknoll: Orbis, 1990) 107–108.

36. Ibid., 108.

37. Mary Potter Engel, "Evil, Sin, and Violation of the Vulnerable," in *Lift Every Voice: Constructing Christian Theologies from the Underside*, ed. by Susan Books Thistlethwaite and Mary Potter Engel (San Francisco: HarperCollins, 1990) 152–164.

38. Ted Peters, *Sin: Radical Evil in Soul and Society* (Grand Rapids: Eerdmans, 1994) 8.

CHAPTER ONE

THE SHRILL VOICE OF THE WOUNDED PARTY

Walter Brueggemann

I

The community that generated and lived in the Old Testament was a community of intense moral passion. In its powerful theological rhetoric, it managed to hold together two insistent ethical claims. First, it bore witness to a sovereign God whose announced purposes aimed to bring every element and detail of the world under God's own sovereign purpose. This sovereign purpose included the *purity* of holiness and *justice* in the neighborhood. The God who enunciated this purpose did so with clarity and solemnity, and with severe sanctions for those who refused this purpose. That is, Israel's moral passion is rooted in the character of God.

Second, this community bore witness to the moral shape and moral reliability of the world that is God's well-ordered creation. The world, they claimed, is not chaotic, anarchic, or nonsensical. It holds together, not by sheer power or domination, but by a moral order that can be known and honored. Those who live inside this moral order that is willed by God benefit from the blessings of God—security, dignity, prosperity, and fruitfulness—all the blessings of a good life. And conversely, those who refuse this moral order or violate it are subject to sanctions, and thereby receive all of the threats of destructiveness—disease, disorder, abandonment, sterility, poverty, and a bad death.

This is a world, so the Old Testament affirms, which is beneficent to its adherents, but severe to its violators. Israel arrived at clarity about a way of life and a way of death, and did not confuse the two. Moreover, Israel understood that there is no compromise or concession about this moral order that is intrinsic to God's creation. Such a characterization of God, world, and human life may evoke in us a sense of the severity of this order, and of God who sanctions it. In the first instance, however, one should observe not the severity of this moral passion, but its reliability. This is a world that can be counted upon. It is, moreover, a world into which one will want to bring children through narration, a world that can be trusted and lived in well. This is a world in which there is no caprice, and in which power or willfulness cannot overturn its moral shape. The fact that this God-ordered world allows no slippage is, of course, part of its problem. But the lack of slippage, before it is a problem, is precisely what commends to us this moral vision.

Israel articulated this God-authorized moral shaping of reality in two ways. First and most obviously, it is the commandments of Mt. Sinai (Ex 20:1–17 and Deut 5:6–21) which articulated the most elemental norms for Israel's moral world. Of the encounter at Sinai, we notice three factors. First, the commands are on God's own lips. These are not the commands of the king or any other human agent. Second, the theophanic prelude of Ex 19:16–25, according to the witness, assures that the commands are rooted and grounded in God's own holiness, out beyond human contrivance. Third, for these commandments, there are no sanctions. They are absolute and disobedience to these commands is not even entertained as thinkable or possible.

Clearly the originary enunciation of moral purpose—behind which one cannot go for explanation—in the Ten Commandments received rich and sustained interpretive expansion in the Old Testament. In every generation, we may suppose, the foundational commands of Yahweh, the God of Israel, needed to be applied, interpreted, and updated.[1] All of these elaborations are assigned in the Old Testament text to Moses, but it is commonly believed that the role of Moses was occupied in each generation by authoritative interpreters, who claimed to be extrapolating what was intended by, and contained, in the initial commands.[2] This expansive interpretation extended, especially in the tradition of Leviticus, to every zone of Israel's worship life, concerning laws of purity, priests, and acts of sacrifice. Correspondingly, in the tradition of Deuteronomy, interpretation expanded into every sphere of "civic" life—political, economic, judicial, and military.

It is evident that two sorts of things happened in the interpretive practice of ongoing Israel. First, every detail of life is brought under the rubric of obedience. There is no facet of life in which the God of Sinai does not have a specific will and purpose. Second, severe sanctions are added to the laws, especially in the curse recitals of Lev 26:14–33 and Deut 28:15–68. In each of these collections, a recital of blessing is given for those who obey (Lev 26:1–13 and Deut 28:1–14). But the positive sections of these two chapters are much briefer than the negative sanctions, and ongoing energy clearly applied primarily to the negative sanctions of curses. In the end, this tradition of commandment came to be summarized in a simple formula of obedience and life, disobedience and death:

> See, I have set before you today life and prosperity, death and adversity. If
> you obey the commandments of the Lord your God that I am command-

ing you today, by loving the Lord your God, walking in his ways, and
observing his commandments, decrees, and ordinances, then you shall live
and become numerous. But if your heart turns away and you do not hear,
but are led astray to bow down to other gods and serve them, I declare to
you today that you shall perish. (Deut 30:15–18)

Israel also devised a second rhetorical system that articulated the moral coherence of the world under the rule of Yahweh. In contrast to the commands of
Sinai, the wisdom tradition was not so severe in its articulation, but it was as
uncompromising in its teaching. The tradition of sapiential reflection, especially
given in the Book of Proverbs, does not appeal directly to the authority of God,
nor to explicit religious sanctions.[3] The teachers of the wisdom tradition, rather,
reflect upon the experience of life, whereby parents, teachers, elders, scribes,
and sages had noticed the kinds of behavior that cause good things to happen,
and conversely, they had noticed over a long period of time, the sorts of conduct that produce bad results. That is, no rewarding or punishing agent (God)
needs to intervene in the process of ethics, for the choices people make seem
to produce by themselves certain outcomes that come along with the choices.

Following Klaus Koch, scholars have hypothesized that there was in ancient
Israel a theory of moral order that noticed a very close connection between
"deed and consequence," so that the linkage between the two, over time, is predictable and inescapable.[4] Thus, for example, laziness results in poverty, having bad
friends produces trouble. These linkages, moreover, are not mere happenstance,
nor can they be understood simply in utilitarian ways. Scholars suggest that this
moral linkage is reflective of creation faith.[5] The Creator God has ordered the
world so that all of life is a series of interrelated components, each of which carries inescapable moral implications. The sapiential tradition is not so heavy-
handed as the tradition of command in enunciating the dangers of destructive
behavior. It is nonetheless as insistent as the tradition of command, in asserting
that consequences of choices and actions are inevitable and nonnegotiable.

Thus wisdom, as a personified voice, speaks in an appeal to its listeners,
who are presumed to be children being inculcated into Israel's deposit of
moral observations:

> And now, my children, listen to me:
> happy are those who keep my ways,
> Hear instruction and be wise,
> and do not neglect it.
> Happy is the one who listens to me,
> watching daily at my gates,
> waiting beside my doors.
> For whoever finds me, finds life
> and obtains favor from the Lord;
> but those who miss me injure themselves;
> all who hate me love death. (Prov 8:32–36)

The one who accepts the guidance of accumulated wisdom and acts accordingly is herself wise. The one who violates this deposit of guidelines to right conduct is not a sinner, but a fool. Such action that violates wisdom is not wrong. It is stupid. The outcome nevertheless is the same as with the violation of the commands of Sinai: death!

These two instructional traditions likely emerge from very different social situations with different agendas, assumptions, and intentions.[6] It is, moreover, very late before the traditions of torah and wisdom are merged, though one can see the tendency toward convergence much earlier.[7] Erhard Gerstenberger, however, has proposed that the two kinds of formulations of moral requirement and moral sanction, for all the difference in their developments, may have the same point of origin. He proposes, moreover, that the sapiential tradition is the antecedent to the Sinai tradition.[8]

Thus it may be the voice of the pater familias who says to the young, "Thou shalt not" (Jer 35:6–7).[9] And it is the "Thou shalt not" of conventional family nurture and discipline that becomes the preferred form of command in the mouth of Yahweh at Sinai. In the end, the communal instruction of Proverbs and the theological insistence of Sinai do converge. Both enunciate moral requirement, without acknowledging any suspicion or reluctance about the moral requirement, its source, its ideological interest, or its intention. Both traditions recognize and insist upon unavoidable sanction, whether imposed by a punishing agent (God), or intrinsic to the act itself. And so both traditions create a world in which the one who violates the commands or departs from established wisdom is clearly in the wrong. That person, in effect, brings down trouble upon himself or herself and upon the community, from which there is no escape. It matters little whether one receives *curse as a sinner* or *consequence as a fool*. The order that promises life is unflinching in meting out deathliness to those who violate, disregard, or mock its requirements.

This account of moral coherence is indeed the stuff of Old Testament faith. It can be given different nuance, but the main line of argument is not in doubt. It is inevitable that such a plot of moral coherence will boldly locate fault, assign blame, and be unblinking in its administration of "justice" to violators. I do believe that in its main force, this cannot be denied. And there is no way to articulate a "doctrine of sin" concerning the Old Testament, apart from this heavy, unaccommodating threat, without cheating.

II

Having said that, it is clear that the community that generated and lived in the Old Testament had to live in the real world. The real world that they inhabited, the same moral world we, their belated heirs inhabit, is not so neat and clean and one-dimensional as these dominant lines of moral coherence might suggest. As a result, one can detect a variety of literary-rhetorical strategies that intend either to open the moral arena of Israel beyond the tight traditions of command and wisdom to allow for the slippages that are inevitable in lived reality, or to

destabilize these high, starchy claims in order to permit less severe ways of thinking. Here I will consider four such strategies, none of which in the end prevail,
but all of which persist in the text of the Old Testament, and by their existence,
deabsolutize the clean "either/or" of Deut 30:15–20 and Prov 8:32–36.

The first of these alternative strategies is found in the Exodus narrative
(Ex 1–15).[10] This narrative functions as Israel's founding act of liturgical imagination.[11] In this well-known, oft-repeated narrative, there are three players,
Yahweh who wills freedom for Israel, Pharaoh who resists the freedom Yahweh
intends, and Israel who is represented by Moses (and Aaron). The fact that there
are three players (instead of the usual two of Sinai and wisdom) already indicates a more complicated plot with much more maneuverability in the moral
conclusions that can be drawn.

In this plot our interest concerns the third party, Israel. About that player
in the narrative, we will ask to what extent Israel is "sinner" and to what extent
"sinned-against." Israel is represented in the narrative by Moses, who is only a
modest actor in the key transactions that take place between Yahweh and
Pharaoh. Israel is in a situation of wretchedness, where it is ruthlessly abused,
and from which it is helpless to extricate itself. What interests us is the fact that
Israel is in this miserable situation through no fault of its own. Israel is not said
to have sinned. Indeed, in Gen 47:13–26, we are given a review of the eco-
nomic-political processes by which such a marginated people as the Hebrews
become slaves, inured to the imperial production system by the brutality of
supply and demand, and by the manipulation of mortgages and taxes.

It is evident that Pharaoh, and his agent Joseph, have acted against the
radical notion of justice fostered in Israel, and have reduced the Israelites to
pawns in the service of imperial projects. As long as the social struggle of the
Israelites involves only two parties, Israel and Pharaoh, Israel is a hopeless, hapless victim of the enormous, ruthless power of Pharaoh, who obeys no law but
his own. Thus Israel is indeed a victim of a social circumstance that happened
through no fault of its own, but it nonetheless suffers mightily at the hands of
the perpetrator, Pharaoh.

The Exodus narrative proper, however, does not get under way until Ex
2:23–25. It is remarkable that in Israel's normative narrative, Yahweh the God
of Israel does not initiate the process of rescue of the slaves. The initiatory act
is taken by the slaves themselves, who "cry out." They do not cry out to anyone in particular. They simply give public voice to their unwarranted pain, and
thereby evoke the interest of Yahweh and mobilize the energy and authority
of Yahweh on their behalf. Throughout the remainder of the narrative that
issues in Israel's freedom (Ex 15:12–18 and 20–10), the primary action is a
struggle between Pharaoh and Yahweh. Pharaoh is cast as the resolute victimizer of Israel, and Yahweh is the champion and advocate of Israel who, through
no fault of its own, is in deep trouble.

There is indeed a sinner in this tale. But it is not Israel. It is Pharaoh.
The sin of Pharaoh is to imagine that he is autonomous, that is, not subject to
the moral restraints of Yahweh, and therefore free to act in his own arrogant,

unrestrained self-interest (cf. Ezek 29:3–7, 31:2–9, and 32:2–16). In the Exodus narrative, Pharaoh is the historical-political embodiment of evil, or in creation language, Pharaoh is the power of chaos, the power that seeks to undo the orderliness of creation.[12] Pharaoh is "the power of sin" that has the capacity to work evil, suffering, and death upon the victim Israel. Yahweh, conversely, is portrayed as the one who actively and powerfully intervenes against this Egyptian embodiment of evil on behalf of Israel.

Everything depends, in this narrative, upon having three parties to the plot. And everything for Israel depends upon Yahweh demonstrating that he is stronger than Pharaoh. No doubt there were those moral teachers, in the service of Pharaoh, who did not reckon with Yahweh as a character in the plot, who thought that the political drama of the empire included only two characters, Pharaoh and Israel. And when there are only two characters, it is simple enough to imagine, with ideological deftness, that Pharaoh is in the right, and that Israel gets what it has coming to it. In such a scenario, Israel suffers because it sins against Pharaoh. Everything depends upon the third character, in order for the Exodus event to be dramatically visible. The Exodus narrative exists in order to assure that Yahweh will be a palpable and available third party in the life and imagination of Israel. It is this third party that makes it possible to see Israel not as sinner, but as sinned-against by Pharaoh. What Israel requires as sinned-against, is not guilt, punishment, and repentance, but an intervening advocate who can and will work justice, and extricate Israel from this unwarranted suffering.

In important ways, the great prophets of Israel continue with the three-character plot of the Exodus. To be sure, the prophets often simply "condemn Israel" as an undifferentiated entity. But more often, they make important social differentiations within Israel. More often they recognize that society is not uniformly bad and under judgment. And so they characteristically address the leadership, the urban elite of the Jerusalem establishment who prey upon the ordinary folk of peasant stock, and who by economic exploitation and juridical manipulation deny a livable life to the marginated, those pushed to the margins of power and dignity.[13]

Robert R. Wilson has suggested that some of the prophets, situated as they are among the socially "peripheral," are indeed advocates for the socially marginated against the monied interest.[14] Thus Isaiah can rail, in sapiential rhetoric, against those

> who join house to house,
> who add field to field,
> Until there is room for no one but you,
> and you are left alone
> in the midst of the land! (Isa 5:8)

Clearly the charge made by the prophet is not aimed at everyone in Israel. For every house that is confiscated, there is a displaced family of unprotected people who are sinned against. And Amos can speak to the powerful in Samaria:

Hear this word, you cows of Bashan
who are on Mount Samaria,
who oppress the poor, who crush the needy,
who say to their husbands. (Amos 4:1)

In the purview of the prophetic poet are the poor and the needy who have not
sinned, but who are sinned-against. Thus the social drama staged by the
prophets, perhaps a miniature replication of the drama of the Exodus, consists
in the ruthless who sin in their acquisitive arrogance, the sinned-against who
suffer at the hands of their exploiters, and Yahweh who is an advocate for the
sinned-against, against the sinners. Again, what is required is enough social differentiation to see that the social drama is a three-player plot. In the Exodus
narrative Pharaoh wanted to exclude Yahweh as a third player, without whom
there would be no Exodus narrative. In the prophets, one propensity is to
ignore the sinned-against and then to assume there are only two parties, Yahweh and sinners. The social differentiation is manifest in the text, but our conventional reductionism tends to collapse the drama. And when such reductionism is practiced, the sinned-against disappear from the plot. The prophets were
evoked in Israel, as was the Exodus narrative evoked in Egypt, precisely by the
presence of the sinned-against, who stand at the center of the drama. Israel regularly celebrates the willingness of Yahweh to stand in transformative solidarity precisely with the sinned-against. That is what justice is about in Israel's
prophetic tradition.

III

We turn now to a second, more difficult, more crucial means whereby the witness of the Old Testament destabalizes the central ethical structures of "sin-punishment" and "deeds-consequences." Any consideration of sin in the Old Testament must of course take on issues rooted in the story of the garden in Gen
2–3, and the subsequent interpretive history of that chapter.

The conventional reading of this subtle narrative directly reinforces the
"sin-punishment" structures of the Book of Deuteronomy. The core story is
not difficult, when taken on its surface reading. The "first couple" is placed in
the loveliness of paradise. They sin by disobeying God's command concerning
the tree of knowledge (Gen 3:6). And so they are, perforce, banished from the
garden as punishment. This simple story line of course has been reinforced by
the assignment of the word *Fall* to this narrative, suggesting that this brave act
of disobedience has a universal dimension to it, whereby all human persons are
guilty, merit punishment, and stand in need of pardon.[15]

It is a truism that this reading of the narrative as "Fall" plays no role in
the Old Testament itself. But in the post-Old Testament period, this "strong
reading" (misreading?) of the text is evident. Thus in 4 Ezra there is a profound
lament over the "human predicament" of sin. And of course in Rom 5:12–21,
Paul escalates the claim of universal guilt out of this narrative. This reading of

the text goes well beyond the claim of the text itself, but it has become the dominant Western reading of the text, so as to establish that sin is, in "Christian realism," definitional for the human person, who is intrinsically guilty.[16]

This reading of Gen 2–3, rooted in Paul, and derivatively in Augustine and Luther, which asserts human culpability at the root of reality, received its most popular and enormously powerful articulations in John Milton's *Paradise Lost* I, 1–4:

> Of man's first disobedience, and the fruit
> Of that forbidden tree, whose mortal taste
> Brought death into the world, and all our woe,
> With loss of Eden. . . .[17]

It is difficult to overestimate the power of this utterance on Western Protestant spirituality, with its inordinate accent on guilt. It is clearly the human person and nothing else, not God, not Satan, who has brought the wretchedness of sin and punishment into the world.

This claim by Milton, however, was a claim barely made by the poet. In *Paradise Lost* I, 27–37, Milton writes:

> Who first seduced them to that foul revolt?
> The infernal serpent; he it was, whose guile
> Stirred up with envy and revenge, deceived
> The mother of mankind, what time his pride
> Had cast him out from Heaven. . . .[18]

In *Christian Doctrine*, however, Milton had written: "This sin was instigated first by the devil. . . . Secondly it was instigated by man's own inconstant nature, which meant that he, like the devil before him, did not stand firm in the truth."[19]

Robert Crosman makes the important observation that Milton uses in one place the word *seduced* and in the other *instigated*, but never *caused*, for *cause* would preclude choice and responsibility. Arthur Sewell has suggested that these several articulations reflect Milton's own conflict with the High Calvinism that yielded such a severe God.[20]

The important point for us, however, is that Milton, in the midst of his classic and influential statement of human sin, guilt, fall, and responsibility, was able to entertain an alternative view. There was on the horizon of Milton a counterview of sin, in which the cause of sin "cannot logically stop until it reaches back to the First Cause, God Himself. . . ."[21] Milton does not take that step. But he is within an ace of it. (It is worth observing that in 2 Sam 24:1, in a context very different from that of Gen 2–3, the Old Testament itself approaches that affirmation, only to draw back in 1 Chr 21, to relieve God of such a burden.) The notion of this tension in Milton suggests that his popular rendering that finally overrides such a possibility is not as settled as it might be.

There is more going on in the narrative than a one-dimensional notion of the Fall might indicate. And of course, it is mind-boggling to ponder the consequences had Milton adjudicated differently.

The awareness of Milton's struggle with the narrative prepares the way for the rereading of this narrative from a very different perspective by Paul Ricoeur.[22] Ricoeur begins with the question, echoing Milton, "What does the serpent signify?"[23] He proposes that the serpent can be understood as "the psychological projection of desire," so that the story invites reflection upon the passion of human desire that drives the story.[24] Such a view of the narrative will leave intact the classic interpretation of "The Fall."

Ricoeur, however goes further, to observe that the serpent is not only "a part of ourselves" but is "also outside." Thus "every individual finds evil *already there*; nobody begins it absolutely."[25] From this awareness, Ricoeur speaks of "the radial externality of evil" of which "man is both author and servant."[26] And from this, says Ricouer, comes later "the great dualisms" that eventuate in the Satanic theme. Ricouer concludes: "man is not the absolute evil one, but the evil one of second rank, the evil one through seduction; he is not *the* Evil One, the Wicked One, substantively, so to speak, but evil, wicked adjectivally; he makes himself wicked by a sort of counter-participation, counter-imitation, by consenting. . . ."[27] This rather subtle point, which seems to build from Milton's use of "seduced," is important to us for two reasons. First, as "author and servant" of evil, the human person is not only understood as perpetrator, but also as victim[28] of the power of sin, responsible, but not completely. And second, the fact that evil is already there means that others, and ultimately God, have "instigated" the production of sin. Now this matter of "author and servant," and perpetrator and victim, is not easy to adjudicate, as it is not clear and obvious for Milton. And indeed, Ricoeur does not blink from recognizing the density of the issue that at its very end implicates God. One cannot ever, in such a reading, exonerate the human agent.

This reading does, however, make clear that in looking seriously at evil and at "the power of sin," one cannot proceed in a simplistic, moralistic fashion, to generate yet more guilt for humans. Humans are from the outset enmeshed in a failure of covetousness, desire, deception, and violence that is already there in the very fabric of creation. Or with John Steinbeck, sin is lying in wait, ready to spring.[29] And therefore the verdict of unmitigated "guilt" so easily given in the classical theological tradition is a misconstrual of the human situation as given in this primal narrative. A true reading of this tale requires a recognition of complexity that softens guilt, allows for a modicum of helplessness in the face of seduction, and dares the notion of some failure already present in creation. Aside from esoteric theological reflections, such a recognition of the cruciality of the serpent may make a practical difference, both in the easement of self-loathing and in the too-ready propensity to blame that so besets our conscience-ridden society.

This subtle strategy of ancient Israel in Gen 2–3 concerning sin recognizes that something has already happened, has always already happened, before we act. This "already happened" illuminates the wretchedness we so habitually choose for ourselves. But it also provides a measure of solace, through the acknowledgment of the larger truth of our theological context. It draws the creation of the serpent, God's most subtle creature and subject, into the crisis. And this prepares us for our next topic.

IV

A third literary-theological strategy that deabsolutizes and perhaps undermines the absolutizing, oversimplified ethical claim of "sin-punishment" and "deeds-consequences" is expressed in the psalms of complaint. This genre of prayer is a dominant one in the spirituality of the Psalter, and yet it ill fits with the classical traditions of theology that focus upon sin and guilt.

The psalm of complaint is the voice of the wounded and weak who cry out in need and pain. This cry is a characteristic element in Israel's piety reflected, as we have seen, in Ex 2:23–25. The cry initiates the Exodus narrative, and mobilizes Yahweh to Yahweh's liberating work on behalf of Israel. In the life and faith of ancient Israel, the wounded and weak did not characteristically submit in silence to their suffering, as though their wound and weakness denied them voice. On the contrary, such circumstance appears to have evoked a vigorous voice of protest which, in its utterance, is a voice of hope that believes that the present circumstance is not only untenable but can and must and will be changed.[30]

Claus Westermann has observed that there are regularly three parties in the prayer of complaint, even as we have suggested in the Exodus narrative.[31] The speaker, God, and the enemy all play a prominent role in these poems.[32] There may indeed be a touch of paranoia about these psalms, for the speaker regularly feels put upon by "an enemy." The identification of the enemy is not obvious, and the identification is not important for our analysis.[33] The enemy may indeed be another (rich? wicked? exploitative?) Israelite. Or it may be an external enemy. Or it may be a suprahuman enemy of some cosmic significance. None of that is specified. What is evident is that the speaker finds himself or herself in a situation of risk, danger, and threat, and has no alternative but to cry out, in an attempt to mobilize God to help.

In an important study of these psalms, Fredrik Lindström has shown that while these psalms reflect great trouble and need, to the point of desperation, there is almost never mention of sin or guilt.[34] That is, the speaker does not entertain the thought that the situation of trouble is to be understood as punishment for sin, and gives no hint of any notion of having sinned. Rather the situation of trouble happens because "an enemy" is on the move, an enemy too powerful for the speaker to resist. And so appeal is made to Yahweh, who is known to be strong enough to resist the enemy and so to save the speaker.

We may see all of these elements in Psalm 7, which we take as representative of the genre. The speaker refers to the threat in a variety of ways: "my pursuers" (v. 1.), "my foe" (v. 4), "the enemy" (v. 5), "my enemies" (v. 6), "the wicked" (v. 9), and "they" (vv. 14–16). The speaker appeals to God to intervene: "save, deliver" (v. 1), "rise up, lift yourself up, awake" (v. 6), and "establish" (v. 9). The speaker, moreover, is clearly innocent:

> O Lord my God, if I have done this,
> if there is wrong in my hands,
> if I have repaid my ally with harm
> or plundered my foe without cause,
> then let the enemy pursue and overtake me,
> trample my life to the ground,
> and lay my soul in dust.
> The Lord judges the peoples;
> judge me, O Lord, according to my righteousness
> and according to the integrity that is in me. (vv. 3–5, 8)

In the theological self-understanding sponsored by the schemes of "sin-punishment" and "deeds-consequences," we might expect the speaker to admit fault, and to seek forgiveness from God. But such a note is completely alien to this prayer and, as Lindstrom has shown, to this entire genre of prayer. This speaker is not a perpetrator, suffering just deserts, but a victim being innocently abused.

The Israelite who lives in and through such a prayer as this lives in a dangerous world. The dangers may be of sickness, or they may be political and military in character. Lindstrom goes further to suggest a more fundamental dualism in the world, in which the power of negation, death, and nihilism takes many forms, but is untamed and is on the loose.[35] In the face of such cosmic negation, the speaker is helpless. Thus Lindström identifies a sweeping cosmic dualism, with a power opposed to Yahweh who is the source of suffering and trouble. In the face of such a threat, only Yahweh is an adequate force to withstand the threat. The power of death advances as it does, not because it is more powerful than Yahweh, but because Yahweh is mistakenly and inexcusably neglectful, inattentive, or absent.

Thus the psalm, the voice of the victim under assault, seeks to get God's attention, to mobilize God to intervene against this ominous threat. When God is actively mobilized, death is sure to be defeated. Given such a way of understanding reality, this tri-part drama suggests that sin is a power, which takes the forms of death, chaos, illness, disorder, and oppression. Sin is not an act taken by the speaker that evokes the power of the Nihil, as though an act per se would evoke all the powers of nihilism. No, rather the power of Nihil is always on the alert to find a place where the power of God is inattentive. When God is absent or inattentive and Nihil advances, the speaker is the hapless victim of such an opening taken by the power of Nihil. The lament psalms insist upon the legitimate claims of the wounded, and are remote from any simplistic moral reductionism that blames the victim. The speaker has a perfect right to expect

God to act in saving ways, and seeks in shrill, demanding speech to move God to act. For if God can be summoned to act, the victim will be freed from the threat of the perpetrator.

V

The ways in which the Old Testament moves against simplistic and absolutizing ethical schemes inevitably culminate in the great poem of Job, which gathers together many of the themes we have already considered. The poem of Job, as Westermann has shown, is the extreme articulation of lament in ancient Israel, in which the weak and wounded find voice against their suffering. The astonishing appearance of the satan in Job 1-2 seems to be an extreme development of the serpent motif.[36] And Gutiérrez's reflection on Job suggests that the themes of injustice and oppression, so central in the Exodus narrative, are again operative here.[37]

The poem of Job features the sufferer Job. "Satan" means "adversary." He is an adversary of the "sin-punishment" scheme. And insofar as God is a function of that system, he is an adversary of God, and will take God to court. Job, the sufferer, protests what appears to him to be his senseless, unjustified suffering. He is willing to suffer, if his suffering is a consequence of his sin, for then it makes moral sense. But he is not told what his sin might be, and never in the poem is there a hint that Job has sinned.

Job's counterpart in the drama are Job's "three friends," who are advocates of the ancient moral schemes to which we have referred. They may be variously understood as proponents of Deuteronomic theology (cf. Deut 30:15–20) or of the domesticated sapiential system of the Book of Proverbs (cf. Prov 8:32–36). Either way, the friends represent the conviction that the world is one of moral coherence and symmetry, and whoever is a victim of suffering (as Job is), is surely a perpetrator of a sin adequate for the punishment inflicted.

The defense of the ethical system on the part of the friends is quite theoretical and untroubled by Job's actual suffering. Their counsel strikes one as condescending and unfeeling:

> Think now, who that was innocent ever perished?
> Or where were the upright cut off? (4:7)
> As for me, I would seek God,
> and to God I would commit my cause. (5:8)
> How happy is the one whom God reproves;
> therefore do not despise the discipline of the Almighty. (5:17)
> If you will seek God
> and make supplication to the Almighty,
> if you are pure and upright,
> surely then he will rouse himself for you
> and restore to you your rightful place. (8:5–6)

The friends believe in and advocate a morally reliable world. The practical consequence of their view is that Job must indeed be guilty of a sin commensurate
with his "punishment."

On his part, the sufferer who finds voice for his hurt is not resistant to
the theory of the friends. Indeed, Job shares their view. He also believes that
suffering is morally situated. But he has no data to relate the theory to his life,
and eventually he begins to doubt and then to reject the theory. He can be sar-
castic to his friends (cf. 12:2, 16:1–5). But his most savage utterances are an
assault upon God, who is absent and silent, and in the end unfair:

> If it is a contest of strength, he is the strong one!
> If it is a matter of justice, who can summon him?
> Though I am innocent, my own mouth would condemn me;
> though I am blameless, he would prove me perverse.
> I am blameless; I do not know myself;
> I loathe my life.
> It is all one; therefore I say,
> He destroys both the blameless and the wicked. (9:19–22)

Job's conclusion is that God is morally indifferent and unreliable, and therefore the entire theory of a moral order to reality, advocated by his friends, is
absurd. Job refuses to admit, without evidence, that he is a sinner justly suffering. Job breaks the comfortable, reassuring linkage of "deeds-consequences."
His great climactic utterance in 31:35–37 is almost Promethean in its defiance
and self-assertion:

> Oh, that I had one to hear me!
> (Here is my signature! Let the Almighty answer me!)
> Oh, that I had the indictment
> written by my adversary!
> Surely I would carry it on my shoulder;
> I would bind it on me like a crown;
> I would give him an account of all my steps;
> Like a prince I would approach him.

This is, so far as he or we or anyone knows, an innocent man whose suffering
makes no sense, and will not be contained in either Deuteronomic or sapiential explanations.

The poem will not leave us there. God must answer. God's answer, however, completely disregards the point of Job's rage, and the domesticated reme-
dies of Job's friends. God's response in the whirlwind is a poem of praise to
God's power (chapters 38–41). Well, of course. God's power has never been in
question (cf. 9:19). Job can sing a marvelous hymn of praise to God's enormous
power (9:4–12) which matches the exuberant doxology of Eliphaz (5:9–16).
But all of that misses the point of the dispute that Job has initiated. Unless of

course the speech of Yahweh resolves the dispute! The poem of Job seems to abandon the idea of moral coherence, which means that Job and his friends, and all of the readers of the poem are left in a world where the category of "sin" is largely dismissed, or in any case moved away from the center of the theological discussion. Thus the poem of Job advances beyond what we have found elsewhere in the Old Testament. In the account of Pharaoh in the Exodus narrative, the serpent in the creation narrative, and the "enemies" in the psalms of complaint, "sin" has to some extent been assigned to someone other than the sufferer. In these cases, the sufferer is the victim of someone else's affront. Here, however, there is no other agent, for not even God is so located, even though Job entertains the notion. Rather the categories of sin and guilt simply evaporate in the face of God's own statement. Job may be a victim. But he is not noticeably a victim of wrongdoing, but only the victim of power that is morally unbridled.

The resolution of the poem of Job, after such a daring foray, is perhaps a bit anemic. We mention two parts of the conclusion. First, Job's "concession speech" is in 42:6. But the statement of Job is notoriously problematic, perhaps made deliberately so by the artist.[38] One cannot determine if Job's final words constitute a genuine repentance and submission, or if they are a mocking way of conceding God's power, without conceding anything of God's right. In any case, they are his final words.

In response, in the prose conclusion, Job receives this verdict from Yahweh:

> my servant Job shall pray for you, for I will accept his prayer not to deal with you according to your folly; for you have not spoken of me what is right, as my servant Job has done. (42:8)

Job, not his friends, has his theological discourse approved by God. Indeed, Job's friends are rebuked by God for engaging in theological "folly." Are the friends rebuked for holding to a moral scheme that God here rejects? It would seem so. In any case, Job is celebrated, seemingly for having pressed his own case against God, for having refused to accept his victimization as morally legitimate, and for having fought through to a new kind of freedom in the face of God. This conclusion removes the faith of Israel as far away as it can be, from the tight moral schemes of the primary ethical systems of the Old Testament.

VI

The four strategies of deabsolutizing and undermining that I have reviewed constitute a formidable challenge to the common propensity to reduce the Old Testament to a system of "sin and punishment." After this review, we may refer to one other facet of Old Testament faith that must be mentioned with reference to our subject, but that must not be mentioned too soon. It is this. The God of the Old Testament is

merciful and gracious,
slow to anger and abounding in steadfast love.
He will not always accuse,
Nor will he keep his anger forever.
He does not deal with us according to our sins,
nor repay us according to our iniquities.
For as the heavens are high above the earth,
so great is his steadfast love toward those who fear him.
as far as the east is from the west,
so far he removes our transgressions from us.
As father has compassion for his children,
so the Lord has compassion for those who fear him.
For he knows how we were made;
He remembers that we are dust. (Ps 103:8–14)

The God of the Old Testament is gracious and capable of forgiveness. And therefore, the vicious cycles of sin, insofar as they are acts of rebellion that generate yet more acts of rebellion, can indeed be broken.

This facet of the character of God in the Old Testament is not so well recognized, especially given Christian stereotypes and caricatures of the Old Testament. Nonetheless, Israel has known, since the time of Moses, that the God of Sinai, the one who gives commands and prescribes sanctions, is a God "merciful and gracious" (Ex 34:6). This marking of God, however, was not plain on the face of it, nor easily and readily given in the midst of harsh sanctions.

Like everything theological in the Old Testament, like everything pertaining to this God, this marking of God had to be contested and struggled for. The context for this disclosure of God in Ex 34:6 is fought through in the aftermath of Ex 32, the narrative of the Golden Calf, and Aaron's savage disregard of Yahweh. Yahweh in great anger is prepared to consume Aaron and his ilk (Ex 32:10), for Yahweh responds in anger when Yahweh's own prerogatives are violated. In the end, there was indeed a great plague upon disobedient Israel (Ex 32:35). In this narrative, we are in the world of retribution, of "sin and punishment," and God will not be mocked.

But there is more to the story. Moses intercedes to Yahweh on behalf of Israel (Ex 32:11–13). Moses asks God to "turn" and to "change your mind." And Yahweh does! It is as though in this crisis, Yahweh must fight through to a new way of being toward Israel. Thus is the midst of enormous anger, at the behest of Moses, Yahweh finally asserts about Yahweh's own self:

The Lord, the Lord,
a God merciful and gracious,
slow to anger,
and abounding in steadfast love and faithfulness,
keeping steadfast love for the thousandth generation,
forgiving iniquity and transgression and sin. . . . (Ex 34:6–7a)

It is in the very character of Yahweh to forgive.

> There is still available to God, to be sure, a destructive alternative:
> yet by means clearing the guilty,
> but visiting the iniquity of the parents
> upon the children
> and the children's children,
> to the third and the fourth generation. (Ex 34:7b)

Which way the future of Israel turns out, in a crisis situation, depends upon Moses, and Moses' daring intervention (Ex 34:8–9). Only in response to the intervention of Moses, comes God's resolve to begin again with Israel (Ex 34:10). We should not miss in this passage the remarkable turn in Yahweh's character. What I prefer to accent, however, is the role of Moses. It is Moses, the quintessential person of God, who must risk God's holiness and summon God to a better way, even though God does not easily turn away from wounding affront.[39] Moses, at great risk to himself, summons God to God's best self. And God, in that moment of Mosaic urging, is able and willing to move to a new beginning. Vicious cycles are broken, because of daring human intervention on the part of those who are perpetrators/victims of destructive behavior.

Now it may be, that after the more daring renderings of the Exodus narrative, the creation story, the lament Psalms, and the poem of Job, focus upon the compassion of God concedes too much to more conventional notions of sin and punishment. The compassion of God, however, is the ultimate deabsolutizing of the "sin-punishment," "deeds-consequences" structures of Israel's faith. The assertion that God does not "keep his anger forever" means that these tight moral calculations are not of ultimate seriousness in the faith of ancient Israel. They are of interest, but only of penultimate interest, and may therefore not be treated in schemes of social interaction as of ultimate importance.

There is no doubt that, theologically, sin is important. Indeed, in terms of social relations, a system of sanctions is an inevitable requirement for the maintenance of social viability. But such modes of discipline are of quite limited interest to this God. To subsume too much of life in such systems is to misconstrue both the character of God and the reality of lived human life. God is not a function of moral sanctions. Well beyond such sanctions, God is the powerful one who resists the power of Nihil. This God is the one who in quite daily ways, "knows how we are made." And this knowledge tends to evoke in God a kind of parental compassion.

This larger sphere of God's goodness is an invitation for a new way with God:

> If you, O Lord, should mark iniquities,
> Lord, who could stand?
> But there is forgiveness with you,
> so that you may be revered. (Ps 130:3–4)

It is also a warning against our excessive valuing of "sin-punishment," "deeds-consequences." Thus Jonah the prophet, for example, knows well that there is much of God beyond a tight system of sanctions. That "beyond" of God greatly upsets Jonah. In the narrative of Jonah, the people of Nineveh had repented, and so had not been punished, as Jonah had hoped. Jonah in a spasm of righteous indignation, assaults God for being gracious: "Is not this what I said while I was still in my own country? That is why I fled to Tarshish at the beginning; for I knew that you are a gracious God and merciful, slow to anger, and abounding in steadfast love, and ready to relent from punishing" (Jon 4:2).[40] There is much of God beyond social control. And in a world such as ours, marked by barbarianism and brutality, driven by fear and by self-loathing, we do well to host that of God that refuses to be held in our explanatory codes. In response to the behavior of Nineveh, Jonah was very angry. But God was not!

NOTES

1. It is evident that the commandments in Israel were nonnegotiable. It is equally evident that they were, in the interpretive process of Israel, endlessly negotiated. See Walter Brueggemann, *Finally Comes the Poet: Daring Speech for Proclamation* (Minneapolis: Fortress Press, 1989) chap. 4; and *Interpretation and Obedience: From Faithful Reading to Faithful Living* (Minneapolis: Fortress Press, 1991) 145–58.

2. Ex 20:18–21 appears to be an anticipation or an authorization for the "office" of Moses. See Hans-Joachim Kraus, *Die prophetische Verkündigung des Rechts in Israel* (TS 51; Zollikon: Evangelischer Verlag, 1957); and James Muilenburg, "The Office of the Prophet in Ancient Israel," in *The Bible in Modern Scholarship*, ed. by J. Philip Hyatt (Nashville: Abingdon Press, 1965) 74–97.

3. On authority in wisdom teaching generally and in Proverbs in particular, see *The Sage in Israel and the Ancient Near East*, ed. by John G. Gammie and Leo G. Perdue (Winona Lake, Ind.: Eisenbrauns, 1990).

4. Klaus Koch, "Is There a Doctrine of Retribution in the Old Testament?" in *Theodicy in the Old Testament*, ed. by James L. Crenshaw (Philadelphia: Fortress Press, 1983) 57–87.

5. The classic statement is that of Walther Zimmerli, "The Place and Limit of Wisdom in the Framework of the Old Testament Theology," *Scottish Journal of Theology* 17 (1964) 148: "Wisdom thinks resolutely within the framework of a theology of creation." For a fuller exposition of the linkage between creation and wisdom, see Hans Heinrich Schmid, *Gerechtigkeit als Weltordnung: Hintergrund und Geschichte des Alttestamentlichen Gerechtigkeitsbegriffes* (Beiträge zur Historischen Theologie 40; Tübingen, Germany: J. C. B. Mohr (Paul Siebeck, 1968).

6. The most likely proposals for the location of wisdom teaching are the family or clan, the school, or the royal court. It now seems evident that there is not sufficient evidence to establish with certainty any of these possible locations, just as there is enough suggestive evidence for each, so that each remains a live option. For a discussion of the

several possible contexts for wisdom instruction and reflection, which are not mutually exclusive, see R. N. Whybray, "The Sage in the Israelite Royal Court" (133–39), Carol R. Fontaine, "The Sage in Family and Tribe" (155–64), and André Lemaire, "The Sage in School and Temple" (165–81), in *Sage in Israel and the Ancient Near East*, ed. by Perdue and Gammi.

7. It is commonly agreed that it is only in the text of Ben Sirach, dated about 180 B.C.E., that wisdom and torah claims converge and are explicitly identified with each other.

8. Erhard Gerstenberger, *Wesen und Herkunft des 'apodiktischen Rechts'* (WMANT 20; Neukirchen-Vluyn: Neukirchener Verlag, 1965).

9. Ibid., 110–117.

10. See my exposition of these matters in *Exodus, New Interpreter's Bible I* (Nashville: Abingdon Press, 1994). See also Brueggemann, "The Exodus Narrative as Israel's Articulation of Faith Development," in *Hope Within History* (Atlanta: John Knox Press, 1987) 7–26.

11. It is important that the material be understood as liturgical, without making historical claims. On the liturgical aspects of the text, see Johannes Pedersen, *Israel: Its Life and Culture III–IV* (Copenhagen: Branner, 1940) 728–737.

12. On Pharaoh and the power of chaos, see Terence E. Fretheim, "The Plagues as Ecological Signs of Historical Disaster," *Journal of Biblical Literature* 110 (1991) 285–296.

13. On the role of the prophet in such "class conflict," Micah may be cited as an exemplary voice. On Micah in this context, see Hans Walter Wolff, "Micah the Moreshite—The Prophet and His Background," in *Israelite Wisdom: Theological and Literary Essays in Honor of Samuel Terrien*, ed. by John G. Gammie et al. (Missoula, Mont.: Scholars Press, 1978) 77–84; and George V. Pixley, "Micah—A Revolutionary," in *The Bible and the Politics of Exegesis: Essays in Honor of Norman K. Gottwald on His Sixty-Fifth Birthday*, ed. by David Jobling et al. (Cleveland: Pilgrim Press, 1991) 53–60.

14. Robert R. Wilson, *Prophecy and Society in Ancient Israel* (Philadelphia: Fortress Press, 1980).

15. It should be noted that the use of the term *pardon* and much of the vocabulary of Western theology has picked up on the juridical cast of much of the Old Testament. While the usages of the Old Testament are quite varied, much of Western theology has been reduced to this single model, which has made it enormously heavy-handed in the production of guilt. For a recent, thoughtful exposition in this theological tradition, see Cornelius Plantenga Jr., "Locked in Sin: The Theology of Corruption," in *Christian Century* (21–28 December 1994) 1218–1222.

16. I leave aside the question of whether Augustine and Luther, in their heavy accent on sin and guilt, misread Paul. See Krister Stendahl, "Paul and the Introspective Conscience of the West," in *Paul Among Christians and Jews and Other Essays* (Philadelphia: Fortress Press, 1977).

17. *John Milton*, ed. by Stephen Orgel and Jonathan Goldberg (New York: Oxford University Press, 1991) 356.

18. Ibid., 356–357.

19. Milton, *Christian Doctrine*, 382–383, as quoted by Robert Crosman, *Reading Paradise Lost* (Bloomington: Indiana University Press, 1980) 25.

20. Arthur Sewell, *A Study of Milton's Christian Doctrine* (London: Oxford University Press, 1939) 80.

21. Crosman, *Reading Paradise Lost*, 25.

22. Paul Ricoeur, *The Symbolism of Evil* (Boston: Beacon, 1967) 252–260.

23. Ibid., 255.

24. Ibid., 257.

25. Ibid.

26. Ibid., 258.

27. Ibid., 259.

28. Ricoeur, in ibid. uses the term *victim*.

29. John Steinbeck, *Five Novels* (New York: Octopus Books, 1988) in *East of Eden*, 685–691 and passim plays with the imagery of sin "crouching" in threat.

30. Erhard Gerstenberger, *Der bittende Mensch: Bittritual und Klagelied des Einzelnen im Alten Testament* (WMANT 51; Neukirchen-Vluyn: Neukirchener Verlag, 1980) has shown how it is that Israel's complaint and protest are in fact acts of hope.

31. Claus Westermann, "Struktur und Geschichte der Klage im Alten Testament," in *Forschung am alten Testament* (ThB 24; München: Chr. Kaiser Verlag, 1964) 269–272.

32. On the drama of complaint as having three members, see my discussion of Ps 9–10 in Walter Brueggemann, "Psalms 9–10: A Counter to Conventional Social Reality," in *The Bible and the Politics of Exegesis*, 3–15.

33. For a complete review of the problem, see Stephen Croft, *The Identity of the Individual in the Psalms* (JSOT Supp. 44; Sheffield, England: Sheffield Academic Press, 1987).

34. Fredrik Lindström, *Suffering and Sin: Interpretation of Illness in the Individual Complaint Psalms* (Coniectanea Biblica Old Testament 37; Stockholm: Almquist and Wiksell, 1994).

35. On the untamed power of the Nihil, see Lindström, *God and the Origin of Evil: A Contextual Analysis of Alleged Monistic Evidence in the Old Testament* (Coniectanea Biblica 21 (Lund, Sweden: Gleerup, 1983); Karl Barth, "God and Nothingness," in *Church Dogmatics III* (Edinburgh: T. and T. Clark, 1960) 289–368; and Jon D. Levenson, *Creation and the Persistence of Evil* (San Francisco: Harper and Row, 1988).

36. Ricoeur, *Symbolism of Evil*, 259, suggests that the serpent in Gen 3 "represents the first landmark along the road of the Satanic theme which, in the Persian epoch, permitted the inclusion of a near-dualism in the faith of Israel."

37. Gustavo Gutiérrez, *On Job: God-Talk and the Suffering of the Innocent*, trans. Matthew J. O'Connell (Maryknoll: Orbis Books, 1987).

38. On the interpretive possibilities in Job 42:6, in addition to the commentaries, see Jack Miles, *God: A Biography* (New York: Knopf, 1995) 425–430.

39. A like role is played by Abraham in the encounter of Gen 18:22–33, though in that narrative the mood does not seem as dangerous and frighted as is the narrative of Ex 32, in which Moses makes an intercession on behalf of Israel.

40. On the subtlety of this text and especially the response of Jonah, see Phyllis Trible, *Rhetorical Criticism: Context, Method, and the Book of Jonah* (Minneapolis: Fortress Press, 1994) 199–204.

CHAPTER TWO

THE BIBLE AND HAN

Andrew Sung Park

INTRODUCTION

The Bible is full of stories of suffering people. Jesus came into the world to set free the wronged from their grief and burden and to forgive the sins of wrongdoers. Between the wronged and wrongdoers, Jesus was primarily concerned about the wronged: "Those who are well have no need of a physician, but those who are sick; I have come to call not the righteous but sinners" (Mk 2:17). Accordingly, the major subject of the Bible was to care for the afflicted, particularly the unjustly oppressed. Thus, it is necessary for Christians to read the Bible chiefly from the viewpoint of the downtrodden.

Traditional Christian theologies, however, have mostly read it from the side of sinners (oppressors), emphasizing Jesus' redemptive work for them. Whenever the powerful exercise control over the interpretation of the Bible, their interpretation is usually bound to be unilateral for them.

In the Hebrew Bible, we find the common theology that legitimates the structure of the society on the one hand and strives to be free of the same theology on the other.[1] In general, the Hebrew Bible can be interpreted either for the dominant or for the downtrodden.

Some books of the Hebrew Bible, however, were definitely written to describe the God who cared for those who experienced oppression, captivity, and other kinds of affliction. When scriptures were used as a tool to oppress the powerless and the poor, which breached Israel's covenant with God, certain prophets arose and proclaimed God's message, advocating the rights of the oppressed against such abuses of power.

In the New Testament, Jesus protested against the oppressive interpretation of the Hebrew Bible from the viewpoint of religious elites, and gave a new

45

interpretation for the powerless, which liberates them from a tyrannical interpretation of the law and ordinances.

As time went by, the powerful came to have control over the interpretation of the Bible, and it was interpreted from their perspective and was used to develop theologies to favor them. Since Constantine the Great converted himself to the "superstitious power" of Christianity, the Bible has been co-opted by the powerful, and Christianity has been the religion of labarum for conquerors.[2]

Since the powerful controlled Christianity and its Bible, their theology has focused on the issue of sin and its forgiveness, overlooking the deep pain of the sinned-against. Whenever the Bible was in the hands of religious leaders and political rulers, its hermeneutic was in danger of being distorted.

We are living in a world of enormous division between rich and poor countries. The United States is the most powerful nation on earth. Its wealth and military strength surpasses that of all mighty nations in history. When these wealthy and well-to-do people interpret the Bible, they tend to comprehend it from their experience.

As the United States and the West control biblical scholarship and theology, their interpretation and theology can easily be that of conquerors.

This chapter is written from the perspective of the sinned-against by focusing on their wounded state of mind, which is called han in Asia. First, I will explain the meaning of han and then read selected biblical accounts from its perspective. I believe that by doing this, new avenues to appropriate interpretations of the Scriptures and theology can be opened to the suffering world. Its starting point is a hermeneutics of the wounded on the traditional interpretations of the Bible. Its premise is that the Bible deals with the reality of the other side of sin, beyond the doctrine of sin.

THE DEFINITION OF HAN

What is han? Han is an intricate concept to define. Let me now explain the notion of han with a poem. The following portrays the han of women under harsh patriarchy:

Gold Chain, Silver Chain

Anonymous

A sigh at midnight
to whom is it addressed?
To have been born a woman
is it sinful to sigh?
No, no more please.
Can it be sinful to be born?
Let's gather all the sighs
and cry out loud.

Dark eyes of the passing girl
are covered with clouds
Today's clouds, rain clouds
snow clouds, black clouds
No, no more please.
Today's clouds can't be lifted,
    just sitting there
Let's take them away
with two arms out-stretched.

In the morning wind, cold wind
a crying grandmother passes by
All the tears she has shed in life
    white tears and black tears.
    No, no more please.
    She wept all her life
    She can't cry any more
Wipe the tears and raise her head.

A baby girl plays in the flower garden.
    Who is running after you?
Binding chains of thousands of years
    gold chains, silver chains
    No, no more please.
    I can only live breaking
    chains of thousands of years
Be courageous, be courageous.[3]

This poem reminds me of a woman whose mother suffered spousal abuse. One night the father battered the poor mother so badly that she escaped to her daughter's house. At night, the daughter could hear her mother's tears through the wall that separated their rooms. This poem represents many mothers' tears and fears. The chains of thousands of years have bound women's souls and have precipitated their moaning. The chains, silver or gold, are the shackles, the tears of thousands of women for thousands of years." It is called "han," the painful scar of the chains impressed against women's necks.

The experience of the powerless, the marginalized, and the voiceless in the world can be summed up as han. Since women have experienced the long suffering of dehumanization, their han is deeper than men's. In Korea, hundreds of years of Confucian oppression have created the sociobiography of women's han.

Han is the suffering of the innocent who are caught in the wicked situation of helplessness. It is the void of the soul that cannot be filled with any superficial patch. This void is the abysmal darkness of wounded human beings.

In other words, han is a physical, mental, and spiritual repercussion to a terrible injustice done to a person, eliciting a deep ache, a wrenching of all the organs, an intense internalized or externalized rage, a vengeful obsession, and the sense of helplessness and hopelessness.

Han can be resolved destructively or constructively. In its destructive resolution, a person of han seeks to avenge one's enemy. In its constructive resolution, the person of han can use it as the source of transforming the root-causes of han.

Where sin is committed, han arises as its corollary. The victims of sin develop han, a deep agonizing pain. They bear excruciating agony and humiliation under oppression, exploitation, abuse, mistreatment, and violation. If their situations do not allow them to change such conditions, they further deepen their han.

HAN IN THE HEBREW BIBLE

Cain and Abel (Gen 4:1–16). From the beginning, han is described in the Hebrew Bible. The story of Cain and Abel is the story of han. The two brothers gave offerings to God. Cain's offering was rejected, while Abel's was accepted. The text is silent on the purposes of their offerings and on the reason for the rejection and acceptance. The response of God, however, generated Cain's anger. Out of his deep jealousy and frustration, Cain struck hard his own brother. Being beaten by Cain, Abel's body responded with convulsion and ceased to move. Cain watched this horrible scene of his brother's last moment. That was the first killing in the Bible.

God was silent at the moment Abel was murdered. God did not intervene! That is the core of han. How can the God of justice be absent in the event of such appalling injustice? Rather, God set a mark on Cain to protect him. A murderer walked out free. The mercy of God conflicts with the justice of God.[4] Anachronistically speaking, God's mercy interrupts criminal justice, social values, and the biblical account *(lex Talionis)*.

Cain created a civilization, but Abel did not. The murderer became the main character of history. This absurd fact of life is the han of the victim's world. The murdered cannot speak! Only Abel's blood cried out to God from the ground (Gen 4:10). The crying-out blood is the voice of han.

Uriah and David (2 Sam 11). While Israel was battling with the Ammonites, David stayed in Jerusalem. From the roof of his house, he saw a woman bathing and had lust for her. He called her and lay with her. When she became pregnant, he recalled the woman's husband, Uriah, from the battle to cover up his sin.

Uriah returned, but refused to go to his own house. Even when David asked him to go to his own house, his loyalty and integrity would not allow him to accept the suggestion and so he slept at the door of the king's house. Having failed in his first plan, David plotted to have him killed. David sent a letter to Joab by the hand of Uriah arranging Uriah's death. Uriah the Hittite was sent to a place of battle where he could not survive. When Uriah was killed along with others, David married Bathsheba.

The faithful, loyal Uriah was betrayed. He lost his wife and his life. No word can express the unfair treatment Uriah received, but han may.

The Aftermath of David's Sin (2 Sam 12:1–18:33). When Nathan reproached David's sin through a parable about a poor and rich herder, David repented of his sin. Nathan said to David that trouble would arise within his house and that the child who is born to him is going to die (vv. 11–14). As Nathan had foretold, the child between David and Uriah's wife died of sickness.

In these plots, we can see that David's sin was forgiven, but he had to pay the price of his sin. First, his price was the death of his son. We might interpret this event as a sin-and-punishment scheme, but David repented his sin and was forgiven. God spared David's life but punished him through the death of his son. This event cannot be explained with a simple theology of retribution. This unresolved dimension of the consequence of sin is han.

Further tragedies struck David's house. David's oldest son Amnon fell in love with his half sister Tamar. Using a trick, Amnon raped Tamar, immediately rejected her, and drove out the crying Tamar from his house. Her brother Absalom comforted her and let her stay at his house. When David heard of this evil, he was angry but did nothing about it because Amnon was his firstborn and he loved him. Such an action of David fostered Absalom's han.

Because of her father's sin, Tamar got the most shameful punishment through her brother (12:10–14). She was violated, was hated, and was expelled from Amnon's house. Worse of all, she was ignored by her own father when the terrible violation struck her.[5] The absence of her father was the real han when she needed him most. Her mother, Maacah, was absent, too. Tamar became a desolate woman, "a woman of sorrows and acquainted with grief."[6] Her father and her mother were silent and absent when she was ravaged. Her unspeakable woundedness cannot be described by any other term but *han*.

Her han was also transmitted to her brother Absalom. For a full two years, he nursed his han against his brother Amnon: "Absalom spoke to Amnon neither good nor bad" (13:22).[7] His han exploded on Amnon and he avenged his sister by killing him. The negative explosion of han seeks to take the life of a han-causing person. The incestuous rape was avenged through fratricide. Here han reproduced the sin of killing.

Third, Absalom revolted against David and almost toppled his dominion. Absalom raped his father's concubines, as Amnon disgraced Tamar. Because of his sin of adultery and murder, David underwent a loss of face by Absalom's rapes, the shameful flight to Transjordan, and Absalom's death. Here the han and sin of the father and the son intersected, mutually reinforced, and produced the series of tragic events, costing so many innocent lives. Caused by David's sin, the vortex of all these tragedies is Tamar's han, which never ceased but increased over the death of her brother.

David's repentance of sin was insufficient to resolve han and the han took its course, demanding its price. The history of Israel was more than the judgment of sin; it included the increment of the punishment of sin in connection with undying han. The simple law of "eye for eye, tooth for tooth" did not work here. Although sin is forgiven, han is not necessarily resolved. In its own terms, han spins entangling with sin, crushing both offenders and victims.

Job. The Book of Job is written to contradict the retributive or the Deuteronomistic theology that holds that suffering is God's punishment for sin. Job undergoes the agony of the bottomless pit that any human being could hardly bear. Worse, his three friends come to visit him and urge him to reveal and repent of his sin. Their theology represents the orthodox theology. Eliphaz accuses Job of culpability. Job rejects the charge and begs for compassion. Bildad indicts him of hypocrisy. Job insists that he has committed no sin and that God is unfair to destroy the righteous and the wicked (9:21–22). Zophar rebukes Job as a liar and a hypocrite. Job rejects his rebuke as banality. Lastly, Elihu appears and pours out his anger at Job for his self-justification. His argument is that God is just and uses suffering as a medium to refine humans, and Job's case was that his iniquity caused his affliction (36:21).[8]

At the end, God speaks to Job out of the whirlwind. God makes two speeches and Job replies to them.[9] God's first speech (38:1–40:2) is inappropriate to Job's question, which is "Why does he suffer such awful tragedies?" God answers him by inquiring whether he comprehends the divine, mysterious power of creation, of which Job's suffering is part. Job replies with silence and never confesses his sin: "See, I am of small account; what shall I answer you? I lay my hand on my mouth. I have spoken once, and I will not answer; twice, but will proceed no further" (40:4–5). He refuses to talk. God's answer was irrelevant to his suffering. His silence is his defiance to such a nonsensical "God-talk," indicating his han.

It is strange that God does not reveal the fact that Job's suffering was just a test initiated by Satan with God's own consent. Even God's second answer discloses none of this fact. This is the han of many suffering victims. They do not know why God does not make known God's hidden code.

God's second speech (40:6–41:34) starts with the questions, "Will you even put me in the wrong? Will you condemn me that you may be justified?" (v. 8). What God is saying in verse 8 is that justice depends on Godself. William Occam (ca. 1280–1349) recapitulates this theology: justice is not what we think of as right but is whatever God does. For Gustavo Gutiérrez, in the beginning Job views God's justice as the retribution of sin. However, in the end Job understands God's justice as God's freedom. Gutiérrez contends that divine justice is divine gratuitousness. To him, the Book of Job centers on the theme of divine *justice* and divine *gratuitousness*.[10] In the rest of the second speech, God stresses the full divine responsibilities, including the creation of the Behemoth (chaos) and the Leviathan (evil).

In his second reply, Job acknowledges divine all-powerfulness and confesses his ignorance. Job obtains no satisfactory explanation for his predicament, yet is satisfied with seeing God personally and he ironically repents of his sin: "Therefore I have uttered what I did not understand, things too wonderful for me, which I did not know. 'Hear, and I will speak; I will question you, and you declare to me.' I had heard of you by the hearing of the ear, but now my eye sees you; therefore I despise myself, and repent in dust and ashes" (42:3b–6). Although Job says that he repents, we do not know of what sin he can repent. The fact that a victim should repent of his or her own wound is han. Here the term *repentance* may not be the best word to apply to Job. He cannot repent of his ignorance, but can only regret it.

Sin usually causes han. Han in turn can regenerate han and sin. Job commits no sin, but agonizes with han. The author of Job tells us that God allows Satan to test Job. Here, a new type of han is introduced. Job's suffering derives from Satan's test. The test for Job was not to refine him, nor to punish him . . . but to confirm Job's voluntary worship of God despite his adversities.

If God did not allow Satan to test Job, Satan's claim would be supported: "Job praises and worships God because it is beneficial." This saying of Satan's is a great warning to the theology of glory, which underpins the notion that we worship God for our own benefits. Here we see the author of Job strongly challenge Protestant theology: "This is to know Christ, to know his benefits" (Melanchthon). Protestant theology is apt to mislead people to misinterpret the doctrine of faith. A distorted Protestant theology asserts that we believe in God because God saves us. The real meaning of the doctrine of justification is whether God saves us or not, we believe in God: "Though he slay me, yet will I trust in him" (13:15, KJV).[11] Our trust or belief is not a bargaining chip with God. Our faith itself is an end, not a means to an end. By faith we wait for the God who never seems to come.

Furthermore, the Book of Job can correct the preoccupation of traditional theologies with the justification or salvation of the sinner (oppressor). Job shifts our focus from a sinner's salvation to the liberation and healing of the han-ridden. Emphasizing the forgiveness of wrongdoers and their justification, traditional theologies have neglected the salvation or wholeness of suffering Jobs.

Theology under God's Wrath. In the end of this epic, God expressed God's anger to Job's three friends, for they had a unilateral theology of retribution with which they afflicted Job. God spoke to Eliphaz: "My wrath is kindled against you and against your two friends; for you have not spoken of me what is right, as my servant Job has" (42:7b). As judgment, God demanded burnt offerings and their apology to Job. They forced an innocent victim to repent of his sin and be saved. Job needed comfort and healing of the han of great tragedies, but they demanded his honest confession of sin.

In pulpits we have preached the one-sided theology of the sin-repentance mode for everyone, including the sinned-against and the wounded: "Repent of your sin and be saved." Toward victims, we have done wrong. The God of Job is angry at this simplistic sin-repentance formula the church has applied to the victims of sin, overlooking their han. It is overdue for us to provide a sensible theology of healing for the victims of sin and tragedy. Our present one-dimensional theology is under God's wrath. Theologians owe burnt offerings to God and our apology to the victims.

Han and Evil. Job's han arises without anyone's sin and the source of han is ambiguous. Here han independent of sin is presented. It is the han of uncertain causality.

There are two types of han: the han caused by sin and the han caused by evil. Job is not a victim of sin, but a victim of han caused by evil.

Evil is not an absolute concept but a relative one. Evil might be interpreted as the privation of good (Plotinus, Augustine, and Thomas Aquinas) or as the fullness of good (Lao Tzu). A definition of evil can be the cosmic element that gives rise to sin and han. Some theologians believe that sin produces evil.[12] No sin, however, involves the evil of Job's suffering. Rather, evil involves the han that Job experiences. Evil in absence of sin is han; han in absence of sin is evil. Sin causes han and evil. Evil can produce han and sin, and han can regenerate evil and sin.

God's Absence and Han. Job's han is God's absence in his suffering. His questions, pain, and agony center on the silence of God in the midst of his suffering and his friends' accusations. His han is caused by Deus Absconditus, the "God of absence." God was unreachable and inaccessible in the time of his trial and suffering. This is the reason why Elie Wiesel defies God's injustice and Richard Rubenstein declares the death of a traditional God.[13] We see this in Jesus: "My God, my God, why have you forsaken me?" a strong protest against God's absence in the midst of the suffering and death of the innocent.

The theophany, however, makes Job realize the fact that God never leaves him alone. God appears in the whirlwind and answers his question through talk. Job's piecing question, however, is more fully answered in the New Testament. The New Testament theophany takes place at the crucifixion. The answer of the cross is that God is not only present in a victim's suffering, but also is fully involved in the suffering, crying out as a victim. Thus, in both the Old Testament and the New Testament, God's appearance resolves the han of victims without solving it.

But, Job's han is not completely resolved. The deaths of his children, the servants, and his own suffering remain painful in his memory. All the potential of his children and the rest were lost forever. These factors elicit his unresolvable han in spite of God's appearance. Each year, forty million of the desperately poor die of hunger, hunger-related diseases, and contaminated drinking water.[14] Their han can never be resolved. Jesus' outcry on the cross is a way of replying to Job's protest. Job's question is, however, repeated over and over again in the soul of the suffering.

HAN IN THE NEW TESTAMENT

Jesus, a carpenter's son, was one of the common people. He interpreted the Hebrew Bible from a commoner's perspective. To locate han in the New Testament, it is necessary for us to walk with Jesus in Palestine. The main attention of his service was given to the people of han. He himself was a man of han. Innocent, yet he was condemned, rejected, despised, and crucified by his own people.

In his hometown, Nazareth, Jesus declared the purpose of his mission: to bring good news to the poor, to proclaim release to the captives and recovery of sight to the blind, to let the oppressed go free, and to proclaim the year of Jubilee (Lk 4:18–19). He knew the agony of the downtrodden at that time. There were many people who sat in darkness and in the region and shadow of death (Mt 4:16). Jesus diagnosed his time and people, and came up with the goal of his ministry, which was to release the downtrodden from their bondages.

The Afflicted: The Theme of the New Testament. The primary reason of Jesus' coming into the world was to bring good news to the afflicted and the sinned-against. Jesus said, "Those who are well have no need of a physician, but those who are sick; I have come to call not the righteous but sinners" (Mk 2:17). Here, "sinners" are not all sinners.

There were two types of sinners in Jewish society at that time. One was a publicly recognized criminal who violated civil laws. The other was a person in a lowly and socially unacceptable occupation.[15] We can differentiate the latter type of so-called sinner into two categories. One is the sinner of dishonorable occupation. The other is the sinner of low status such as the sick or the poor. Jesus' followers in general were the disreputable, the uneducated, and the ignorant, whose religious ignorance and moral behavior were problematic to their access to salvation, according to the public view of the time.[16] They were publicans and sinners (Mk 2:16), prostitutes (Mt 21:32), or the sick. They were simply called "sinners" (Mk 2:17 Lk 7:37, 39).

The sinners of the first category were involved in despised occupations. Some examples were herders, tax collectors, and publicans.[17] Others were sinners because of the unclean or ill-smelling nature of their jobs (e.g., butchers, tanners, and coppersmiths). They were alienated and could not partake in worship.[18]

The sinners of the second category were the sick people who could not fulfill the duties of the law. As we have seen in Job, the theology that treated sickness as the consequence of sin was widespread in Judaism (Ps 73, Jn 9, Mk 2:5). Thus, the blind, the lepers, the mentally disturbed, and the hemorrhagic were particularly regarded as either unclean or cursed by God.[19] The sick were not transgressors, but those who were condemned by the religious leaders. Jesus was their friend.

Most poor and powerless people were called "sinners" by the religious leaders because poverty prevented them from observing the Sabbath or the law of purification. The *am ha'arez* were the uneducated and the ignorant, whose lack of religious knowledge and moral practice stood in the way of their entrée to salvation.[20] During the Babylonian exile, the cream of society was taken as captives; the common people that were left behind became heterogeneous. These people were called the "*am ha'arez*," the people of land. From the time of Ezra, the term was used to designate a low class of people who were ignorant of the law. Rabbinic Judaism used the term to refer to the poor and the powerless, who were despised and marginalized.[21]

Jesus came into the world to take their infirmities and to bear their grief (cf. Mt 8:7). He had compassion for the crowds "because they were harassed and helpless" (Mt 9:36). His proclamation was good news for the han-ridden. In Jesus' eyes, the righteous were the actual sinners who had to repent of their sin of self-righteousness, religious persecution, and ostentation. In contrast to the religious leaders and scribes, Jesus invited the han-ridden—the despised, the sick, and the poor—to rest: "Come to me, all you that are weary and are carrying heavy burdens, and I will give you rest" (Mt 11:28). Their burden was double: public contempt and the hopelessness of attaining God's salvation.[22] They were not in fact sinners, but were the sinned-against by the oppressive religious leaders and their legal system.

This implies that these so-called sinners needed solace, healing, and liberation, not repentance. Jesus used all his measures, including miracles, to heal the wounded from their suffering, oppression, and affliction. Contrary to our present theology that is basically engaged with sinners' sin and salvation, Jesus' teaching centered on comforting and healing the wounded and sinned-against.

The Lord's Prayer. Jesus taught this prayer to his followers. There are the two forms of the Lord's Prayer: Matthew's and Luke's. Since Luke's version is shorter and thus may be more likely original, we will focus on it.[23] "Father, hallowed be your name. Your kingdom come. Give us each day our daily bread. And forgive us our sins, for we ourselves forgive everyone indebted to us. And do not bring us to the time of trial" (Lk 11:2–5). In the prayer, petitioners were the han-ridden: the poor, the sinned-against, and the tempted. They were the poor who had to worry about the next day's meals. In regards to whether "daily bread" refers to necessary bread (today's) or bread for the "coming day," the latter is more appropriate because an Aramaic translation of Matthew explicates it that way.[24]

Jesus' audience was largely the hungry, the tired, and the poor. Sometimes, the crowd that followed him could not afford food for three days (Mt 15:32–39). In Luke, the Sermon on the Plain was directed to those whom Jesus cared for: "Blessed are you who are poor, for yours is the kingdom of God. Blessed are you who are hungry now, for you will be filled. Blessed are you who weep now, for you will laugh. But woe to you who are rich, for you have received your consolation. Woe to you who are full now, for you will be hungry" (Lk 6:20–25). Jesus clearly sided with the poor. Understanding their life-situation of poverty, oppression, and misery, Jesus taught this prayer to his followers.

In fact, to the rich, reciting the Lord's Prayer can be awkward. While they have stored surplus food for many days, how can they pray for the next day's meal? Their prayer cannot be answered. The Lord's Prayer is superfluous for the wealthy and only can mean one thing: relinquishing their accumulated wealth to the destitute.

For the affluent, a saving element in the prayer is "Give *us* this day *our* daily bread." By saying "us" and "our" daily bread, the rich can commit themselves to working with the hungry in fighting against hunger and poverty. Until the time when everybody is being fed, they can earnestly press themselves toward it.

It is easy to notice that Jesus taught this prayer to those who were chiefly sinned-against, since the sinned-against were those who could forgive their oppressors' sin. The readiness to forgive was the indispensable condition of all prayers in Jesus' teaching.[25] For the forgiving of the injustice of the oppressors precedes the forgiveness of God for the oppressed. Jesus' other teachings on prayer also focused on victims (Mt 5:44 Lk 6:28). Had Jesus been concerned about the oppressors, he would have said in the prayer that you must ask the forgiveness of others (your victims) prior to asking God's forgiveness.[26]

Jesus further taught his followers to ask not to be brought to the time of trial. The term *trial* is from the Greek *peirasmos* (temptation).[27] In the first century, temptations and trials included apostasy caused by the hardship of discipleship. We should note that Jesus did not instruct his audience to avoid sins, but temptations. The oppressors also face temptations, but in this context, the oppressed stand before trials and temptation. In general, sin is of tempters, whereas trials are of the tempted. Jesus addresses this ("Lead us not into temptation") to protect the harassed from possible dangers and victimization.

The Lord's Prayer is for the people of han—particularly the poor, the sinned-against, and the tempted. When the rich and offenders recite the Lord's Prayer, it should be reinterpreted from the other end. For the rich and offenders, it might mean the following: "Our God. . . . Use us to help the hungry prepare for their daily bread. Forgive our trespasses and persuade our victims to forgive our trespasses. Lead us not into tempting others, but deliver us from evil-doing." By focusing on the well-being of the poor, the rich and offenders can be the answer of their victims' Lord's Prayer.

Healing a Paralytic (Mk 2:1–12). At Capernaum, four people brought to Jesus a paralytic man by creating a hole in the roof of the house where Jesus was and lowering down the mat on which the man lay. Seeing their faith, Jesus healed the paralytic by saying, "Son, your sins are forgiven" (v. 5). When some scribes questioned in their hearts about his authority to forgive sin, Jesus said to them, "Which is easier, to say to the paralytic, 'Your sins are forgiven', or to say, 'stand up and take your mat and walk'?" (v. 9). And then, he said to the young man to stand up, take his mat, and go home. The paralytic did as Jesus said.

In this conversation, even though Jesus said that his sins were forgiven, the term *sin* should be recast. As we have seen in Job, the Israelites connected suffering or sickness with sin. To them, any sin provoked divine wrath, which caused sickness. Thus, the Israelites believed that the forgiveness of sin precedes restoration from sickness. Sometimes it may be true that sin can generate sicknesses, but most of the time, ailments create false sin-consciousness.

The young man must have suffered from sin-consciousness. His sin could cause his sickness, but in reverse, his sickness could generate his false sin-consciousness. It is more likely that his condition was the latter. The reason for this is the following: sin requires repentance and without repentance, sin cannot be absolved. In the case of this young man, his sins were forgiven without either confession of sin or repentance of sin. This indicates that he committed no sin to repent of. Subsequently, Jesus asked which is easier: "Your sins are forgiven" or "Stand up and take your mat and walk." To the young man, the pronouncement of the forgiveness of sin is much easier to understand and accept than the command of "stand up and walk." Jesus' declaration of the forgiveness without demanding repentance indicates that he was not concerned about the young man's sin but about his false sin-consciousness. This is the reason why Jesus treated the forgiveness of his sin as equivalent to "standing up and going home" with his own mat. "Standing up and going home" was letting go of his false sin-consciousness.

Unlike the case of the adulteress (Jn 8:11), Jesus did not command him not to sin anymore. Considering this, we can come to realize that this person's problem was not sin, but his false sin-consciousness caused by his sickness.

Releasing him from the false sin-consciousness, Jesus healed this han-ridden paralytic. This healing event concurs with the story of Job in terms of defying the theology of retribution. Sin and human suffering are not necessarily interlocked in the cycle of cause and effect.

In our churches, we see many victims with broken spirits, victims of sexual abuse, racial discrimination, and economic exploitation. Rather than demand repentance of their sins, Jesus would pronounce the words of comfort: "Stand up, take your mat of han, and go home." For Jesus, releasing people from their han is more urgent than dealing with their sin.

The Execution of Jesus (Mk 15:25–39). Jesus disputed the unilateral interpretation of the sin-penalty model. This is clearly shown in the incident of the healing of the blind man (Jn 9:1–41). When the disciples saw a blind man from birth, they raised the question whether his blindness was caused by his own sin or by his parents'. Although the retribution (Deuteronomical) theology was confronted by the Book of Job, the idea of sickness as God's punishment was prevalent in Jesus' time. Jesus rejected the Deuteronomical theology by saying that his blindness was neither caused by his sin nor by his parents', but for the manifestation of God's work. By flatly denying the popular belief of the sin-sickness model, Jesus opened up the possibility of a new interpretation on suffering.

Yet such mentality of the sin-penalty theology has not disappeared from the Christian church. Our traditional interpretations on Jesus' crucifixion show this fact. Even though Jesus did not die naturally, but was executed by the Romans and Jewish leaders, the church has interpreted the execution as his death. Furthermore, the church has understood his execution in the mode of the sin-suffering thinking: "People sinned and he died for their sins." This formula is the exact mode of the retribution thinking: since people sinned against God, someone should pay for it. Jesus' death is the penalty of people's sin (the substitution theory).

Does God really require people to pay back for their iniquities? Does God have to let God's own Son be killed as the penalty of peoples' sin? Letting alone the issue of child abuse, we see little grace and forgiveness of God in this mode of thinking. If God cannot forgive sinners without the violent execution of Jesus, that God is neither gracious nor merciful, but retributive. In reality, our God surpasses the sin-penalty model as we have just seen. Toward the suffering humanity, God is greatly merciful.

If we take Jesus' execution as propitiation, it will be hard for us to defend it thoroughly. Let's assume that Jesus died to forgive the sin of people. Then such a death is only for those who had lived unto Jesus' time, because it is absurd that God should forgive sins that have not yet been committed. If Jesus died to forgive the sins of all people, including future generations, people after Jesus should be carefree from sin because Jesus has already paid for their sins. In addition, there is no need of repentance because our sins were forgiven through Jesus' death. It is inappropriate that God punished Jesus for the sins that people will commit in the future and that they need no repentance of their sin.

The execution of Jesus defies the sin-suffering theology, expressing God's han caused by human sins. Jesus did not know sin, yet knew han thorough and thorough. Jesus' last cry was a victim's outcry in han: "My God, my God, why have you forsaken me?" (Mk 15:34). The cross represents the many innocent victims who suffer injustice, oppression, and the retributive interpretation of suffering. It is the symbol of God's han. Jesus' cross is great advocacy for the victims of abuse, violence, and unjust oppression, opposing abusive power unto death. The victims would be healed in his solidary woundedness with them and would be vindicated by the power of the cross that demands offenders to repent of their sins.

CONCLUSION

We have reviewed the Bible and its theology from the perspective of the sinned-against in light of han. The Bible is for both sinners and the sinned-against. However, the Bible, particularly the New Testament, was primarily written for the community of faith that was persecuted and sinned-against. If we want to have a more holistic interpretation, it is critical to read the Bible from their perspectives. The notion of han may contribute to such an effort to see biblical truth from such perspectives, complementing the doctrine of sin. This notion may free people from the unilateral interpretation of the sin-penalty scheme and provide an alternative theological mode of interpretation for victims—Job, the paralyzed young man, the blind man, and Jesus of the cross. Imposing the sin-penalty formula upon the victims of sin is grave injustice. By naming the reality of han, we can begin to heal the victims of sin rather than condemn them. Such a move will start off a new journey to a theology of han-liberation.

NOTES

1. Cf. Walter Brueggemann, *Old Testament Theology: Essays on Structure, Theme, and Text*, ed. by Patrick D. Miller (Minneapolis: Fortress Press, 1992) 1–21.

2. The labarum is the symbol of the cross with which Constantine won his battles.

3. Sun-ai Lee and Don Luce, eds., *The Wish: Poems of Contemporary Korea*, trans. by Lee (New York: Friendship Press, 1983) 14.

4. Cf. Bill Moyers, "The First Murder," in *Genesis: A Living Conversation*. 16 October 1996. PBS series.

5. Amnon was a victim of his father's sin, too. His rape derived from David's adultery. This might be the reason why David was quiet about the rape incident, believing that it was God's punishment for his sin and crime.

6. Phyllis Trible, *Texts of Terror: Literary-Feminist Reading of Biblical Narratives* (Philadelphia: Fortress Press, 1984) 36.

7. NRSV. Hereafter, all biblical quotes will be from the NRSV unless otherwise mentioned.

8. Most scholars believe that the speeches of Elihu were inserted between the Dialogues and God's answer by someone later on. This is why God refers only to the three friends and does not mention Elihu. Solomon B. Freehof, *Book of Job: A Commentary* (New York: Union of American Hebrew Congregations, 1958) 235.

9. According to a larger number of scholar only part of God's speeches was written by the original author and that most of chapters 40 and 41 were later additions. The two descriptions of the Behemoth and the Leviathan were independent nature poems and were added later to the original divine speech. Ibid.

10. Gustavo Gutiérrez, *On Job: God-Talk and the Suffering of the Innocent*, trans. by Matthew J. O'Connell (Maryknoll: Orbis, 1987) 82.

11. "See, he will kill me; I have no hope" (NRSV). It is debatable whether the translation of KJV is right. Whatever its original intent may be, my point is that faith means unconditional trust.

12. Schleiermacher believed that. Also, see Ted Peters, *Sin: Radical Evil in Soul and Society* (Grand Rapids: Eerdmans, 1994) 7–9.

13. Elie Wiesel, *Messengers of God*, trans. by Marion Wiesel (New York: Random, 1976); Richard Rubenstein, *The Cunning of History* (New York: Harper Colophon Books, 1978).

14. G. Tyler Miller, *Living in the Environment: Principles, Connections, and Solutions,* 8th ed. (Belmont, Calif.: Wadsworth Publishing Co., 1994) 10.

15. Joachim Jeremias, *Jerusalem at Jesus Time* (Philadelphia: Fortress Press, 1969), cited in Byung-mu Ahn, "Jesus and the Minjung," in *Minjung Theology: People as the Subjects of History*, ed. by CTC-CCC (Maryknoll: Orbis, 1981) 143.

16. Joachim Jeremias, *New Testament Theology* (New York: Scribner, 1971) 112.

17. Herders were accused of driving their herds onto others' land and stealing the produce of the herd. The publicans were particularly outlawed. They were *toll* collectors (*môk^esâ*), different from *tax* collectors (*gabbâyâ*). While tax collectors as state officials took

in the direct taxes, the toll collectors were subtenants of the rich toll farmers, who had to extract the agreed amount plus their additional profit. They often capitalized on public ignorance of the scale of tolls to bring money into their pockets during the tax season (Lk 3:12 f). The civil rights of the publicans were denied, and they were deprived of their rights to be witnesses. Jeremias, *New Testament Theology*, 109–110.

18. Ahn, "Jesus and the Minjung," 144.

19. Ibid.

20. Jeremias, *New Testament Theology*, 112.

21. Ahn, "Jesus and the Minjung," 150.

22. Jeremiah, *New Testament Theology*, 113.

23. Jeremias, *The Lord's Prayer*, trans. by John Reumann (Philadelphia: Fortress Press, 1964) 10–12.

24. Eduard Schweizer, *The Good News According to Matthew*, trans. by David Green (Atlanta: John Knox Press, 1975) 153. He further explains that when the prayer was said at an early hour, "daily bread" meant the bread of the same day; otherwise, it referred to tomorrow. According to Jerome, the Gospel of the Nazareans, which is lost, used the term *mahar*. W. Foerster concludes that *mahar*, "tomorrow," is the Aramaic express standing behind the Greek *epiousios* (Foerster, "*Epiousios*," in Gerhard Kittel, *Theological Dictionary of the New Testament*, trans. and ed. by Geoffrey W. Bromiley [Grand Rapids: Eerdmans, 1964], II:590–599). To Jerome, the "bread for tomorrow" was not referring to earthly bread but to the bread of life. In the early church the eschatological understanding of "bread of life," "heavenly manna," and "bread of the age of salvation" was familiar, if not the leading interpretation of "bread for tomorrow" (Jeremias, *Lord's Prayer*, 25). We cannot exclusively spiritualize or materialize the petition for tomorrow's bread, but include both. However, its primary intention was to ask daily bread for tomorrow.

25. Jeremias, *New Testament Theology*, 192.

26. Considering Jesus' teaching that focuses human relationships before our relationship with God (Mt 5:23–24), we can see that oppressors need to ask forgiveness from their victims before asking God's forgiveness.

27. This part echoes a very ancient Jewish evening prayer:

> Lead me not into the power of transgression,
> And bring me not into the power of sin,
> And not into the power of iniquity,
> And not into the power of temptation,
> And not into the power of anything shameful
> ([Jeremias, *Lord's Prayer*, 30)

The meaning of this evening prayer was to protect early Christians from the power of sin, temptation, and anything shameful.

CHAPTER THREE

THE ALIENATION OF ALIENATION

Justo L. González

As I consider the general theme of this book, sin and alienation, the first thought that comes to mind is the need to clarify what one means by "alienation." Indeed, in its common usage in North American white culture, alienation is understood mostly in its psychological dimensions, having to do with how one relates to oneself and to others. One is inwardly alienated if one is not at one with one's identity. One is alienated from others if there is a rupture in relationship or communication. One is alienated from God if one does not know or does not accept God's love.

The counterpart to this understanding of sin as alienation is salvation as reconciliation. Indeed, the antidote to every level of alienation thus understood is the restoration of communication and relationship. If one is alienated within oneself, common wisdom says that it is a matter of "getting in touch" with oneself. If one is alienated from God, what one has to do is come to understand and accept God's love, thus healing the breech in communication and relationship with God.

There is much to be said for this understanding of sin as alienation and salvation as reconciliation. It certainly takes into account the manner in which sin works on a person's self-identity, on one's relationships with others, and even on one's relationship to God.

Yet, this understanding of alienation in such psychological terms can also be seen and criticized as one more step in the internalization and individualization of sin. And these in turn are two of the main reasons why it is so difficult for Christians today to speak of sin in terms that are pertinent to the many forms in which alienation is experienced.

By the individualization of sin, I mean the tendency, begun at a very early time in the history of the Christian church, and accelerated as the church became more closely associated with the structures of power, to speak of sin in terms of something an individual does. It is from that perspective that it becomes customary to use such phrases as: "It is a sin to. . . ." (steal, lie, commit adultery, etc.); and "Is it a sin to? . . ." In other words, what we have here is an atomization of reality into a series of individuals, and the further atomization of the individual into a series of acts. The consequences of this may be seen in Western theology in the development of the penitential system, which in a nut-shell is a system whereby individuals, by means of particular acts of penitence and reparation, are relieved from at least part of the consequences of particular acts considered to be sins. In the penitential system, and particularly in confes-sion, one does not focus on the structural dimensions of sin, nor even on one's own sinfulness, but rather on disconnected acts of sin.

It may be argued that Pelagianism consists precisely in this atomization of reality and of human nature. It has been suggested[1] that Pelagius was dis-turbed by the implications of Manicheism, which held that good and evil are based on the very nature of eternal principles, and that therefore the evil nature can do no good, nor the good nature any evil. Such moral determinism Pelag-ius saw as a corrupting influence, which made sin both unavoidable and excus-able. Therefore, he set out to develop a system in which it was clear that the human will was free to choose both good and evil at each moment, and that this freedom was not destroyed by any previous action, nor by the nature or condition of the will.

What is ultimately unacceptable about Pelagianism—and also what makes it most attractive—is the notion that life consists of a series of points of decision to which one comes with total freedom from other decisions and lim-itations. At each of those points of decision I have a good and an evil choice: one is sin; the other is not. Obviously, such atomization of reality was unac-ceptable to Augustine, and should be unacceptable to anyone who has any notion of the interconnection of reality, so that I am not able to make decisions apart from either my own past or from the actual structures of sin around me.

Clearly, the privatization of sin and the atomization of reality plays into the hands of the powerful, to the detriment of the powerless. If sin is an individual matter, and the best way to analyze reality is as a series of discon-nected decisions, the sin of the powerful is no different than the sin of the powerless. In each case, sin consists in making the wrong choice, and has lit-tle to do with the complex web of human relations in which the powerful exploit the powerless.

By the internalization of sin I mean the process whereby it is made to reside only or primarily in the will—and, because this process follows the individualization of sin, in the will of the individual. While Augustine was able to see the dangers in the atomization of life proposed by Pelagius, his own understanding of sin is a landmark in the process of its internalization. Partly due to the influence of Neoplatonism, Augustine sees reality as a great and hierarchical chain of being.[2] There is nothing wrong with the hierarchy, which is part of the very nature of things. Within that hierarchy, the human will may direct the mind toward its proper object, God, or toward the lesser creatures. To do the latter is sin. Naturally, such sin results in a series of sinful acts—theft, violence, and adultery. But sin resides in the will rather than in the act itself. Furthermore, in the mind itself there is a proper hierarchy, in which the intellect is to reign supreme; but the will has the power to depose the intellect from that place, and that is the nature of sin.[3] Thus, while Augustine saw clearly that sin goes far beyond individual acts or decisions, and therefore argued quite vehemently and convincingly that the human will in the present condition is not able to avoid sin,[4] his own internalization of sin, making it reside exclusively in the will, made it difficult for him to see the structural dimensions of sin—at least, those dimensions that go beyond the damage it has done to the human will. No matter whether bound or free, the will has become the main seat of sin.

The result of this internalization of sin is a long tradition that insists that what makes an action sinful is its intention. Hence Abelard's argument, that if a man shoots an arrow at a deer, and by mistake hits another man, he has not committed homicide.[5] Significantly, many in Abelard's time warned against the dangers of such doctrine.[6] And even more significantly, very few today would find fault with it. To me, that is an indication of how far the internalization of sin has gone. Is sin so limited to the will and the intention that it is impossible to sin unknowingly or unwillingly? Were the atrocities of the Spanish conquistadores not sinful, because they thought they were serving Christ? Was the taking of the lands from the native inhabitants of North America not sinful, because those who did it thought they were serving God? Are the consequences of neoliberal capitalism in Central America or in the Philippines not sinful, because investors in richer countries are not aware of those consequences?

Clearly, if that is the case, then ignorance is a value to be sought, for it also preserves innocence and avoids sin. Is that not the reason why so many in the churches in the United States do not wish to be told of the nefarious consequences of neoliberal capitalism on other parts of the world? If they do not know, they preserve their innocence and they are innocent; they cannot be sinning—or at least, so they think.[7]

It is interesting to look at Anselm in this context, and at the manner in which he speaks of the consequences of sin being determined by the dignity of the offended. While there is much to be said against such notions, apparently derived from Germanic notions of Wergild,[8] there is an important insight here that must not be missed. Sin is not measured only in terms of the inner intention of the sinner; it is also measured in terms of the sinned against. Sin is not only in the will of the sinner; it is also "out there." And this to such an extent that Anselm argues that the gravity of sin has to do, not only with the decision of the will, but also with its gravity in terms of what it does "out there"—in the case of his argument in *Cur Deus homo*, what it does to God's honor.

We tend to think that the problem with this notion is that it measures sin, not on the basis of the sinner's actions or intentions, but on the basis of the one whom sin offends. Part of the reason why we think in such terms is precisely the internalization of the notion of sin. If sin is an internal and individual matter, clearly its gravity has nothing to do with the one whom it offends or hurts. I would suggest, however, that the problem with Anselm's proposition is not that it places sin "out there," in the hurt of the offended. The problem is rather with Anselm's understanding of the hierarchy of being, which he derives from a combination of Augustinian/neo-Platonist notions of ontological hierarchy and feudal social hierarchy.

On the matter of the objective nature of sin, and the necessity to measure it in terms of the offended or the sinned-against, Anselm is right. Somehow, Pizarros' massacre at Cajamarca, or the slave trade that resulted in so much tragedy and oppression, must be judged more severely than a petty theft at a store—even though both are motivated by the same greed. Certainly motivation plays a role in sin; but the outward results of sin are not mere consequences; they too are part of the sin, and must be judged as such. Thus, Anselm's dictum, that the guilt of an offense is measured by the dignity of the offended, is not altogether wrong.

The point at which one must take issue with Anselm is not his "objective" understanding of sin, but rather his hierarchical understanding of reality.[9] According to Anselm's worldview, there is an entire hierarchy of being and of authority, and God stands at the top of both. The consequence of this is that those entities that in the hierarchy of being are higher up are more like God, and therefore more valuable. And, likewise, those people whose standing in the hierarchy of power is high are closer to God, and therefore more worthy. When applied to the notion of sin, this belief leads to the conclusion that to sin against one's feudal lord is worse than to sin against one's neighbor, and that the sin of a peasant against a lord is a more grievous matter than the sin of a lord against a peasant.

If, however, we turn this hierarchy upside down, according to Gospel principles, the result will be quite startling. Clearly, in the Gospels—and indeed in the entire Bible—we are told that God stands closer to the disenfranchised than to the powerful. The Old Testament says much more of God's special protection for the widow, the orphan, the poor, and the sojourner, than of God's special protection for the king or the Temple. Jesus made it quite clear that if one wishes to be close to him, what one must do is not to work one's way up in the hierarchy of society (or of being), but rather to work one's way down, to meet him in those whom the world would consider the least. When asked about who would be the greatest in the Reign of God, he took a child, put him in the center, and declared that whoever receives one of these little ones receives him. (In the interpretation of this passage, it is important to set aside our modern, sometimes romanticized views of the innocence of children, and understand that the reason why Jesus puts the child at the center is not due to his innocence, but due to his powerlessness. He moves the child from the periphery of attention and concern to the center, and invites his followers to do likewise with any whom the world considers peripheral.) And, in speaking of the final judgment, he declared that those who serve those others who are considered the least, that is, the prisoner, the hungry, the thirsty, the naked, the foreigner, and the sick, serve him. In other words, that in this strange "hierarchy" of the Gospel, God does not stand at the top. God stands at the bottom. And any who would serve God and meet God must do so, not at the top, but at the bottom.

If one then combines this Gospel "hierarchy" (would it be better, taking some license with the etymological origin of the word *hierarchy*, to speak of a "lowerarchy"?) with what Anselm says about the gravity of sin having to do with the "dignity" or the standing of the offended or the hurt, it follows that the more disenfranchised and defenseless the sinned against, the graver the sin. The sin of David against Uriah and Betsheba is compounded by the fact that as compared to David, they were powerless. That is part of the point that Nathan makes in his famous parable of the rich man who ordered that his poor neighbor's favorite ewe lamb be slaughtered. The sins that take place in today's society against the powerless and disenfranchised are much more serious than the sins that take place against the established order and the privilege of the rich and the powerful.

The reasons why such views are not commonly preached or taught should be obvious. If the hierarchy of sin is parallel to the hierarchy of the social order, it follows that to question or to challenge the existing order is a grave sin—one that becomes graver as the challenge reaches higher in that order. If, on the other hand, the "hierarchy" by which sin is measured is the Gospel "hierarchy" in which the last are first, and the least the greatest, then the very notion of sin becomes subversive.

Thus, one manner in which much traditional Christian teaching has managed to avoid the charge—and the reality—of being subversive is precisely by the individualization and the internalization of sin.

This internalization of sin has an ideological function—using the term *ideology* in the sense of a construct by which society justifies its own interests, particularly those of the status quo. This is made clear when we realize that in common usage there is one point at which the societal dimensions of sin are preserved. That point is the common assumption, in most of our churches, that crime is always a sin. Needless to say, societies cannot subsist without some measure of order, and therefore quite often a crime against the rules of that society is also a sin against its members. But we must not take for granted that such is always the case. It may be the order itself that is sinful, and rebellion or resistance against it may be justified as an act of holiness.

There is, however, one step further in the process of the internalization of sin that has become typical of the second half of the twentieth century. That is the psychologization of sin. One of the great discoveries of the twentieth century, beginning with the groundbreaking work of Sigmund Freud, has been the complexity of the human psyche and its workings. We now know that our motivations are not always—perhaps rather, are always not—what they seem or what we ourselves believe they are. We also know that much of our oppression is self-perpetuated, through the internalization of past experiences and perceptions, as well as of social values and mores that may well go unchallenged. We have come to the point where we are beginning to learn ways to liberate people from some of these inner oppressions through psychotherapy and even by means of drugs. All of this is true and valuable. It represents significant breakthroughs in the possibility to heal much human pain and dysfunction. At the same time, however, these very breakthroughs have tempted theologians as well as psychologists to reduce their understanding of sin to that which can be expressed, explained, and treated on the basis of psychological theory and psychotherapeutic practice. The result is what could properly be called "the alienation of alienation."

As I stated at the very beginning of this chapter, in our North American context "alienation" is often understood primarily, and sometimes even exclusively, in terms of its psychological dimensions. The remedy for such alienation is reconciliation, usually understood in terms of what one can do in order to be reconciled with the conflicting forces within oneself, as well as with others (including God) from whom one has been alienated.

While there are several objections that could be raised against such a therapeutic approach to sin and alienation, probably the most damaging is that it tends to obliterate the difference between the sinner and those against whom sin is committed. When I first studied pastoral counseling, many in the field seemed to be saying that the purpose of such counseling was to help people who for one reason or another were maladjusted. This included people who found they could not function in society, as well as people who were alienated from themselves. Thus, it was taken for granted that if someone was maladjusted and alienated, this was mostly that person's responsibility, and that my task in counseling was to help that person deal with the. inner forces of alienation.

Fairly soon, however, I discovered that most of the people with whom I interacted as a pastor or a counselor had good reason to be maladjusted. Perhaps from the point of view of society at large, it was they who were maladjusted and alienated; but from the point of view of justice and love, it was in the society, rather than in them, that maladjustment was to be found. Perhaps some of the white men who wrote my textbooks on pastoral counseling, who had fulfilling jobs and a fairly secure income, and who still found themselves unhappy and dissatisfied, had reason to believe that maladjustment is a matter of inner attitude, to be resolved by means of a therapeutic approach. Perhaps the demon they had to conquer was their own alienation from themselves, from others, and from God. But the poor widow with four children and three jobs who came to tell me that she did not know how she would be able to cope when next month's rent came due, was not maladjusted. The demon that she was facing had little to do with her own psychological alienation, and much to do with a society alienated from her. Were I to attempt to deal with her in therapeutic terms, I would be laying on her the blame for her own pain and oppression.

That is why we must beware of the alienation of alienation. In its full sense, "alienation" is not purely psychological nor internal. In forensic terms, to "alienate" means to make another's—to sell, give away, yield, or surrender something to another person. And this too is part of what the early church understood the human predicament to be. As I read early Christian theology, the human predicament is not simply that we have become dysfunctional and divided within ourselves, nor even that we stand in enmity before God and others, but also that we are "alienated," that we have become the property of another who is not God, nor ourselves. And, since only God is our rightful owner, and we are God's stewards, this alienation is a theft or usurpation. Our problem is not that we do not understand. Our problem is not that we have become maladjusted. Our problem is not that we ought to feel or to act otherwise. Our problem is alienation in the most radical sense: slavery.

In its strict sense, to be alienated means to belong to another who is not the rightful owner. In the early church, this was a common understanding of sin and the human predicament. original sin did not become an inherited fault until Tertullian suggested such an interpretation, and then Augustine popularized it to such an extent that in the Western tradition it became the dominant and almost sole understanding of original sin. In many earlier Christian writers, original sin is the condition in which we find ourselves because we are born into a humanity that has become enslaved to the powers of evil. It clearly is thus that Irenaeus understands original sin when he declares, for instance, that "we were all brought into servitude by our first parents."[10] Furthermore, this is not limited to something that our mythological first parents did. It is also something to which various generations add. This is, for instance, the manner in which Irenaeus interprets the passage in Exodus about the golden calf. By submitting to the calf, and by desiring to return to Egypt, the people in fact made themselves slaves again, and thus added to the bondage that is common to all humanity.[11] In other words, that the bondage of original sin is not merely something that happened in a bygone *urgeschichtliche* time, but also something to which humanity adds by its own creation of structures of oppression and submission to them.

Without such understanding of the nature of sin as bondage it is difficult to understand what Ephesians means when it affirms that Jesus "made captivity itself a captive,"[12] or indeed the entire Book of Revelation.

The alienation that stands at the heart of sin is not purely inner nor merely psychological alienation. It is not even alienation in the sense of estrangement from God. It is also and foremost alienation in the sense of subjection to entities and structures whose very power is an usurpation. Thus, when speaking of sin and alienation, it seems necessary to add to the common psychological dimensions of *alienation* those that have to do with the use of that term in relation to property rights. In this sense, to "alienate" is to convey or transfer to another rights of property, by sale, gift, or any other means—including deceit and theft. When thus joined to the notion of sin, alienation is an usurpation of rights, leading to an improper subjection of one part of creation to another.

In early Christian theology, this is most often expressed in terms of the subjection of humanity to the Devil. In the theology of Irenaeus, for instance, the power of angels over human beings was supposed to be temporary, for humans were like princes being tutored by the angels until they could inherit the glory of their Creator and Parent. The Devil, one of those angels, has wrongly usurped authority over humanity, and must be defeated and deposed so that humanity will be free to grow again as it was intended, toward the image and likeness of God.[13] It is for this reason that, when speaking of the work of Christ, Irenaeus says that "forgiving the ones whose sin had made them captive, he broke their chains"[14] and that "he restored freedom to humanity.[15] Using twentieth-century language, one could say that what Jesus did was mount a successful revolution against the Devil and his usurpation.

However, the usurpation that is at the root of sin is not merely "spiritual." It is not just that the Devil or some other unseen power has gained control of humanity. It is also that some very concrete and very visible powers have gained control of that which is not rightfully theirs. This too is alienation, perhaps not in the sense of estrangement. but certainly in the sense of becoming another's.

In this sense, political oppression is one of the many forms that sin manifests itself in alienation. The oppressed have been alienated by the oppressors, who are in fact usurpers over them. The same is true of sexual oppression, class oppression, and economic oppression. All of them involve forms of alienation, not merely in the sense that they result in estrangement among persons, but especially in the sense that they constitute an usurpation.

Actually, much of what we sometimes attribute to alienation only in the psychological sense is also related to alienation in the forensic/property sense. Thus, for instance, when we today speak of the ecological crisis we often say that its roots lie in humanity's alienation from the earth. What is usually meant by this is that we have so distanced ourselves from the earth and from nature in general that we view them as an "other," and that in this estrangement from our physical roots in the earth we come to see nature as an enemy to conquer. This is certainly true. But there is also another sense in which the earth has been alienated that is also responsible for the ecological crisis. The earth has been alienated in that, precisely as a manifestation of sin, some people have claimed it for themselves as a private property. This is a theme that is seldom discussed in churches today, but that was paramount in early Christian writers. A few quotations from Ambrose of Milan suffice to show the tenor of much early Christian thought on the matter:

> Why do you drive out of their inheritance people whose nature is the same as yours, claiming for yourselves alone the possession of the land? The land was made to be common to all, the poor and the rich. Why do you, oh rich, claim for yourselves alone the right to the land?[16]

> The world has been made for all, and a few of you rich try to keep it for yourselves. For not only the ownership of the land, but even the sky, the air, and the sea, a few rich people claim for themselves.[17] God our Lord willed this land to be the common possession of all and give its fruit to all. But greed distributed the right of possessions.[18]

What all of this shows is that for a theologian such as Ambrose, the "alienation" of the earth was not simply that we have become psychologically or emotionally estranged from it—true as that may be—but rather that it has been acquired by masters who do not use it for its proper end. It has been "alienated" in the forensic sense.

It is precisely because when relating it to sin we seldom speak of "alienation" in this forensic sense, as related to issues of property and power, that we must call attention to "the alienation of alienation," and to the loss this implies. When "alienation" is understood almost exclusively in terms of estrangement from God, from oneself, and from others, we are all on the same side of the divide. That is an important element of the doctrine of sin that must not be forgotten: we are all sinners. But when "alienation" is understood also in the forensic sense, then there are alienators and alienatees, those who commit the sin and those who are sinned-against. Now not all sin is the same, as when sin is made to reside in the intention. Now there are degrees and varieties of sin. As with Anselm, the degree of the sin is closely related, not with who sins, but rather with who is sinned-against. The lower in the scale of power the sinned-against is, the greater the sin. The higher in that scale the sinner is, the greater the sin.

It is when we understand the alienation connected with sin in this forensic sense, and the hierarchy of God's concern as the reverse of the human hierarchy of power, that we really understand why an author such as James can write:

> Come now, you rich people, weep and wail for the miseries that are coming to you. Your riches have rotted, and your clothes are moth-eaten. Your gold and silver have rusted, and their rust will be evidence against you, and it will eat your flesh like fire. You have laid up treasure for the last days. Listen! The wages of the laborers who mowed your fields, which you kept back by fraud, cry out, and the cries of the harvesters have reached the ears of the Lord of hosts. (5:1–4)

Perhaps a fuller understanding of alienation, including both its psychological/emotional and its forensic/property dimensions would help us appreciate many other portions of scripture that are currently neglected.

NOTES

1. Torgny Bohlin, *Die Theologie des Pelagius und ihre Genesis* (Uppsala, Sweden: Lundequist, 1957).

2. Perhaps the best place to study this hierarchical understanding of being, and how it affects Augustine's view of good and evil, is his treatise *De natura boni*, where he clearly states that a being of a higher order, even when corrupted, is better than a being of a lower order *(De nat. boni* 5). Although Augustine does not draw the consequences of such views for the social order, they would later provide theological justification for many a social hierarchy, including that of feudalism.

3. *De lib. arb.* 16.34.

4. On this score, the classical reference is *De correp. et grat.* 12.

5. See P. L. Williams, *The Moral Theology of Abelard* (Lanham, Md.: University Press of America, 1980).

6. Bernard of Clairvaux, for instance, asked if this meant that, if those who crucified Christ did so out of ignorance, they committed no sin (P.L. 182:1064).

7. Is it partly for that reason that elsewhere I have proposed that we must begin to uncover the "guilty innocence" that in our society is often the handmaiden of injustice. *Mañana: Christian Theology from a Hispanic Perspective* (Nashville: Abingdon, 1990) 38–41.

8. There are many studies on the matter. See James C. Russell, *The Germanization of Early Medieval Christianity: A Sociohistorical Approach to Religious Transformation* (New York: Oxford University Press, 1994) 170. See also the numerous bibliographical entries in this book.

9. The conservative thrust of such hierarchical understanding, and how it was used to reinforce the existing order, may be seen clearly in several passages of *Cur Deus homo.* One such example: "Truly, when any creature keeps the order [or station] to which it has been assigned, be it through an act of nature or through a rational act, it may be said that it obeys and serves God." *Cur Deus homo* 15.

10. *Adv. haer.* 4.22.1.

11. *Adv. haer.* 4.15.1.

12. Ef. 4.8.

13. I have developed this aspect of Irenaeus' theology, and contrasted it with the theological positions that we tend to take for granted, in *Christian Thought Revisited: Three Types of Theology* (Nashville: Abingdon, 1989).

14. *Adv. haer.* 3.9.3.

15. *Adv. haer.* 3.5.2.

16. Tract. in *ep. Io. ad Parth.* 31.5.

17. Ibid., 61.16.

18. *In Psal,* 124.2.

CHAPTER FOUR

FOR SHAME, FOR SHAME, THE SHAME OF IT ALL:
POSTURES OF REFUSAL AND THE BROKEN HEART

Susan L. Nelson

Although Freddy was the first grandchild I knew to be hit by Mr. Barnes, it was not difficult to extrapolate the old man's expectations; Freddy was to realize that the blow itself completed his grandfather's direct role and now he had to assume the responsibility of punishing himself more, until even the tiniest impulse to repeat the offense was routed and destroyed.
—Kaye Gibbons, Sights Unseen

In her novel *Sights Unseen* Kaye Gibbons gives us a small vignette on shame. Freddy Barnes, the protagonist's brother was, at the time of this scene, an adolescent stretching to be seen as a grown man. He kept to himself as boys growing into men do. He shaved; he drove cars; he practiced a haughty distance from his sister. But, at age eighteen he made the mistake one day not only of teasing his twelve-year-old sister who had just become sick and vomited the contents of her lunch over the side of the deck of the family's beach cottage, but of doing so within the hearing and sight of his stern grandfather. Mr. Barnes, witnessing the event from below the deck, called Freddy to him, reprimanded him within the hearing of his little sister, slapped him across the face hard enough to raise a welt, and reduced him to a sniveling child who only wanted to hide his face. As his sister, Hattie, later reflects upon the event: *"I remember thinking how big he [Freddy] was to have been slapped. I did not understand the full meanings of the words "degraded" and "humiliated," but that must have been how Freddy felt to have Mr. Barnes slap him in the face over so small a sin as teasing a little sister"* (134). In this small vignette Gibbons not only chronicles a shaming incident in the life of Freddy, but shares her observation that such incidents have grave implications

71

beyond their initial moment. Mr. Barnes's intent in slapping Freddy (the narrator understands) is precisely so that Freddy will be shamed into not behaving in the same manner again. So painful was the slap, that Freddy is to learn never to act in a way that will provoke such humiliation. He is to internalize his grandfather's aversion to a certain range of behaviors (a range that Mr. Barnes seems to understand as dangerous within himself), link it to his experience of degradation, take responsibility for monitoring his own behavior, and bind that type of behavior away within himself where it will cause no further harm. The intent, we are told, is that Freddy will even learn to punish himself. This self-punishment serves as a way to avert shame-inducing behavior. It is also a means to protect himself from further humiliation at the hand of his grandfather.

In this story we are introduced to shame and to the way in which it wounds and then binds those who are shamed. We also learn that such behavior has implications for how those who are shamed choose to construct themselves and to negotiate their futures. In a rather minor but extremely painful event, the perpetrator of a "small sin" becomes a victim and learns postures of defense and self-punishment that will shape himself and any relationships he might form in the future. The grandfather's intent in such humiliation is precisely that Freddy be formed in this way and no longer bully his little sister. In actuality, however, Freddy has learned *to* bully (slap across the face) those whose behavior mirrors bullying behaviors of his own. His self-punishing posture has implications of alienation not only for him (as he struggles to bind away certain behaviors that in actuality were more benign than the slap they instigated) but also for others as he will be tempted to replicate his grandfather's act in the humiliation of others. Thus we can see how a shaming incident (surely the grandfather could have handled the situation in a less caustic and humiliating manner) can fester into a wound which, untended, can grow into a posture toward the world that is less than friendly—that we might even call "sin."

THE HUMAN CONDITION AND THE TRAGIC TRAJECTORY OF SIN

The human condition, as the story of Mr. Barnes and Hattie and Freddy has in some way inferred, is structured with ambiguities. It has opportunities but also limits. It is laced with vulnerabilities, disappointments, and joys, and with times when (perhaps as in the case of Mr. Barnes) our best intentions (to affect his grandson's behavior for the better) turn back on themselves. It offers challenge and achievement, and experiences of fear and missing the mark. It is fraught with the tension between our most basic relationality, our need for one another and our desire to have another look upon us and love us, and our desire to be independent "persons in our own right." In it we know the joy of face-to-face encounter, the satisfaction of loving as well as the thrill of being loved, and the shocking ruptures of death, disappointment in love, and loss.

Human sin, modern theologians have told us, is forged in the crucible of the human condition. This is the initial insight of Søren Kierkegaard,[1] developed by Reinhold Niebuhr and more recently elaborated upon by the theologian Edward Farley: that life itself is so structured that it presents human creatures in our finitude and freedom with a condition of anxiety that begs for resolution. It pulls and tears at human beings, on the one hand threatening our sense of well-being and survival, while on the other throwing us off-center by the weight of its freedom and possibility. It has to it what Farley has called a "timbre of discontent."[2] And sin is the way we seek to secure ourselves by making some less-than-ultimate aspect of our life the source of our ultimate security. Sin turns some appropriate opportunity for relative securing (family, job, home, loving relationship, ideology, and even religion) into something it by definition cannot be, thereby distorting our ability to appreciate that opportunity for the limited securing and delight it actually can bring. Sin is the human response to a creation that feels less than secure. It reflects an understandable human desire for "safe passage,"[3]—for security in a world that ultimately offers none.

Sin is also more than single acts of securing. It is a response which, made repeatedly, slowly sediments into postures of self-securing from which it becomes more and more difficult to choose not to sin. We can define sin in this sense with Farley[4] as the human refusal of our humanity. It is the refusal to accept our human condition with all the opportunities, limits, relationality, vulnerabilities, and anxieties that are intrinsic to it, and the practice of securing ourselves in ways that are idolatrous.

Just as life offers human beings many possibilities to fulfill ourselves, so sin can be various in form. It can range from the traditional form of sin as pride, to what I have called elsewhere the sin of "hiding."[5] It can be a refusal of vulnerability; and it can be the loss of ourselves in relationality. Life challenges us to live within the parameters of finitude and freedom and to trust in the source of this life to ultimately secure us. Sin is a refusal of that trust.[6] Understood in this way, sin has three aspects: it is the refusal of our human condition that results in postures of refusal that have grave implications for ourselves, others, and the world.

But, are all postures of refusal best named sin? In this chapter I argue that there are situations of alienation within the range of human experience that look like the "postures of refusal" we have called "sin." But these alienations follow a sinful trajectory other than the one just outlined. These postures of refusal are born not by a refusal of our human condition, but rather out of an historical experience of *being refused*.

The thesis I wish to explore is that the theological category of sin is not adequate to describe the full range of human alienations. The Christian tradition has maintained that sin is the problem from which human beings need redemption and that the cross is the locus of that salvation. I argue that human beings suffer not only sin, but also the experience of being refused (sinned-against). Contemporary theologians have developed a range of terms to describe this experience of being refused.[7] I will speak about this experience under the category of brokenheartedness first suggested by Rita Nakashima Brock.[8]

First, then, the category of brokenheartedness emerges from the fact that human beings are by nature very vulnerable. Despite our cultural mythology that posits and values self-made men and women, human beings are intrinsically relational: we are born from the coming together of two persons; we are dependent on others to welcome us, feed and protect us, and to teach us the ways of the world. As object relation psychology maintains,[9] we even build ourselves out of relationships, learning through them who we are, and taking from them bundles of experience that we fashion into our response to the world that is our very self. This relationality is basic to who we are and is an important piece in understanding how we come to fashion for ourselves postures of refusal to protect and secure ourselves.

Second, while postures of refusal may well be inevitable to the human condition (Augustine said that human beings cannot not sin), some postures of refusal are born not of an initial refusal of our human condition (as our description of the "tragic trajectory of sin" might suggest) but rather of actual experiences of being refused. Given the basic relationality of our condition, ruptures in relationship are not insignificant. They can wound and, when not healed, fester into a brokenheartedness that can become a core experience to our being. When we look at sinful behavior and postures of refusal then we must consider the possibility that brokenheartedness may lie at its root.

Third, language of sin and self-blame often attach themselves to experiences of being refused and the resulting postures of refusal. But such use of the language of sin in these cases is at best ambiguous. On the one hand, as in the case of Freddy's teasing of his little sister, it may describe what was a sinful activity and what may persist as refusing engagement of others and the world. On the other, the language of sin might be better understood as a meaning-making narrative, a defensive measure that has developed around the original experience of refusal perhaps to explain the pain of a shaming incident and the sense of degradation that accompanies such an event, thus blaming the victim of such violation. This narrative can be created by the perpetrator. Often, however, it is constructed by a child who, without help, is unable to see that their wounding was not their "fault" or (as in Freddy's case) was out of proportion to the weight of their misdemeanor, and to feel the pain of the betrayal that such wounding often indicates. This structure of meaning then serves both to rationalize the wounding and giving it meaning (it didn't come from nowhere "I deserve what I got"). It also camouflages the origination of the posture of refusal in a heartbreaking experience of being refused, an experience that is then buried beneath the layers of consciousness. This fact then either makes the uncritical use of the language of sin for such situations problematic if not totally inappropriate, or as Brock suggests reflects that the category of sin actually names a *symptom* of underlying damage.[10]

Fourth, while persons whose postures of refusal are born of a broken heart may actually participate as perpetrators in ongoing situations of refusal (e.g., battered children becoming batterers; those wounded by trusted others refuse to risk the vulnerability of their basic relationality) and thus can be said to be guilty of sin, their "salvation" or "reconciliation" entails not only repentance and the receiving of forgiveness (where appropriate), but *more basically* a process of healing that includes remembering their experience of being refused, grieving their loss, accepting their vulnerability, forgiving themselves for being so vulnerable, seeking restitution (where possible), and learning to reconnect and trust again. Where theologies have focused on sin as *the* problem of human alienation, they have failed to address these situations of broken-heartedness and to offer healing and hope to the brokenhearted. They have also, perhaps inadvertently, compounded the confusion and brokenheartedness of those who have been refused by reinforcing their sometimes inappropriate construal of themselves as wretched sinners.

Examples of being refused are manifold in human history. Rigidly defined gender roles refuse men and women the fullness of their being. Sexism devalues women *and* men. Racist institutions refuse the full humanity of the dominating as well as the oppressed group. Economic systems exploit workers. Imperialist activities rob a conquered people of their identity and freedom.[11] Child and sexual abuse robs people of their very subjectivity. Dysfunctional family systems and shaming parenting and teaching techniques (e.g., that described by Gibbons) refuse children their full range of behaviors.[12] In order to focus our conversation about the experience of being refused and the questions it raises for the adequacy of sin language to describe all situations of alienation, I will direct our discussion to one type of refusing situation: the phenomenon of shame.

SHAME: THE BROKEN TIE THAT BINDS

We all have painful memories of moments when we, perhaps like Freddy, felt deeply shamed. A child sneaks a cookie from the cookie jar, is caught in the act, and cannot raise his eyes to look into those of his mother. A new student realizes after ten minutes of a class that she is in the wrong classroom but is too embarrassed to ask for help. A choir member gets so drawn into the passion of a special piece, that he forgets to heed a measure rest and wants to sink through the floor when his is the only voice singing. A new professor asks a woman sitting at the secretary's desk to type a letter for her, only to later realize that the woman was not the new secretary but a fellow professor she had yet to meet. A teacher punishes the whole class for a mistake we alone have made. The experience of shame is the deeply painful experience of being "seen through," of being judged in some way inadequate, or of being seen (or seeing oneself) as out of congruence with a certain situation.

Our self-help literatures have taught us to make a distinction between shame and guilt. Guilt, we are told, is feeling bad for something we have done. Shame, on the other hand, is feeling bad for who we are (or are not). To put it another way, to experience shame is to feel that we (or parts of ourselves) *are* bad. It is the experience of not only making a mistake, but also fearing that mistakes reveal something deficient about ourselves: that we, in the very core of our being, *are* mistakes.

Since the human condition is laced with ambiguity and limit, we are by definition unable to control or anticipate the events of our lives. Since we are relational beings, our reactions to one another *do* matter. We do long to see on someone's face a delight in seeing our face and are hurt when that delight is absent. Human beings inevitably disappoint and are disappointed by one another. Situations do from time to time take us by surprise. We do not always know all the "rules of the game" or where we, in or freedom, might appropriately choose to challenge them. Shame, thus, is simply a possibility given to the human experience.

Some have argued[13] that while shame is always a painful experience, it can also be helpful. It can teach us when we have pushed a limit too far for our own well being or beyond the stretch of protective social norms. A group of children tease one other, but stop when one of their number is overcome with tears. Shame can tell us when we are frightened or unsure about ourselves in a certain situation, perhaps indicating that we are not yet ready to venture in this way. For instance, an adolescent, uncomfortable with the attention focused on her when she tries on a sophisticated party dress, chooses not to go to the formal dance, but rather attends a rock concert, where she feels more comfortable in her jeans and flannel shirt. Shame reminds us (when we have the composure to reflect on the experience) how important it is to be graciously received by another, and how fragile our expectations and relationships can be.

While shame can be said to be a piece of the human experience, the shame I am focusing on is not this experience of shame, but shame that has become what John Bradshaw has called "toxic,"[14] shame as the experience of being refused that sediments into postures of protection and refusal that are binding to the human being. Toxic shame is more damaging than a single shaming experience. It is a state of alienation born when shame experiences have been particularly devastating (as in the case of rape or incest or the slap on the face Freddy suffered), or chronic (where one never heals from an experience of shame but, through repetition, experiences shame as "the way things are" or "who I really am"). It results when shaming tactics are used repeatedly as a tool for control, when the system in which we live is "shame-based" (one that indoctrinates people as to their unworthiness or that always needs to blame someone or something when anything goes "wrong"), or when the person who shames us is a very significant other in our pantheon of relationships. This shame reflects not only the external shaming incident(s), but also an internalizing process that is both inner and outer, as the shamed person repeats over and over again to him or herself the sense that "I am inadequate," or as she develops compensating strategies in order to avoid being shamed again (the monitoring and self-punishment Gibbons points to). As Gershen Kaufman describes the experience:

> All of us embrace a common humanity in which we search for meaning in living, for essentially belonging with others, and for valuing of who we are as unique individuals. We need to feel that we are worthwhile in some especial way, as well as whole inside. We yearn to feel that our lives are useful, that what we do and who we are do matter. Yet times come upon us

when doubt creeps inside, as if an inner voice whispers despair. Suddenly, we find ourselves questioning our very worth or adequacy. It may come in any number of ways: "I can't relate to people." "I'm a failure." "Nobody could possibly love me." "I'm inadequate as a man or as a mother [sic]." When we have begun to doubt ourselves, and in this way to question the very fabric of our lives, secretly we feel to blame; the deficiency lies within ourselves alone. Where once we stood secure in our personhood, now we feel a mounting inner anguish, a sickness of the soul. This is shame.[15]

To know shame is to experience ourselves as deficient and ultimately rejectable. The posture of alienation that is toxic shame is the process of internalizing that shame and developing protective strategies to defend ourselves from ever being shamed again. In this process, what was an experience of shame becomes core to our experience of who we are. If sin is to refuse our human condition and to seek to secure ourselves and protect our future, then shame is born of being refused and is reflected in the sense of being "defective," in the corresponding dread that there is no future for "me" (at least as "I" am), and in strategies and postures that seek to defend the self against further shaming incidents.[16]

THE SPIRAL OF SHAME

Being together is knowing
even if what we know
is that we cannot really be together
caught in the teeth of the machinery
of the wrong moments of our lives.

A clear umbilicus
goes out invisible between,
thread we spin fluid and finer than hair
but strong enough to hang a bridge on.

That bridge will be there
a blacklight rainbow arching out of your skull
whenever you need
whenever you can open your eyes and want
to walk upon it.

Nobody can live on a bridge
or plant potatoes
but it is fine for comings and goings,
meetings, partings, and long views,
and a real connection to someplace else
where you may
in the crazy weathers of struggle
now and again want to be.

Marge Piercy, "Bridging"[17]

How does this experience of toxic shame come about? Kaufman in *Shame:The Power of Caring* chronicles the development of shame from initial experiences between persons to the binding and paralyzing condition it can become. Kaufman's description of the process of shame is built on presuppositions about the human condition that mirror the human condition as described earlier as the context out of which human sin is born.

To be human, Kaufman first assumes, is to be deeply relational. Human persons need others. We need to be wanted and loved, *and* we need to love and to have our love accepted by others. This assumption informs Kaufman's understanding of shame as "the power of caring." Shame might not be such a powerful experience if human beings did not care so much or desire other's care. Shame we might say is formed in the arms of love. Human beings reach out to each other for affirmation, for connection, out of a desire to love. We build bridges of interconnection, bridges that are the basis for trust and vulnerability. Bridges allow us to reveal ourselves to one another and thus to have reasonable expectations for one another. Human beings are bridge builders and shame is the result of broken bridges.

Second, human beings not only build bridges to others, but Kaufman assumes we also build bridges within ourselves. Humans are about the task of forming an identity: a relationship with ourselves. This relationship is shaped out of the experiences we have with others. It is informed by a process of identification whereby we learn to treat ourselves as others treat us.[18] Schooled in the experience of respect, where we are treated as a separate individuals worthy of love and where our attempts at loving others are valued and received, we learn self-respect. Schooled in the experience of shame, where we are repeatedly shamed and learn that we (or parts of ourselves) are shameful, we learn not self-respect but self-refusal.

Third, to be human, Kaufman argues, is to have needs, feelings, and drives, all of which are normal to the human experience. All of which, he reminds us, are in need of validation from significant others. This is most especially true for children who need the security/affirmation of parents' acceptance in order to know and accept these needs, feelings, and drives, all of which are vulnerable (through failing to garner the needed validation or through attracting actual rejection) to being named shameful and thus worthy of rejection. We learn through shame then to bind rejected feelings, needs, and drives to shame and, in hope of avoiding further shameful experiences, to cast these feelings, needs, and desires out of the realm of conscious awareness. We learn to hide parts of ourselves, hiding them even from ourselves. To be human, then, is to have the possibility of refusing parts of ourselves and binding those parts away, thus living in active refusal of ourselves.

Fourth, if to be human is to relational, to be about the much needed task of building bridges (as Piercy envisions in her poem, taking the filaments of connection between people and building upon them substantial bridges of interconnection, bridges strong enough to come back and forth upon), then to be human is also to know the reality of broken bridges. No human connection is "perfect." All relationships must be worked at. Given the finitude and the ambiguity of the human situation, given the fact that our needs often conflict and that our energies give out and that we cannot always be "present" to one another as we would like, broken bridges are a regular part of the human situation. Because for Kaufman, the source of human shame is inter-personal, resulting from the breaking of the human bridge, shame is a "given" to the human situation.

Fifth, the difference between shame as a given to the human situation and shame as the debilitating, spiraling experience of toxic shame is how we react to the shaming incident(s). To be human is not only to build bridges and to experience them as crumbling as we experience disappointment and even more intentional hurt from one another. It is also to know the possibility of reconciliation. Broken bridges can be mended. Breaking bridges, having them broken on us, and then having them mended is part of the human experience informing our ability to hope and our confidence in ourselves and others. It is when bridges are broken and not attended to that, Kaufman argues, shame provides the seeds for greater disruption in the human experience. When we are shamed, we know disappointment and a sense of being exposed. When we experience shame as if we are the only ones to ever experience such shame, as if this exposure has revealed us to be radically unacceptable to other human persons, then shame is an experience of radical isolation. When bridges are rebuilt, we learn that we are not radically isolated and unacceptable, and that disappointments, while being part of life, are not the final word.

But if to be human is to build bridges and to know broken bridges and to heal as bridges are mended and we learn to trust others and ourselves, to hope, and to know that broken bridges are not the final word, *then*, sixth, to be human is also to know the possibility that our shame might not be healed. Broken bridges can be left unattended, and we can be left alone in our feelings of unworthiness. When bridges are not restored, then we live in the danger of greater alienation as our sense of ourselves as unacceptable (worthy only of refusal) and isolated, left unattended, can be amplified by a growing sense of powerlessness to change our situation, and an internalization of the shaming process where we can, now without the need of another, experience an inner replay of shameful moments, making increasingly greater efforts to keep hidden and separate those parts of ourselves that would trigger such pain.

If shame is formed in the arms of love and created when our human bridges inevitably are broken, then finally shame and the process of refusal and alienation it describes is also informed by our human proclivity to blame ourselves when broken bridges occur. This affect is especially evident in children who, out of love for their parents (or for other significant adults) and out of a need to see those adults as essentially loving, will blame themselves for a broken connection. Seeing themselves as the cause of their shame rather than seeing that adults can disappoint and even be intentionally hurtful (as Mr. Barnes was), children can develop unreasonable expectations for themselves, their children, and those they love. Thus shame is enhanced by the proclivity to blame ourselves, to see ourselves as a problem and thus rejectable, and to continue the act of rejection by persisting in refusing ourselves (or those "problematic" parts of ourselves). This process, of course, can be amplified when the relational system in which the person abides is, in actuality, one that finds the need to blame others when an unacceptable event occurs.[19]

The process of toxic shame continues onward and inward from initial experiences of shame when these initial shaming experiences are left unhealed, are internalized, and when it is those experiences that we predominately depend upon to name ourselves, to shape our expectations for ourselves, and to inform the ways in which we related to ourselves, to others, and to our world. In this process we name parts of ourselves as shameful, refuse them (as they might have been refused or as we assume that they were the cause of our refusal), and hide them from sight. We can become vigilant in watching ourselves, and repeat the drama of shame within ourselves, with or without the trigger of an external event. Kaufman describes this experience of internalization, as one that may begin at an early age and become part of our unconscious perception of ourselves, affecting the way we treat ourselves and others. Disengaged in our consciousness from its interpersonal, historical, source, shame becomes formative for our self-identity. With toxic shame buried deep in our unconscious, we can forget that it was *learned*, that it resulted from painful experiences of refusal and broken bridges, and that is not a "given" or essential part (even though it may have become a central part) of our human nature.

While shame can be internalized as a toxic part of our human identity, the process of shame is further complicated as we take various defensive measures to protect against further shaming events. These defenses, often directed at others who might shame us, can also be turned against those parts of ourselves that generate shame within us. Kaufman's list of defensive measures include rage, contempt, striving for power, striving for perfection, transfer of blame, and internal withdrawal (79–97). Furious over being disappointed, hurt, and exposed, we can lash out in rage at the offending/offended other or at ourselves (or at other potential offending others) for "causing" the experience. Seeking to protect our wounded selves, we can turn on others or parts of ourselves with contempt. Striving to avoid being shamed by others, we can seek to gain maximum control over our lives and the lives of others. (For instance, we can seek to move up the hierarchical ladder, where we can always have someone else to blame when things go wrong.) Desiring to compensate for underlying feelings of defectiveness, we can strive to be perfect so that we cannot be shamed. This is a doomed process at best since perfection is elusive to human creatures, and fooling ourselves into thinking we might attain perfection, actually can make us more vulnerable to shaming.[20] In order to free ourselves from culpability, we can learn to blame others or parts of ourselves, thus encouraging an environment of blame. Rather than risk further exposure, we can withdraw within ourselves, protecting ourselves from being seen (through), hiding behind masks of shame.[21]

We can see that the defenses against shame hold the possibility for further disruption of the fabric of human connection: they threaten bridges to others and within ourselves. They can even disrupt our relationships with our children (and grandchildren) passing onto them (as Mr. Barnes sought to do) a legacy of shame. But while human response to shame (which is itself a reflection of the spiraling of toxic shame) can and often does perpetuate patterns of shaming, broken relationship, and refusal, it is important to remember that these defenses are *survival* mechanisms. Born for interconnection with others, in shame humans beings build distorted relationships. Born for "heart,"[22] we shape relationships out of brokenheartedness. (Perhaps, as one develops more less-flexible scar tissue, we might even say such relationships are shaped out of *hard-heartedness.*) But if defenses are the cause of hurt to others and ourselves, if they reflect a posture of refusal with which we meet ourselves, others, and the world, and if these postures have grave implications for ourselves, others, and our world, they are born in prior experiences of hurt, refusal, and shame. While this does not make the intentional harming of another person or oneself acceptable (not even as in the case of Mr. Barnes when it is intended for the other's well-being), it does help us understand the origin of some of the refusing ways in which we do treat one other.

We can conclude that shame is a human experience that results when human bridges are broken, when we are overtly shamed by another as well as when our simple expectations for a relationship are left unmet, when we experience ourselves or parts of ourselves as refused by another, and that affects the way we feel about and treat ourselves and others. Through the internalization of shame, the building up of defenses (which can become postures of refusal), and the continuation of that refusal upon others and ourselves, an initial rupture in relationship spirials in to create greater rupture.

"BLEST BE THE TIE THAT BINDS . . ."
HEALING BROKEN BRIDGES

Shame is the painful human experience of being exposed, rejected, and disappointed. It is a process wherein we learn to think of ourselves (or parts of ourselves) as shameful, perhaps sinful, and worthy of refusal that both are the result *of* and result in the breaking of relational bridges (within ourselves and between others and ourselves). Rebuilding broken bridges and returning parts of ourselves to ourselves is the task of Kaufman's healing work. Healing rebuilds bridges, turns shame binds that cut us off from parts of ourselves and others into ties that bind us together with others in the human community, and builds a community that realizes that disappointments and broken bridges are a part of life, that hurt, shame, and refusal are structured into the world as we receive it, *and* that those ruptures, refusals, and disappointments do not have to isolate a person from the human family.

The process of healing from shame through the mending of bridges is complicated by the intricacies of the shaming process itself. As noted earlier, when shame has become a part of our identity, we have often forgotten both the interpersonal origin of the shame (we have come, perhaps, to believe that *"I am shameful!" "I am the worst of sinners."*) and the parts of ourselves that we have bound off in an effort to avoid further shaming experiences. The process of healing, then, is a journey of remembering what has been forgotten, restoring our knowledge of our shamefulness to its correct historical place of origin. It is a re-membering of ourselves, a bringing together, a reconciliation and acceptance, of what has been refused and bound apart.

The process of healing is one of returning to the original rupturing experience(s), seeing what has (actually) happened (perhaps Mr. Barnes was really reacting to a refused part of himself that he saw projected upon Freddy), and feeling the hurt and grieve the pain and humiliation of that incident, allowing it to be a part of our *past* history. Because the originating coparticipant in the breaking of the interpersonal bridge may no longer be accessible to those who would heal, the process of healing from shame may entail finding a new "other" who we can trust to accompany us in this process. In this process of bridging with our past, we can also learn, by journeying and building new bridges with new significant others, that bridges *do* break (for they do and will break with this new significant other) and *can* be healed. These are lessons we did not learn earlier when attention was not given to our brokenness and hurt. This means we must learn to be willing to trust another again, to care, and to risk more broken bridges. This is not an easy task. But, how else can we learn that life both breaks and can be healed? How else can we learn to hope? How else can we learn new ways to perceive ourselves and the world?

Because the originating interpersonal experiences of shame are often hidden from consciousness, healing entails uncovering them, exposing them to the light. Healing thus comes through risking the reexperiencing of the shaming experience and the pain it brought. We come to new life, then, by journeying through the darkness. However, whereas we might have first hidden in shame, cutting ourselves off from others, healing comes from allowing an other to see our shame and from being accepted as we are seen. Whereas shame isolates, in the healing process we are no longer alone. For the coparticipant in this process (the therapist, minister, friend), this may mean getting "into the mud" with the person bound by shame (becoming flesh and dwelling with the other), confessing that they also know moments of shame, and acknowledging that their feelings are part of the human situation, thus challenging the myth of isolation.

POSTURES OF REFUSAL AND THE BROKEN HEART

Are all postures of refusal best defined and addressed as sin? In what ways can those who have been refused, who then (as in the case of toxic shame) assume postures of refusal that may include narratives about their own sinfulness and blame for their pain, be said to be sinful? Is it possible to be both the victim of someone's (or some system's) sin (and thus not to blame), and yet culpable for the postures of refusal and defensive measures that may perpetrate further refusal? Our brief exploration of Kaufman's work on shame has given us several clues as to how theologians can interpret postures of refusal and the damage they both may reflect and perpetrate.

First, we have seen not only that human beings are inherently relational, that we build and depend upon inter- and intrapersonal bridges, but that our relationality makes us very vulnerable to wounding, to situations of disappointment and refusal. Since this wounding/refusal can result in postures of refusal that look very much like the postures of refusal we have named sin, we can assume that human relationality and the vulnerability it entails needs to be a factor in our discussion about sin. If sin is our human attempt to secure ourselves inappropriately, then wounding and refusal can enhance our need to be secure and our reluctance to trust in anything more than our own abilities.

Second, while both sin and shame may look alike in that both assume postures of refusal and self-securing that can have grave implications for others, ourselves, and our world, they claim different places of origin. Since some postures of refusal may reflect not an initial will to be like God (as sin has classically been understood), but a broken heart, we must be discerning in the way we approach situations where people treat each other in sinful ways. While we can assume that all acts of violation need to be seen as the sin against another (or the self) that they are, they then could also be an expression of a broken heart. As such, their actions need to be stopped and judged, while they themselves are treated with a tender but firm respect that can help to bring the brokenheartedness to the surface where it can be healed.

Third, we must be equally discerning in listening to people speak about their sense of their own sinfulness. If narratives of self-blame and unworthiness can develop to cover over initial experiences of refusal, then in talking about themselves as wretched sinners, people may be reflecting a false construal of a situation in which they were sinned-against. We might sit with a new curiosity as congregations sing about God's amazing grace that "saved a wretch like me" and wonder just what is the wretchedness that each person is singing about. And we might wonder if words of forgiveness and assurance of pardon are the right words of salvation for everyone. Do we need to have not only times of confession, but periods of remembering, rage, lamentation, sorrow, restitution, and reconciliation? Will we find that confession of sin, and healing of brokenheartedness, are companion postures—that sometimes those who wound others (as Mr. Barnes wounded Freddy) are unable to see the full impact of their refusals until they can bear the reality of their own woundedness?

Finally, if postures of refusal are sometimes born of original experiences of being refused, then it is possible to understand how postures of refusal can be passed on from generation to generation (as indeed Mr. Barnes attempted to do with Freddy). If it is possible that some postures of refusal are born of deprivation (being refused) rather than depravity (an inborn tendency to refuse), this raises some interesting questions for the classic doctrine of original sin. Is it possible that some of our focus on original sin (as a defect of the will that is passed on congenitally from generation to generation) would be more appropriately named original shame?[23] If so, then we might understand how human sin (postures of refusal) can be passed on not by an inherited depravity, but through our human vulnerability to being refused, through actual ruptures of the interpersonal bridge that are left unattended, and through the repetition of refusals that are an expression of that unhealed wound. Original sin/refusal would not then be inherent to the human condition and core to our being, but the result of an historical event. Human vulnerability to refusal, however, would be inherent—as would the fact that unhealed refusals often are repeated upon others and the self.

In our postmodern world, we are often aware that human innocence is a myth.[24] If the classic doctrine of original sin captured this insight in its belief that humanity has fallen so that we cannot choose not to sin, postmodern theologians argue that so interwoven and ambiguous is our human condition, that all of our actions have implications for others. Even our best intentions can have harmful repercussions for some other aspect of creation—and we are not innocent. Recognizing our human vulnerability to refusals, acknowledging that broken bridges and hurt seem to be endemic to creation as we know it, accepting that sometimes our sinful behavior—while hurtful and thus evil—can be born of a broken heart, alerts us to the complexity that confronts us when we would talk about human sinfulness. It also offers us a challenge that if we would be more attentive to the relationships that are core to our being, if we would work with the consciousness that ambiguity and conflict happen in the human situation but that they can be attended to and healed (even if they can never be made perfect), if we know that sometimes people assume postures of refusal born of a broken heart, then we might be that much more able to participate effectively in the healing of the world. If the world is ultimately beyond our abilities to heal, then at least we will have a new perspective from which to know how truly amazing is the grace that not only forgives sinful wretches but also heals and binds up the brokenhearted and will not abandon them to their shame. That is a reality worthy of our awe and praise.

NOTES

Kaye Gibbons, *Sights Unseen* (New York: Putnam, 1995).

1. Søren Kierkegaard, *The Concept of Anxiety,* trans. by R. Thome and A. B. Anderson, (Princeton: Princeton University Press, 1980); and Kierkegaard, *The Sickness Unto Death,* trans. by Walter Lowrie (Princeton: Princeton University Press, 1951).

2. Edward Farley, *Good and Evil: Interpreting a Human Condition* (Minneapolis: Fortress, 1990) 123.

3. See the film *Safe Passages* for a look at how one family tangles with the realities of the limits of the human situation to find security for its members. Inevitably, they come to the awareness that we are not able to guarantee safe passage after all.

4. Farley, *Good and Evil*, 119–138.

5. See Susan L. Nelson (Dunfee), "The Sin of Hiding: A Feminist Critique of Reinhold Niebuhr's Sin of Pride" in *Soundings* (Fall 1982) 316–327.

6. Farley calls this process the tendency to see the vulnerability of creation as something "sporadic and accidental" and "contingent" rather than accepting it as "necessary and inescapable." Ibid., 132.

7. Mary Potter Engel speaks of this experience as "evil." Wendy Farley calls it "radical suffering." Andrew Sung Park refers to it as "han."

8. See Rita Nakashima Brock, *Journeys by Heart: A Christology of Erotic Power* (New York: Crossroads, 1988) for a more in-depth discussion of brokenheartedness and how it is born of (and is thus a symptom of) the relationality and resulting vulnerability that are endemic to the human condition. Brock argues that what the tradition has named "original sin" is actually the damage that is passed on from generation to generation not through conception and birth but through the wounding that is all but inevitable to the human situation—especially for Brock as that human experience has been organized in patriarchal families.

9. For example, for an exploration of how our first bond forms the basis for future relationships and extensive notes on the development of object relations theory see Jessica Benjamin, *The Bonds of Love* (New York: Pantheon, 1988).

10. Brock, *Journeys by Heart*.

11. See Park, *The Wounded Heart of God* (Nashville: Abingdon Press, 1993), for a discussion of han that results from such situations.

12. See Nelson, *Healing the Broken Heart: A Conversation about Sin, Healing, and the Broken Heart* (St. Louis: Chalice, 1998) for a more detailed discussion of family systems that refuse children their full range of experience.

13. John Bradshaw, for instance, makes this point in his description of good shame. See Bradshaw, *Healing the Shame that Binds You* (Deerfield Beach, Fla.: Health Communications) 3–9.

14. Ibid., 9 f.

15. Gershen Kaufman, *Shame: The Power of Caring* (Rochester, Vt.: Schenkman Books, 1992) vii. Kaufman's work has been the most informative one for this chapter, especially since he focuses on the rupture of the relational bridge as the source of shame.

16. I have made a distinction between sin and shame. For a provocative discussion of the relationship between sin and despair—how despair is both sin and yet not sin but sickness, see Mary Louise Bringle's *Despair: Sickness or Sin?* (Nashville: Abingdon Press, 1990).

17. Marge Piercy, *Circles on the Water: Selected Poems of Marge Piercy* (New York: Knopf, 1982) 107.

18. It is worth noting here the *reversal* of the logic in the threefold love command Christ gives his followers. Love of God and others, in Christ's command, are to be modeled upon our love for ourselves. In Kaufman's model, we learn to love ourselves as we are loved—to show ourselves the respect we have seen modeled in the way others respect us, themselves, and others.

19. Blaming, of course, can also be projected outward toward others. As we shall see, blaming others (or split-off parts of ourselves) can be a defensive strategy against greater shame. This does not negate the point made here, however, that part of the shaming process is blaming and that blaming is often directed at ourselves.

20. This drive for perfection can also tie love and acceptance to performance (am I good enough?) and actually works to erode further human relating.

21. See L. Wurmser, *The Masks of Shame* (Baltimore: Johns Hopkins University Press, 1981).

22. See Brock, *Journeys by Heart*. *Heart* is her word for human connection and joy at life just as *brokenheartedness* is the term she develops to describe the wounding (e.g., by shame or, as she argues, by patriarchal patterns of childrearing) that damage and persist within that heart.

23. See Laurel Arthur Burton's "Original Sin or Original Shame," *Quarterly Review* (Winter 1988–1989) 31–41; as well as Donald Capps's studies of Augustine that suggest that Augustine, the author of the doctrine of original sin, was himself the victim of shaming incidents in his youth. See "The Scourge of Shame and the Silencing of Adeodatus," and "Augustine as Narcissist: Of Grandiosity and Shame," in *The Hunger of the Heart: Reflections on the Confessions of Augustine*, ed. by Capps and James E. Dittes (West Lafayette, Ind.: Society for the Scientific Study of Religion, 1990) 69–92.

24. See Kathleen M. Sands, *Escape from Paradise* (Minneapolis: Fortress, 1994), for an exploration of the complexity and ambiguity of creation that makes it impossible for people not to be complicit in the suffering of the world.

CHAPTER FIVE

BEYOND "THE ADDICT'S EXCUSE":
SIN, PUBLIC ADDICTION, AND ECCLESIAL RECOVERY

Ched Myers

> So the people worked all day and night and all the next day, gath-
> ering the quails; the least anyone gathered was ten homers. . . . But
> while the meat was still between their teeth, before it was con-
> sumed, the anger of G-d was kindled against the people, and G-d
> struck them with a very great plague. So that place was called
> *Kibroth-hattaavah* (which means, "the graves of craving").
>   —Num 11:32–34

> The great obstacle is simply this: the conviction that we cannot
> change because we are dependent upon what is wrong. But that is
> the addict's excuse, and we know that it will not do.
>   —Wendell Berry

"The vocabulary of Christian faith suffers from misunderstanding at every
turn, but no one term is as badly understood in both society and church as the
little word, 'sin,'" writes the Canadian theologian Douglas John Hall.[1] Most
modern critics of Christianity would concur. Dour Christian discourses of sin
have been favorite targets of the culture of narcissism. For such critics, however, the problem lies in churchly concepts of sin that are too severe, too
absolute, and too ubiquitous—in short, too *big*. Hall's argument, however, is
that the notions of sin circulating in the North American churches persist in
being too *small*.

A fatal mistake is made, Hall contends, whenever the church switches its
focus from *sin*, a matter pertaining to the human condition, to *sins*, transgressions to be cataloged and controlled: "The individualism fostered by pietistic

and liberal expressions of Protestantism has greatly aggravated the tendency to identity sin with negative qualities (sins)—specifically, negative *personal* failings."[2]

Dominant culture Christianity in the United States has indeed domesticated the language of sin. Conservatives tend to focus upon personal morality while equivocating about structural and historical manifestations of human alienation. Such religion continues to prosper in our social context because its essential individualism is congruent with the privatizing culture of late capitalism. Liberals, meanwhile, having assimilated into the optimistic secular myth of progress, tend to be embarrassed by the rhetoric of sin. Exceptions were the "social gospel" and "neo-orthodoxy" movements in this century, which attempted to reassert the public and political character of sin. Both movements remained, however, steeped in theologies of historical entitlement, and excluded from their critique not only their own gender, race, and class privileges but also the essential superiority of the American national project.

The problem is that neither privatistic nor positivistic theologies can account for the horrors of the twentieth century. It is not surprising, then, that in the last quarter century it has been Third World liberation theologians, working in contexts of severe human oppression and violence, who have consistently articulated an enlarged discourse of sin. Gustavo Gutierrez, for example, writes: "Sin is evident in oppressive structures, in the exploitation of man by man, in the domination and slavery of peoples, races, and social classes. Sin appears, therefore, as the fundamental alienation, the root of a situation of injustice and exploitation."[3] Recently Third World theologians have directed their reflections on sin specifically toward the First World church. The "Road to Damascus" Kairos document, for example, denounces "the sin of idolatry . . . that serves the total war being waged against the people, leading to the death and destruction of our communities."[4]

But such pointed appeals from the Third World have made relatively little impact upon mainstream churches in the United States. If anything, these churches are increasingly defensive, reflecting the dominant culture's anxieties as the national dream of ever-expanding political hegemony and ever-increasing economic affluence fades.[5] Thus while most middle-class people now intuit that they can no longer count on upward mobility for their children, their tendency is to channel their resentment toward the poor rather than trying to understand *why* the concentration of wealth is intensifying.[6] Indeed, the more social and economic systems are restructured at home and abroad to benefit capital—at the expense of the workplace, the neighborhood, and the home—the more First World churches seem to retreat into an obsession with personal sins.

Despite a growing sense that our exploitation of the earth is unsustainable, there are few serious, popular efforts to curtail the consumption that makes this exploitation both profitable and inevitable. Affluent North Americans are increasingly unable to stop their self-defeating, neurotic responses to a way of life that is out of control. We have become externally reliant upon a socioeconomic system that destroys the land, exhausts its resources, and alienates and exploits human labor: "The steps we have taken to quell the anxiety," writes Paul Wachtel "have actually exacerbated our sense of insecurity and—by ironic logic familiar to the student of neuroses—have thereby called forth still more of the same kind of efforts and thus still more undermining of security and still further acceleration of a one-sided and self-defeating pattern."[7]

In his classic *Whatever Became of Sin?*, psychologist Karl Menninger caricatured this kind of "American progress":

> We glowed; we gloried; we prospered; we preempted; we evicted; we extended; we consolidated; we succeeded! We shut our eyes to all that was unpleasant about these words and these processes. We were too busy to discern the misery created everywhere, too smug to see the devastation we were wreaking, too greedy to recognize the waste and the inequity and the ugliness and the immorality. . . . Suddenly we awoke from our pleasant dreams with a fearful realization that *something was wrong*.[8]

What is wrong, says Wendell Berry plainly, is that "we all live by robbing nature, but our standard of living demands that the robbery shall continue."[9] We are so internally captive to our illusions, excesses, and appetites that we can no longer *imagine* the world differently—and our little theologies of sin can't explain why. Berry, however, has this suggestion: we are using "the addict's excuse, and we know that it will not do."[10]

SIN AS ADDICTION

If a representative analogue for sin in a Third World context is *oppression*—the inability to say yes to life because of deprivation and injustice-then a corresponding First World analogue may well be *addiction* as the inability to say no because of captivity to pathological desires. "Empire," wrote the historian William Appleman Williams, "is the child of an inability or an unwillingness to live within one's own means; empire as a way of life is predicated upon having more than one needs."[11] An apt biblical metaphor for this condition might well be the alternative account of the manna story found in Num 11. Indeed, addiction is a kind of deadly "too muchness," in which we hoard the gifts of creation and overconsume in defiance of Exodus 15's express instruction to limit consumption based on need and to distribute the goods equitably.[12] The Numbers version of the manna tale captures perfectly the "plague": in our anxiety over the possibility of scarcity and our lust for gratification, we gorge ourselves to death (Num. 11:34). Yet today it is the poor who precede us to the "graves of craving" that our addictions have dug.

There have been three recent notable attempts by North American theologians to reflect on addiction as an analogy for sin. Psychologist Gerald May's *Addiction and Grace* sees addiction as universal in the human experience, and thus as a primary metaphor for alienation:[13] "We succumb because the energy of our desire becomes attached, nailed, to specific behaviors, objects, or people. *Attachment*, then, is the process that enslaves desire and creates the state of addiction."[14] May identifies two classes of addiction—the *attractive* (which attaches compulsion) and the *aversive* (which attaches repulsion)—and explores their psychological, neurological, and theological character.

Reformed theologian Cornelius Plantinga, in *Not the Way It's Supposed to Be* acknowledges the condition of addiction as *tragic*: "Like the fallenness of the human race, the chaos of addiction comes out of particular human character and sin but also out of the temptations and disorganizing forces resident in an addict's home and neighborhood and maybe even in her genes. The serpent is both within and without."[15]

Catholic moral theologian Patrick McCormick's *Sin as Addiction* considers the traditional "stain" and "crime" models of sin, and then proposes a "disease" model that allows us to move from punitive to therapeutic strategies of intervention.[16] He defines addiction as "a pathological relationship with a (normally) mood altering substance or process":

> [It] promises the "user" a consistent, dependable and repeatable solution to the anxieties and pains of life. . . . As the person becomes more and more immersed in and dependent upon this substance or process he/she experience himself/herself as less free, more compulsive. At the same time the addictive process begins to produce tangible and painful side-effects or consequences. More of the substance or process is required to kill the pain. . . . The solution has become the problem, but continues to be employed as if it were a solution. In order to continue the use of the addiction solution and maintain the addictive belief system the person must now engage in all sorts of denial and deception to ignore its counter-productivity and painfulness. . . . The addiction operates as a chronic and progressive disease, disintegrating the physical, spiritual, emotional and psychological life of the person, leading inevitably to insanity and/or death.[17]

McCormick contends that addiction has significant "theological likenesses." It arises from a "denial of creatureliness," our inability/unwillingness to live within limits, seeking instead the omnipotence promised by the delusional attachment. It represents also a denial of the Creator by its idolatrous fixation on the addictive object. Addiction seduces with the promise of liberation from pain, only to deliver progressive enslavement, which it masks through a delusional world of Denial. It is sustained through a web of lies: "The Devil is a murderer from the beginning . . . a liar and the father of lies" (Jn 8:44).

There are several compelling reasons why the addiction model can help restore a more comprehensive discourse—and more specifically a political theology—of sin in the North American context. First, personal addiction in North America today is epidemic. One must ask what social forces engender and sustain the current high levels of substance abuse and compulsive behavior among the populace. At the same time, the recovery movement (particularly Twelve-Step programs) is probably the most widespread form of individual and group transformative work current in the culture, cutting across gender, race, and class lines.[18] McCormick points out that the classic models of sin have been defined and adjudicated by professional clerics, judges, and psychologists, whereas the diagnosis of addiction and the practice of recovery has largely been the domain of *addicts themselves*. The ubiquity of the addiction/recovery phenomena represents a sociocultural gestalt that cries out for theological reflection.

Second, addiction offers a more complex view of evil than a moral anthropology that presumes that humans make "free" choices. Because the addict in denial cannot "see" her addiction, though surrounded and consumed by it, moral exhortation alone is impotent to change her behavior. Addiction is understood as a captivity, which means the addict is victim as well as victimizer. The recovering addict, consequently, must address both his *injury* and his *culpability*. On one hand he must seek to understand how severance from his true self—because of life-texts of abandonment, violation, poverty, and so forth—generated the void that addiction tried to fill. On the other hand addicts must also "confront the damage they have caused, to accept the consequences of their addiction and to shoulder responsibility for all their actions."[19]

Third, the model of addiction moves beyond behavioral symptomology ("sins") to a radical analysis of dysfunction as a way of life ("sin"). This emphasizes the predatory, lethal, and even demonic nature of sin. Addiction spirals exponentially toward destruction: "No matter how they start, addictions eventually center in distress and in the self-defeating choice of an agent to relieve the distress. In fact, trying to cure distress with the same thing that caused it is typically the mechanism that closes the trap on an addict."[20] It has been noted before that the apostle Paul's meditation on the enslaving power of sin in Romans sounds to modern ears like someone wrestling with the advanced stages of addiction: "I am sold under sin. I do not understand my own actions. For I do not do what I want, but I do the very thing I hate . . . I see in my limbs another law at war with the law of my mind, making me captive to the law of sin that dwells in my limbs. Wretched man that I am! Who will rescue me from this body of death?" (Rom 7:14 f, 23 f). Unlike the "sins" that moral philosophies seek to manage, the wages of addiction are *death* (Rom. 6:23).

The problem with the addiction model as it is understood by most First World psychological and religious professionals is that it has, like our theologies of sin, been domesticated as a strictly personal pathology. The social implications of the model are rarely addressed. While the role of the addict's family system is acknowledged, the role of the economic or political system is not. But addiction is biologically and socially *systemic*, both in its genesis and maintenance. Human appetites and deficits, engendered by the society at large, are exploited by addictive substances and relationships, which means that addiction has a complex personal and collective *history*. The addicted personality is embedded in social networks of complicity, as McCormick recognizes: "The burgeoning data on co-dependence, co-addiction, addictive families and addictive societies provides verifiable evidence concerning the ways in which addiction operates on the personal, familial and societal levels as well as the manner in which addiction is communicated from generation to generation."[21]

Anne Wilson Schaef has pioneered the application of the addiction model to organizations[22] and to society as a whole.[23] Her work has spawned other efforts to relate the model to the economy[24] and to other cultural strata such as education and religion.[25] I agree with this emerging literature that we should view the personal and political dimensions of addiction as ultimately inseparable.

DIAGNOSING PUBLIC ADDICTION

For purposes of the following discussion I will refer to individual pathology as "household addiction," recognizing the essentially domestic locus and often covert nature of the behavior. Collective pathology, on the other hand, I will call "public addiction." This not only underlines its social character, but also acknowledges that the addictive behavior can be engaged in quite publicly—indeed it is often *rewarded* by the body politic. McCormick names several examples in the First World context of what I am calling "public addiction": consumerism, colonialism, militarism, and sexism.[26] I will now focus on what might be the most obvious case: consumerism.

In the United States, individuals and households are relentlessly seduced by the promises and the products of consumer culture. Our desires often become so attached to commodities that we are truly possessed by our possessions—we simply *must* have the new dress, the nicer home, or the computer upgrade. Many consumer products themselves are manufactured to breed psychological and/or physiological dependence: titillating soap operas, sugar-filled fast food, and the planned obsolescence of virtually everything.[27]

Huge marketing apparatuses, in turn, both create and sustain the addiction by creating a vast, intense universe of artificial needs. Popular cultural forms such as music, art, and storytelling are put at the service of commercial marketing—a long-standing corporate design, argues Stuart Ewen, to "transform the consciousness of a proletariat into that of a consumeriat."[28] Advertising is a relentless aural and visual onslaught upon our consciousness with objectified texts and alluring subtexts that we cannot help but absorb. "Why ask why?" taunts a popular current beer commercial: the perfect mantra for an addicted consumeriat that passively ingests the aggressive marketing discourses that seek to form us economically, socially, politically and spiritually.[29]

Capitalism triumphs, warned Herbert Marcuse in *One Dimensional Man: Studies in the Ideology of Advanced Industrial Society*, when "people recognize themselves in their commodities": "Free choice among a wide variety of goods and services does not signify freedom if these goods and services sustain social controls over a life of toil and fear—that is, they sustain alienation. And the spontaneous reproduction of superimposed needs by the individual does not establish autonomy; it only testifies to the efficacy of the controls."[30] When the opportunity to choose between twenty varieties of deodorants becomes our working definition of freedom, and we no longer experience cognitive dissonance when Budweiser sponsors spots on "responsible drinking," our identity as a consumeriat has truly been consum-mated.[31] This collective condition reflects the compulsive and delusive nature of addiction.

Plantinga lists eight dynamics characteristic of the phenomena of addiction (though he cautions against attempting a "neat taxonomy"[32]). Let us test the culture of consumerism against this list, using brief, suggestive examples from both the household and public spheres:

ADDICTIVE DYNAMIC	HOUSEHOLD SPHERE	PUBLIC SPHERE
Pleasurable and habit-forming behavior that escalates tolerance and desire	Instant gratification of a product purchased	Short-term benefits of economic growth reflected in corporate profits, glut of investment capital, falling consumer prices
Unpleasant aftereffects of such behavior, e.g., withdrawal and self-reproch	Struggle to pay for products bought on credit	Unemployment, inflation, tightening of credit
Vows to moderate/quit, followed by relapses and attendant distress	Unsuccessful attempts to resist further overextensions; desires rekindled by next product "improvement"	Adjustments in interest rates and money supplies
Easing distress with new rounds of same or "companion" addictive behavior	Working harder to earn more to pay bills and enable more purchases	Renewed economic growth will solve all problems (tax cuts, wage freezes, public subsidy of new development)
Deterioration of work and relationships with accompanying denial and deception	Debt mounts, creditors demand payment and refuse to admit overextension	Capital flight, erosion of labor codes, corporate domination of local communities
Preoccupation then obsession with addictive substance	Increasingly desperate efforts to increase income or restructure credit; money fetishism and gambling	Subordination of social and political issues to need for economic growth; speculative and high-risk financial transactions, volatile markets; rewarding debt through credit ratings; deficit financing
Compulsivity in addiction; will is enfeebled	Inability to reduce material expectations, mortgaging of assets	Refusal to question basic economic structures; sacrificing rights and public assets to private corporate interests
Drawing others into web of addiction = codependence	Complicity of family, banks, and employers with financial demise of consumer addict	Globalized system of resource and labor exploitation and profiteering via "structural adjustment"

While these correlations are neither precise nor comprehensive, they do suggest that the addiction model can illumine individual and collective economic behavior.

McCormick identifies a further key dynamic in the destructive spiral of addiction: the pendulum of manic omnipotence in the fixation/attachment phase, and of depressive impotence in the "crash" phase.[33] One can see this same dynamic in the national mood swings that correspond to perceptions concerning the ebb and flow of the economy. Skyrocketing personal salaries for major CEOs and entertainers are watched by a mostly underemployed and under-compensated working class with envious fascination (publicly lionized grandiosity) while those on public assistance or the homeless or immigrants are scapegoated (publicly "split-off" depression).[34] The addiction prevents people from seeing that both manic and depressive manifestations are signs that the *system* isn't working.

The private and public compulsion of consumerism drives an economy which, as Barbara Brandt has shown, also keeps us addicted to work and to money.[35] A wasteful, growth-dependent economy is unsustainable in the long run, whether the limits are determined by ozone depletion, aquifer contamination, fossil fuel shortages, the trash crisis, or any other combination of ecological indices.[36] The only question is how long this complex addicting and addictive system can perpetuate itself before the organism collapses.

In the meantime, however, not only is this economy slowly but surely destroying the environment it mercilessly utilizes, but also the human societies it purportedly serves, by intensifying the stratification of wealth and the exploitation of human labor.[37] This latter phenomenon is both domestic and international. Writing in the *Los Angeles Times*, Jeff Gates summarizes the economic polarization in the United States over the last decade:

> The financial wealth of the top 1% of Americans now exceeds the combined net worth of the bottom 95%. . . . The wealth of the Forbes 400 richest Americans grew by an average $940 million each over the past two years (topping a combined $1 trillion). That's while the modest net worth of the bottom 40% shrunk by 80% between 1983 and 1995. . . . Eighty-six percent of stock market gains between 1989 and 1997 were harvested by the top 10% of households, while fully 42% flowed to the topmost 1%.[38]

Accompanying this dysfunctional distribution of wealth are a whole array of pathological behaviors, which fetishize not only commodities, but also money itself, whether through the public lionizing of the lifestyles of the rich and famous or through the stunning recent growth in the gambling industry.[39]

In the international political economy, Walden Bello characterizes the First World as draining the Third World: "Draconian policies of debt collection produced a staggering net transfer of financial resources—$155 billion—from the South to the North between 1984 and 1990."[40] This pillage is accomplished primarily through global policies of "structural adjustment" that have been devastating for the poor, both at home and abroad.[41] Sin-as-addiction among the haves, we must conclude, makes sin-as-oppression inevitable among the have-nots.

CONVERSION AS RECOVERY

What might it mean, wonders Hall, for dominant culture Christians in North American to rediscover "a hamartiology (doctrine of sin) that was truly—and not just rhetorically—biblical"?[42] In the prophetic traditions of the Bible, the discourse of sin and repentance go together. The prophetic call to repent implied a negation of continuity with the historical project of Israel, insofar as this project was predicated upon illusions of a benign national past and an equally benign future (see e.g., Isa 6 and Jer 7).

Standing firmly within this tradition of "harsh love" was the late Second Temple prophet John the Baptist. According to the ancient historian Josephus, John was a militant Jewish nationalist who objected to the Hellenistic alliances of the Judean client-king Herod Antipas. According to the gospels, however, his preaching relentlessly attacked Judean ideologies of entitlement: "Who warned you of the wrath to come? Bear fruits that befit repentance! Do not begin to say to yourselves, "We have Abraham as our ancestor," for I tell you God is able from these stones to raise up children to Abraham" (Lk 3:7 f). This discourse offers a *radical* analysis of the system: "Even now the ax is laid to the *root* of the trees" (Lk 3:9). It is not a moral exhortation to "be better" but a historical *ultimatum.* This challenge is not primarily directed to individuals, but to a *people.* Our historical project is headed toward destruction, it claims; we must *turn around and move in the opposite direction.* The synoptic gospels all portray Jesus of Nazareth as taking up this same message of John after the authorities had silenced the Baptist (Mk 1:14 f par).

A discourse of repentance that calls for radical *discontinuity* with the social, economic, and political order enjoys little hospitality today among the dominant culture churches of the United States. The reason is simple: for those entitled within the system, the greatest social value is *continuity.* From their perspective the system *works:* it has no fatal contradictions; it perpetuates itself; it even grows and spreads. This is why *conversion*—a theme once taken seriously by nineteenth-century Protestantism—is today either wholly marginalized (by liberal Protestants) or wholly spiritualized (by evangelicals). Repentance as discontinuity resonates strongly, however, with *those in recovery from addiction.* What might we learn from them?

The Twelve-Step movement has emerged over the last half-century as a genuinely popular insurrection against the epidemic of household addiction in the First World. Alcoholics Anonymous was developed in relationship to the pietistic Protestantism of the "Oxford Movement" of the 1930s.[43] These origins explain the Twelve-Step tradition's oft-noted congruence with the theology of conversion, but also caution us to beware of its limitations.

Because the Twelve-Step tradition has worked within the privatizing religio-psychological paradigms of capitalist modernity, it has tended to give nonpolitical, personal definitions of recovery. The systemic character of our public addiction, however, warns us against individualistic notions of recovery. If I am liberated from household addiction, but ignore the social and political expressions of, or contributors to, that addiction, I have only learned to function better in a pathological public system. What are needed instead are *collective* and *long-term* disciplines of "turning around."

Still, I believe the Twelve-Step tradition reflects three important insights for a theology of addiction and recovery. First, it is a "conversionist" model. *Step One*, as essential as it is uncomfortable, is the acknowledgment that the addictive system that controls me is destructive to me and to all those around me. To be liberated from the nihilistic logic of that system I must

appeal to and yield to a "Higher Power" (*Two and Three*);

accept my culpability in that system and "confess" it to others (*Four and Five*);

seek to "repent" of those practices (*Six and Seven*);

make reparation to those I've wronged (*Eight and Nine*).

The Twelve-Step process assumes that because the addictive system cannot be reformed, we must struggle to live in radical discontinuity with it. In this sense it is "apocalyptic": it seeks to overthrow the dominating system and concedes that the power to do so must come from "outside."

The aim is, in other words, nothing less than revolutionary transformation. As the recovering addict becomes stronger he invites other family members (as well as other addicts) to join in the insurrection against dysfunctional behavior so that the family system as a whole may be transformed. This insight need only be politicized. As Herbert Marcuse put it in his classic *Essay on Liberation*: "'Voluntary' servitude (voluntary inasmuch as it is introjected into the individuals), which justifies the benevolent masters, can be broken only through a political practice which reaches the roots of containment and contentment. . . . Such a practice involves a break with the familiar, the routine ways of seeing, hearing, feeling, understanding things so that the organism may become receptive to the potential forms of a nonaggressive, nonexploitive world."[44]

The second key insight of the Twelve-Step process—particularly for North Americans—is that it begins with our *own* experience of pain, oppression, culpability, and responsibility. An abstract analysis of the system is impotent; we are the *subjects* of the struggle for social change. This is crucial if we are to take seriously what Marcuse and other New Left thinkers called the "social psychosis of mass capitalist culture" as it relates to Marx's theory of alienation. The commodification of life demonstrated the "irresistible tendency toward the universalization of alienation . . . turning all human subjects into passive spectators of their own alienated existence."[45] More recently Michael Lerner has described this as the "surplus powerlessness" of capitalist individualism.[46]

The field of popular education has shown that if people perceive themselves to be powerless, they must be engaged at the level of their own experience if they are going to be animated toward change.[47] This is what popular theater practitioner Augusto Boal calls moving from spectating to "spec-acting."[48] It is true that in capitalist formations the focus on oneself risks degenerating into *subjectivism*, a danger we have noted already in both religious and therapeutic culture, including Twelve-Step programs.[49] But we cannot avoid this error by falling into the opposite trap, which concludes that structural problems are so vast and remote that "nothing I can do will make any difference." We must acknowledge and understand how we are part of the addictive system (complicity) and how it is part of us (internalization). This allows us to recognize the power of the system over us (our addiction) in a way that does not concede impotence or resignation (the addict's excuse).

The third, and perhaps most important, aspect of the Twelve-Step recovery process is its recognition of the necessity of an ongoing community of accountability and support in sustaining resistance to the addictive system. However great our internal opposition to recovery may be, the *external* opposition will be much more formidable, because the status quo always attempts to constrain fundamental changes in the system. In the family system, those who hold power are invariably the ones who, while rhetorically affirming the addict's quest for recovery, refuse to acknowledge their own complicity. Such "conserve-atism" is often desperate to maintain the family *ideal* (how it views itself) and *reputation* (how it is viewed in the community). As the recovering addict tries to stand her ground while refusing to cooperate with old family patterns, the alternative community of recovery becomes crucial as a place of understanding, identity, and support.

This is, of course, much more difficult in the case of public addiction, because it means breaking with the national "family" and its myths. Moreover, there is no socially constructed "shame" when it comes to consumption-addiction in this culture the way there is with, for example, alcoholism. Because the economic, social, and ideological mechanisms of seduction in the dominant culture are so powerful, and the mechanisms of repression so potentially vicious, a community of resistance and alternative consciousness-formation becomes key to a strategy of recovery from public addiction. If our diagnosis of the sociopolitical pathologies that define life in the United States were clearer, our recovery groups would necessarily become more "politicized"—as basic Christian communities in the Third World long ago discovered.

In sum, the traditional bourgeois Protestant notion of sin as moral failure simply cannot explain why it is so difficult for church members to confront public addiction such as consumerism in capitalist culture. Liberals have discovered that people do not "reform their behavior" just because they are so exhorted, even when it is argued that it is in their self-interest to change. Evangelicals have discovered that highly emotive "experiences of salvation" prove to be inadequate for the long-term struggle against the "old self" in a society that rewards pathological behavior. Perhaps then a First World theology of sin should reconsider the congruence between the old biblical language and the new discourse of the Twelve-Step tradition, in order to explore repentance as a *strategy of intervention* in an addictive system and conversion as a *strategy of recovery*.[50]

COMMUNITIES OF RESISTANCE AND RECOVERY

It is probably fair to say that most churches in the United States today have at least one Twelve-Step group meeting in their halls during the week. What might it take for our churches to *themselves* become communities of discontinuity with public addiction? First we need to name our sinful condition clearly. Consumerism, to take our example, is mildly scolded in our churches on occasion, but hardly considered to be a deadly *addiction!* To propose it as such would obviously provoke congregational opposition. This would not in most cases be attributable to any deep commitment to consumerist values and practices, however. Rather the objection would be that issues of economic culture are simply too large for regular church folk to deal with. Where, after all, would we *begin?*

We must recognize this as a socialized response. We have been formed to believe that we cannot make any real "difference" in the economic system unless we are powerful politicians, bankers, or corporate chiefs. Insofar as it concerns the structural imperatives of capitalism regarding profit, production, and power this is, unfortunately, all too true:

> When we consider where we experience some degree of freedom, we always find it exists within a broader framework over which we have no control. We are like the little child who is free to run away from home but not free to leave the block. The environment is a conspicuous example. We can recycle paper and other waste materials, but industrial America fouls the environment in ways we seem helpless to restrain. In large measure it is the nature and dynamic of the economic order that controls the framework within which we can make only rather inconsequential decisions.[51]

But this truth strips us of our illusion that we are somehow *not* entrapped in an addictive system (Step One!).[52] It thus presents us with two, somewhat paradoxical challenges.

On one hand it means that there is no such thing as strictly "personal liberation" from public addiction, a delusion that capitalist culture promotes vigorously. Just as credulous consumers imagine that a racy sports car will "set them free," so do many disaffected individuals imagine that they can disconnect from the dominant culture by wearing thrift store clothes or by fleeing the city. But private strategies of defection only strengthen a system whose purpose is to privatize the consciousness of the consumeriat. Our practices of recovery must address the *public* character of the addiction and must therefore include disciplines of collective analysis and action.

On the other hand, we are not absolved of individual responsibility. Just because we cannot *personally* change a system does not mean we have ceased to exist as moral and political agents. This is precisely the erasure capitalism seeks: to convince us that socioeconomic processes are so complex and cosmic that we, as isolated producers/consumers, are absolved of all obligation to think critically or to act discontinuously.[53] But this reflects the late stages of addiction: total capitulation to the structural imperatives of the system. Privatization and exoneration are the warp and woof of denial in public addiction; to embrace both culpability and responsibility, therefore, is to begin to unravel the whole cloth. A community of recovery reasserts responsibility *and* repoliticizes it, empowering members to take steps in their political bodies to resist the imperatives and expectations of the addictive body politic in the *actual* social, political economic spaces of their lives.

This requires us to reimagine the church not as a venue for religious entertainment (in which most attendees are essentially spectators) but as a committed community of recovering addicts (in which each member is a "spec-actor" struggling for sobriety). A quarter century ago Brazilian theologian Rubem Alvez called for precisely such a restoration of the church: "What the biblical sociology of liberation tells us through the symbol of community is unequivocal: the creative event cuts its way through the social inertia by creating *counter culture*."[54] This conviction has in each era of Christendom inspired renewal movements to attempt to disestablish the church and to find ways to live discontinuously from the dominant culture, from the early monastic movement to Franciscanism, and from the Anabaptists to nineteenth-century Christian socialist communitarians. In our time it has spawned base community movements throughout the Third World[55] and less widespread but no less important First World experiments with alternative forms of church.[56]

Countercultural movements have failed, contended Alvez, whenever they lacked both "communal discipline" and "political practice." The ancient metaphor for such discipline, Gerald May reminds us, is *asceticism* (from the Greek *askeeo*, "to exercise"): "Any struggle with addiction is a desert because it involves deprivation," he writes. "With major addictions . . . the desert can grow to encompass all of life: every habit may be exposed to the searing, purifying sun; every false prop is vulnerable to relinquishment; and one can be left truly dependent upon the grace of God for sustenance."[57] What "ascetic" disciplines might the church as a community of recovery from public addiction practice and promote?

REVISING THE EVANGELICAL DISCIPLINES

A fruitful beginning place might be to reappropriate the three great "evangelical disciplines" articulated in the old monastic Rule of St. Benedict (490–543 C.E.): poverty, chastity, and obedience. The early monks understood three key things about "civilization":

1. It is built upon the concentration of wealth and exploitation. If their communities were to repent they must become self-sufficient as possible.

2. The root of wealth-concentration is private property. If they wanted to resist the "temptations of the world" they must renounce exclusive ownership.

3. The exploitation of human labor is the root of all alienation (Marx later rediscovered this). If their communities were to restore human dignity they must practice manual (i.e., unalienated) labor.

For the first monastic communities the vow of "poverty" actually intended to inspire a social model that would *eradicate* poverty.

Today North Americans "spend $5 billion a year on special diets to lower their calorie consumption, while the world's poorest 400 million people are so undernourished they are likely to suffer stunted growth, mental retardation, or death," writes Alan Durning.[58] The affluent clearly need disciplines different than compulsive diets and obsessive gym workouts, which only mask the addiction to consumerism! The vow of poverty today might represent the equivalent of Steps One through Three in the Twelve-Step tradition. To recognize our public addiction to economic privilege and power means keeping the dysfunctional and deadly disparity of wealth always in view, and daily deciding to "turn over" our economic lives to the alternative reality of the divine "Great Economy" of grace.[59]

Three household disciplines of "economic sobriety" come to mind. The "simple living" movement has been well-documented.[60] As a spiritual discipline, so-called "downward mobility" is necessary but not sufficient, as it too easily can remain a private (and for many, a privileged) strategy. Groups such as the Ministry of Money have developed processes specifically for affluent people, including exposure tours to poor countries and suggestions for personal economic partnerships. Other groups are trying to help individuals and churches invest responsibly, particularly given the need for capital in poor neighborhoods. Building local organizations that promote economic sharing, on the other hand, takes us more into the public struggle. Experiments in alternative economics range from communal common purses to community credit unions. Collectivist living and cohousing arrangements, while difficult to sustain under capitalism, nevertheless encourage the recovery of traditional practices of extended family and hospitality that have atrophied in modern urban culture. Cooperative work strikes at the heart of alienated and alienating wage-labor, as do some of the emerging "green" and socially responsible business practices.[61] Land trusts and agricultural or environmental conservancies represent an alternative to private ownership, and community money systems and the burgeoning Community Supported Agriculture movement address the challenge of "recommunitizing" the marketplace.

An even better discipline of recovery is making *ourselves* available to the poor. People of privilege should socially relocate to live and work in proximity to disenfranchised people not primarily in order to "help," as in the old missionary model, but in order to view the world *from that space.* We thus avoid liberal abstractions about poverty and begin to build relationships with poor people. I have found community among the very folk against whom I had been "insulated" by my suburban, middle-class upbringing. The longer we are rooted in such neighborhoods the more the issues so familiar to the poor become our own. Our work then moves from "aid" to "alliance," from sympathy to solidarity.

Such disciplines expressing a "vow of poverty" no more make us poor than do those of an institutionalized monk today. But they do create the conditions for engagement with bigger structural issues, because our awareness of public addiction is heightened in direct proportion to our *actual* discontinuity with it. Lifestyle changes are not a political *solution* to anything, but can represent a political *question* to everything. As Marcuse put it: "No matter how great the distance between the middle-class revolt in the metropoles and the life-and-death struggle of the wretched of the earth—common to them is the depth of the Refusal."[63]

Behind traditional vows of "chastity" lay the early monks' profound appreciation of the fundamental connection between flesh and spirit. Economic practices, like sexuality, are not inherently evil; they are intrinsic to our humanity. But our appetite—economic and sexual—are exploited mercilessly by the highly sophisticated techniques of seduction in capitalist culture. Recovery thus also involves a kind of "consumer celibacy" toward commodity fetishism. Rather than yielding to the promises and obfuscation of marketers, we reassert responsibility for what we buy, investigating what conditions the product was made under, who profits from it, what its environmental impact is, and so on.[64] This represents Steps Four through Seven: the ongoing struggle to remove the addictive behavior from our lives.

In this case, chastity is not a private vow, but a discipline of collective accountability. We middle-class people are hostages to deeply ingrained assumptions about private ownership, freedom, and control. This extends not only to material things but also to use of time, space, vocational options, and above all, decision making. Nothing challenges our socialization into the fictive autonomy of the consumer more viscerally than accountability for how we earn and how we spend, because we *actually* (not hypothetically) have to give up private control. More accurately, however, we are *taking* back control from the expectations of the market. Such disciplines are the only way to discover how deeply we are possessed by our possessions, and the most effective means of facilitating recovery.

The vow of "obedience" was understood by the monks to represent single-minded attentiveness to the will of God. Here it means living in fidelity to the Great Economy. This requires both a defensive strategy of noncooperation with the social and economic imperatives of the public addiction, and an offensive strategy of engagement with the political Powers. War tax resistance, for example, is a household spiritual discipline of refusing to cooperate with the political economy of militarism, and an act of citizenship responsibility some of us believe to be more meaningful than voting.[65] Because public addiction is legal, the vow of obedience may often lead to civil *disobedience*. There is a growing movement around Sabbath-keeping that is trying to reassert the healing (and subversive) character of regular rhythms of rest and "nonproductivity" for both individuals[66] and for society.[67]

Offensive strategies require us to move beyond household-based lifestyle changes to political action. This includes promoting economic literacy at the grassroots and organizing consumer education and actions, from boycotts to shareholder protests. A Catholic priest was acquitted by a Chicago jury in 1990 after a campaign of defacing neighborhood billboards advertising alcohol and tobacco products that ravage the lives of so many in his urban, working-class, black and Latino parish. In South Central Los Angeles churches and community groups organized to prohibit the rebuilding of liquor stores after the 1992 uprising, and ended up fighting a white political establishment "under the influence" of the powerful alcohol lobby.[68] Other strategies include participation in labor organizing such as the nationally spreading "Living Wage Campaign," zoning battles, class-action lawsuits, and of course political lobbying. There are many consumer, public interest, and corporate watchdog organizations that would welcome the support of churches, such as Corporate Watch (*www.corpwatch.org*) and the Alliance for Democracy (*www.igc.org/alliance*). The historic disruption of the World Trade Organization by a broad coalition of grassroots advocacy groups in Seattle in late 1999 served as a hopeful wake-up call for populist struggle for global economic justice in the new millennium.

Steps Eight and Nine demand *reparation*, the most demanding discipline of obedience in the economic sphere. For those of the dominant culture, resisting addiction to immediate entitlements does little to deconstruct generations of inheritance upon which privilege is based. Reparation means exploring meaningful ways to redistribute wealth and power in conversation with those who have been disinherited, in order to create justice in the present and to heal past injustices. Sadly, for all our talk of reconciliation, we First World Christians have not seriously grappled with the tasks of reparative politics. The historical victims of oppression, however, have.

Many Third World countries, for whom the legacy of colonialism is continued indebtedness, are calling for debt forgiveness.[69] Another example is the National Coalition for Redress/Reparations, a successful decade-long campaign by Japanese Americans to get the U.S. government to apologize for the wartime internment of more than 120,000 Japanese Americans, and to provide symbolic redress to surviving internees:[70] "America had sinned, had been sinning for nearly a century, and the wages of sin is spiritual death," wrote a survivor Edison Tomimaro Uno. "Racism, economic and political opportunism were the root causes of this crime. . . . The Japanese American heritage is no exception to the experience of all minorities and oppressed people who know the bitter sting and enduring stigma of hate, fear and despair in a land of abundance. . . . Justice was trampled upon, and it is a responsibility all Americans must share."[71]

The struggle of Japanese Americans gave new impetus to the long-ignored National Coalition of Blacks for Reparations in America. And the oldest wound on the continent, the dispossession of Native America, is also beginning to be addressed, whether through efforts at the United Nations to catalog treaty violations against indigenous people by national governments worldwide[72] or in denominational apologies to native peoples for the oppressive legacy of Christian missionaries.[73] While restorative gestures are necessarily *symbolic* to some degree, this does not mean that they cannot also be *substantive*. In fact, they must be; psychologists point out that in order for reparation to be therapeutic for the culpable party, it must be *felt*. Perhaps the best current example of reparative struggle is the worldwide "Jubilee 2000" movement, calling for debt reduction/write-off for the most heavily indebted nations (*www.j2000usa.org*). Without disciplines of reparation, the rhetoric of reconciliation and recovery among First World churches will remain empty. And the longer we opt for cheap grace, the more costly real forgiveness will become. For the sin of First World addiction and Third World oppression are bound inextricably together in our common history.

The types of new evangelical disciplines just overviewed are hard work, and we are forever *reverting* rather than *converting*! We soon learn the truth of Jesus' parable about casting out one unclean spirit only to have "seven spirits more evil than itself return" (Lk 11:24 f). Recovery is like peeling an onion: each layer of internalized capitalism we remove brings more tears. That is why disciplines of economic celibacy demand both greater pastoral sophistication and contemplative commitments in our faith communities. Neither politics nor piety can substitute for the authentic inward journey here (Step Eleven).

"America is in deep trouble," writes anthropologist Marvin Harris, "but let no one suppose that our plight cannot get a whole lot worse."[74] With reactionary politics again on the rise, we who are entitled will face an ever-starker choice between the path of feeding public addiction or breaking it. It is likely that few members of the dominant culture in North America will want to walk the difficult path of recovery, especially when that demands costly reparation. Our churches, on the other hand, with their tradition of repentance, conversion, and the evangelical disciplines, are uniquely situated to shatter the denial, name the addiction, and model the practice of sobriety. Only as we become communities of resistance and recovery can we truly proclaim the good news to both the addicted and the oppressed that "the Spirit of life in Christ Jesus has set us free from the rule of sin and death" (Rom 8:2).

NOTES

1. Douglas John Hall, "The Political Consequences of Misconceiving Sin," *The Witness* (March 1995) 8 ff.

2. Ibid.

3. Gustavo Gutiérrez, *A Theology of Liberation: History, Politics, and Salvation*, trans. by Sister Caridad Inda and John Eagleson (Maryknoll: Orbis Books, 1973) 175 f.

4. Robert McAfee Brown, *Kairos: Three Prophetic Challenges to the Church* (Grand Rapids: Eerdmans, 1990) 125.

5. Ched Myers, "God Speed the Year of Jubilee: The Biblical Vision of Sabbath Economics," *Sojourners* (May–June 1990), 3 ff.

6. Chuck Collins, Betsy Leondar-Wright, and Holly Sklar, *Shifting Fortunes: The Perils of the Growing American Wealth Gap* (Boston: United for a Fair Economy, 1999).

7. Paul Wachtel, *The Poverty of Affluence: A Psychological Portrait of the American Way of Life* (Philadelphia: New Society Publishers, 1989) 60.

8. Karl Menninger, *Whatever Became of Sin?* (New York: Hawthorn Books, 1973) 4 f.

9. Wendell Berry, "The Futility of Global Thinking" *Harper's* (September 1989) 19.

10. Ibid.

11. William Appleman Williams, *Empire as a Way of Life* (New York: Oxford University Press, 1980) 31.

12. Myers, "God Speed the Year of Jubile."

13. Gerald May, *Addiction and Grace* (San Francisco: Harper and Row, 1998).

14. Ibid., 14.

15. Cornelius Plantinga Jr., *Not the Way It's Supposed to Be: A Breviary of Sin* (Grand Rapid: Eerdmans, 1995) 139 f.

16. Patrick McCormick, *Sin as Addiction* (New York: Paulist Press, 1989).

17. Ibid., 150 f.

18. Elaine Emeth, "Recovery and the Christian: A Bibliographic Essay on Addiction," *Sojourners* (December 1990) 40 ff.

19. Ellen McGuire, "A Place Called Hope," *The Nation* (28 December 1992) 822.

20. Plantinga, *Not the Way it's Supposed to Be*, 131.

21. Patrick McCormick, *Sin as Addiction*, 147.

22. Anne Wilson Schaef and Diane Fassel, *The Addictive Organization* (San Francisco: Harper and Row, 1988).

23. Schaef, *When Society Becomes an Addict* (San Francisco: Harper and Row, 1987).

24. Barbara Brandt, *Whole Life Economics: Revaluing Daily Life* (Philadelphia: New Society Publishers, 1995).

25. Denise Breton and Christopher Largent, *The Paradigm Conspiracy* (Center City, Minn.: Hazelden, 1996).

26. McCormick, *Sin as Addiction*, 163 ff.

27. Marvin Harris, *America Now: The Anthropology of a Changing Culture* (New York: Simon and Schuster, 1981) 17 ff.; and Wachtel, *Poverty of Affluence*, 31 ff.

28. Stuart Ewen, "Living by Design," *Art in America* (June 1990) 69 ff.

29. John Kavanaugh, *Following Christ in a Consumer Society: The Spirituality of Cultural Resistance*, 2d ed. (Maryknoll: Orbis, 1992) 21 ff.

30. Herbert Marcuse, *One Dimensional Man: Studies in the Ideology of Advanced Industrial Society* (Boston: Beacon, 1964) 8.

31. For a trenchant critique of the ways in which commodity "fetishism" has colonized our unconscious see Frederic Jameson's *Postmodernism, or the Cultural Logic of Late Capitalism* (Durham, N.C.: Duke University Press, 1991).

32. Plantinga, *Not the Way It's Supposed to Be*, 145.

33. McCormick, *Sin as Addiction*, 152 f.

34. This pendulum is almost exactly parallel to the "control/release" dynamic identified by Merle A. Fossum and Marilyn J. Mason, *Facing Shame: Families in Recovery* (New York: Norton, 1986) in their analysis of shame-bound systems (see also Susan L. Nelson's piece in this book). I have explored the national swing from grandiosity to depression in relation to the Gulf War from the perspective of social psychology (see Myers, *Who Will Roll Away the Stone? Discipleship Queries for the First World Christians* (Maryknoll: Orbis, 1994) 90 ff. Brandt has analyzed the same phenomenon in terms of American "business cycles" over the last century and a half in *Whole Life Economics*, 62 ff.

35. Brandt, *Whole Life Economics*, 60 ff.

36. Two of these examples will suffice. The *Los Angeles Times* reported on 23 February 2000 that "earlier this year, a blue-ribbon panel of climate experts commissioned by the National Academy of Sciences quashed most lingering doubts by calling global warming over the past 100 years 'undoubtedly real'" (A16). Most of the doubts have been generated by studies funded by the fossil fuel industry. Similarly, the *New York Times* reported on 6 January 2000, that despite strenuous public subsidy and encouragement, mandatory and voluntary recycling programs are not reducing the volume of trash nearly enough to head off serious crisis in the coming years ("Recyclers Are Saying: 'Bin There, Done That,'" A1). For overviews of current global ecological issues, see Donella Meadows, Dennis Meadows, and Jorgen Randers, *Beyond the Limits* (Post Hills, Vt.:Chelsea Green, 1992); and Bruce Brown, *Marx, Freud, and the Critique of Everyday Life: Toward a Permanent Cultural Revolution* (New York: Monthly Review Press, 2000).

37. Jeremy Brecher and Tim Costello, *Global Village or Global Pillage: Economic Reconstruction from the Bottom Up* (Boston: South End Press, 1994).

38. Jeff Gates, *Los Angeles Times*, 12 January 2000, B4.

39. Jean Kilbourne has been on the forefront of analyzing the cultural impact of advertising and commodity fetishism, particularly on women. See Kilbourne, *Deadly Persuasion: Why Women and Girls Must Fight the Addictive Power of Advertising* (New York: Free Press, 1999). Gambling is one of the fastest growing sectors in the U.S. economy, currently estimated to be a sixty-billion-dollar industry. All but a handful of states now have lotteries, while it is estimated that currently some fifteen million people gamble online, with industry analysts predicting that revenues from this sector will grow from one to ten billion dollars over the next three years. The National Gambling Impact Study Commission placed the number of compulsive gamblers at 5.5 million, more than the nation's rolls of hard-core drug users. Meanwhile, the recent explosion of television game shows such as *Do You Want to Be a Millionaire* reflect the insatiable public appetite for diversions which, like gambling, essentially play with money with the promise of instant wealth. See Philip Slater, *Wealth Addiction* (New York: Dutton, 1983).

40. Walden Bello, "Global Economic Counterrevolution: In the North-South Confrontation, Its Apocalypse or Solidarity," *Christianity and Crisis* (17 February 1992) 36 ff.

41. Structural adjustment includes "reducing the state's role in the economy, lowering barriers to imports, removing restrictions of foreign investment, eliminating subsidies for local industries, reducing spending for social welfare, cutting wages, devaluing currency, and emphasizing production for export rather than for local consumption" (ibid., 37). In other words, it means trying to unloose the manic phase of the economy and severely control the depressive phase. As social, economic, and political conditions have deteriorated among the poor the predictable result has been massive human displacement on a global scale. Perhaps, writes Bello, it is the homeless, the undocumented migrants, and the political and economic refugees "who most clearly perceive the truth about structural adjustment: it was intended not as a transition to prosperity but as a permanent condition of economic suffering to ensure that the South would never rise again to challenge the North" (ibid., 38).

42. Hall, "The Political Consequences of Misconceiving Sin," 8 f.

43. Ernest Kurtz, *A. A.: The Story* (San Francisco: Harper and Row, 1988).

44. Herbert Marcuse, *An Essay on Liberation* (Boston: Beacon, 1969) 6.

45. Brown, *Marx, Freud, and the Critique of Everyday Life*, 13 f.

46. Michael Lerner, *Surplus Powerlessness: The Psychodynamics of Everyday Life . . . and the Pscychology of Individual and Social Transformation* (Atlantic Highlands, N.J.: Humanities Press International, 1991). See also Christopher Lasch, *The Minimal Self: Psychic Survival in Troubled Times* (New York: Norton, 1984).

47. Paulo Freire, *Pedagogy of the Oppressed*, trans. by M. Ramos, reprint (New York: Continuum, 1992).

48. Augusto Boal, *Games for Actors and Non-Actors*, trans. by A. Jackson (New York: Routledge, 1992).

49. See J. Hunter, "Subjectivization and the New Evangelical Theodicy," *Journal for the Scientific Study of Religion* 21, no. 2, 39ff.

50. There are of course critics of the addiction/recovery model, from both the left and the right (see Peele, "Ain't Misbehavin': Addiction Has Become an All-Purpose Excuse," *The Sciences* [July–August 1989] 14 ff.; and *Utne Reader*, "Are You Addicted to Addiction," special issue [November–December 1988] 51 ff.). Feminist critiques of the Twelve-Step tradition should in particular be taken into account. Some women have objected to the program's emphasis upon Divine dependence, calling for "rational recovery." See Charlotte Davis Kasl, *Women, Sex and Addiction: A Search for Love and Power* (San Francisco: Harper and Row, 1990); and Plantinga's interesting rejoinder in *Not the Way It's Supposed to Be*, 142 ff). Others see the codependency movement spreading a "victim mentality" and the "politics of powerlessness." See Wendy Kaminer, *I'm Dysfunctional, You're Dysfunctional: The Recovery Movement and Other Self-Help Fashions* (New York: Addison-Wesley, 1992). Still others are concerned that the model ignores the gendered construction and social context of addiction. See Marguerite Babcock and Christine McKay, *Challenging Codependency: Feminist Critiques* (Toronto: University of Toronto Press, 1995).

51. Paul King, Kent Maynard, and David Woodyard, *Risking Liberation: Middle Class Powerlessness and Social Heroism* (Philadelphia: John Knox Press, 1988) 150.

52. Except, of course, the choice we make as consumers between products, which is made to be all-important. Even this is an illusion, however: "In the competitive capi-

talist system the consumer is not the master he is made out to be in the paradigms of economic theory and in the ideology of day-to-day politics," writes Jens Harms. "It is the producer who is sovereign, with the technological structure determining the production plans (in "Bourgeois Idealism and Capitalist Production: Changes in Consumer Behavior-The Way to a Human Society," paper for the Commission on Churches' Participation in Development, World Council of Churches, Geneva, 1977, 12). Since we have only the fiction of choice anyway, to stop "choosing" (e.g., refusing brand loyalty and finding alternative markets) becomes the only genuine choice.

53. A classic example of how systemic irresponsibility is transformed into pandemic exoneration can be see in the design, manufacturing, and deployment of sophisticated nuclear weaponry. Despite its impact on our economy—including our personal tax obligations—most of us not directly involved in this massive national project do not consider ourselves morally culpable. Yet those who *are* directly involved generally feel no greater sense of agency: not design engineers, nor those working the assembly line, nor those in the military bureaucracy, nor those in the missile silo—not even the policymakers. For a dramatic story of this phenomenon see Barry Siegel, "Showdown at Rocky Flats," *Los Angeles Times Magazine*, 8 August and 15 August 1993.

54. Rubem Alvez, *Tomorrow's Child* (New York: Harper and Row, 1972) 202.

55. Dominique Barbe, *Grace and Power: Base Communities and Nonviolence in Brazil*, trans. by J. P. Brown (Maryknoll: Orbis Books, 1987).

56. See Thomas Rausch, *Radical Christian Communities* (Collegeville, Minn.: Liturgical Press, 1990); David Clark, *Basic Communities: Towards an Alternative Society* (London: SPCK, 1977); and Myers, *Who Will Roll Away the Stone?* 178 ff.

57. May, *Addiction and Grace*, 135.

58. Alan Durning, "Life on the Brink" The World's Poor Became Poorer and More Numerous During the 1980s," *Absolute Poverty* (March–April) 22 ff.

59. See Myers, *Who Will Roll Away the Stone*, 168 ff. and Myers, "God Speed the Year of Jubilee."

60. See Mary A. Neal, *A Socio-theology of Letting Go: The Role of a First World Church Facing Third World Peoples* (New York: Paulist Press, 1977); and Adam Daniel Finnerty, *No More Plastic Jesus: Global Justice and Christian Lifestyle* (New York: Dutton, 1977).

61. David Batstone, "What's Your Price: Ten Principles for Saving a Corporate Soul," *Sojourners* (January–February 2000).

62. See Susan Meeker-Lowry, *Invested in the Common Good* (Philadelphia: New Society Publishers, 1995); and Michael Kinsley, *The Economic Renewal Guide: A Collaborative Process for Sustainable Community Development* (Boulder: Rocky Mountain Institute, 1997). Three of the best sources for finding resources on all these issues and initiatives are Alternatives for Simple Living (*www.SimpleLiving.org*); the Center for a New American Dream in Washington D.C.; and *Yes: A Journal of Positive Futures.*

63. Marcuse, *Essay on Liberation*, 6.

64. See, for instance, the excellent work on youth, identity, and consumerism by Kalle Lasn, *Culture Jam: The Uncooling of America* (New York: Eagle Brook, 1999); and Kilbourne, *Deadly Persuasion.*

65. William Durland, *People Pay for Peace: A Military Tax Refusal Guide for Radical Religious Pacifists and People of Conscience* (Colorado Springs: Center Peace Publishers, 1982).

66. Wayne Muller, *Sabbath, Restoring the Sacred Rhythm of Rest* (New York: Bantam Books, 1999).

67. See the recent "Free Time/Free People project, Shalomctr@aol.com.

68. Myers, *Who Will Roll Away the Stone?* 64 ff. and 291 ff.

69. Paul Vallely, *Bad Samaritans.*

70. See Vinton Deming, "Japanese American Internment: A Retrospective," special issue, *Friends Journal* 38, no. 11 (November 1992).

71. Edison Tomimaro Uno, Introduction to Richard and Maisie Conrat, *Executive Order 9066: The Internment of 110,000 Japanese Americans.* Los Angeles: UCLA Asian American Studies Center, 15 f.

72. See M. Annette Jaimes, *The State of Native America: Genocide, Colonization and Resistance* (Boston: South End Press, 1992).

73. Perhaps the most interesting and substantive example has been the United Church of Christ deliberations regarding apologies and reparations to native Hawaiians. See the record compiled by Kaleo Patterson, ed., "Apologies and Resolutions: After 100 Years, Hawaiian Sovereignty (August 1989–May 1994)," Honolulu: Hawaii Ecumenical Coalition, 1993.

74. Marvin Harris, *America Now: The Anthropology of a Changing Culture* (New York: Simon and Schuster, 1981) 174.

CHAPTER SIX

RECONSTRUCTING THE DOCTRINE OF SIN

Theodore W. Jennings Jr.

In the past few years a revolution has been brewing in theology as voices hereto-fore silenced or marginalized begin to make themselves heard in the work of the construction and reconstruction of Christian doctrine.[1] To many observers the contemporary theological scene appears chaotic, characterized by an unruly multiplicity of theological voices representing perspectives not easily assimilated into the framework of earlier theological discussion. Yet this very plurality may also be viewed as having positive significance for the reinvention of the doctrinal mediation of the gospel. The pluralizing of theological options is the consequence of an opening to the insights and perceptions of those who have been excluded from the process of constructing theological discourse. As such it promises a new birth of speech, especially theological speech, in our time.

One of the areas in which the task of the reconstruction of theological discourse has become most acute is with respect to the doctrine of sin. For it is increasingly clear that the hegemony of Euramerican males drawn from the influential classes has greatly skewed our understanding of the brokenness and bondage[3] of the human situation to which the gospel of redemption is a response.

In order to critique or reform the doctrine of sin it is important to understand its proper function within a grammar of theological discourse.[4] For Christian discourse the category of sin designates what might be termed the *shadow side of salvation* or *redemption*. That is, it designates that deformation of the human condition to which the mission of God as announced and enacted by Jesus is an effective response.

In the formulation of this doctrine then it is essential to ask, what is it about the human condition that provokes or evokes the action of God in Christ? What is the need to which this action corresponds, the question to which it is the answer, the disease of which it is the cure?

Thus the doctrine of sin is always correlative to some hope or certainty of fundamental or radical transformation. Indeed it is this prospect of transformation that casts into relief and puts in focus those aspects of the human condition that require that transformation. To this extent the anticipation of redemption is prior to, and negatively constituitive of, the disclosure or analysis of salient aspects of the human predicament that are to be transformed.

But this most elementary feature of the "grammar of faith" is regularly forgotten and, in consequence, the doctrine of sin comes to be deployed in ways that separate it from the good news of divine redemptive activity.

In this chapter I want to focus on some of the ways in which the doctrine of sin has been deformed to become, instead of the countersign of the hope of radical transformation, a mechanism of social control. The doctrine of sin comes to be a way of maintaining a social status quo (of which religion becomes the sanctifying legitimation) instead of a diagnosis of the radical transformation announced and promised in the gospel.

The issues I will raise therefore concern the deployment of doctrine in the interests of the power arrangements of this world; power arrangements that benefit the few, including the few who have heretofore been permitted to engage in theological discourse. By uncovering some of the strategies of social control that have been operative in the traditional construction of the doctrine of sin I hope the various proposals for the reconstruction of this doctrine will be seen in a new and more hopeful light.

THE POWER TO PARDON

In order to clarify in a preliminary way the contrast I have in mind between the use of talk of sin as a mechanism of social control and the use of the same term to announce the breaking open of these systems I turn to a story from the Gospels:

> And just then some people were carrying a paralyzed man lying on a bed. When Jesus saw their faith, he said to the paralytic, "Take heart, son, your sins are forgiven." Then some of the scribes said to themselves, "This man is blaspheming." But Jesus, perceiving their thoughts, said, "Why do you think evil in your hearts? for which is easier, to say, 'Your sins are forgiven' or to say, 'Stand up and walk'? But so that you may know that the Human[5] has authority on earth to forgive sins"—he then said to the paralytic— "Stand up, take your bed and go to your home." And he stood up and went to his home. When the crowds saw it, they were filled with awe, and they glorified God, who had given such authority to human beings. (Mt 9:2–8)

In some ways the version of the same story in the Gospel of Mark is even more dramatic for there the friends of the paralytic actually tear the roof off the house in order to bring their friend's predicament to the attention of Jesus (Mk 2:1–12; see Lk 5:17–26).

The story demonstrates two opposing ways of deploying talk of sin. In the case of the interaction between Jesus, the paralytic, and the paralytic's friends, "sin" serves to indicate the paralysis that is in the process of being over-come. The urgent and audacious hope of the friends, the intervention of Jesus, and the subsequent wholeness of the man present one context for talk of sin: the context of hoped for and actualized transformation. The discourse of the religious experts however integrates talk of sin into a mechanism of social control. They claim that sin cannot be addressed by people but only by God. But this also means that it can only be addressed through the mediation of the religious institutions that control access to the divine. Thus the act of Jesus is blasphemy because it bypasses the mechanisms of social control that are in the hands of the religious establishment. The concern of this religious establishment is not the immediate and direct relief of the human predicament but the manipulation of this predicament for purposes of maintaining power within the world as it is.

In this case the crowds who are witnesses to this confrontation between disparate ways of deploying talk of sin are rendered momentarily speechless (awed) because they recognize that (all) ordinary human beings have the power and authority to announce and enact the radical transformation indicated by the coming of the reign of God. In these circumstances there is no need whatever for recourse to temple and priest, ritual and sacrifice. Redemption is available to all and is mediated by all. In this way the religious establishment that is all too susceptible to manipulation by social, economic, and political forces is circumvented and transformation is experienced as radically available and as already overthrowing the paralyzing effect of the alliance between religion and worldly power. Thus the stunned awe of the masses gives way to an exuberant praise of God.

There are a number of ways in which talk of sin has been extracted from a liberative discourse and integrated into a mechanism for social control manipulated by structures of domination and division. In this chapter I want to focus on seven of these.

VERTICALIZING OF SIN

One of the most remarkable but seldom remarked upon features of NT ethical discourse is the way in which the decalogue is appropriated. A consistent feature of this appropriation whether in words attributed to Jesus (e.g., Mk 10:19, Mt 19:18–19, or Lk 18:20) or in the rhetoric of Paul (e.g., Rom 13:9) is the omission of what tradition calls the "first table"; those commandments that treat specifically of our relation to God and to the sphere of the sacred as such (e.g., the Sabbath). Instead, those commandments dealing with our relationship to one another take over the whole commandment. We may call this the "humanization" or "horizontalization" of the moral imperative and thus of the category of sin.

This is, of course, a continuation and intensification of the insistence of the prophets that YHWH does not require sacrifice, Sabbath, or fasting but justice for the poor, the widow, the orphan, the immigrant, and all who are vulnerable to the rapacity of the powerful and prosperous. On this view then sin

consists in what is done to the neighbor; it refers to the affliction and humiliation of the most vulnerable in our midst.

Precisely this point of view also comes to expression not only in the
humanistic appropriation of the decalogue but in the insistence that the relation to God is determined by our relation to the brother and sister (1 Jn 4:20),
the neighbor, and the least of these (Mt 25:31–46).

Now within this context the cry, "Against you, you only have I sinned"
may function to underscore the seriousness of the violation of the other person.
For this, precisely as the violation of the neighbor, is therefore and thereby a violation of the divine will for justice and thus a violation of the holiness of God.

But in fact the emphasis upon the violation of God more often serves to
divert attention away from the concrete violation of the neighbor and to dis-
place horizontal with vertical responsibilities. One consequence is that sin
comes to be highlighted as the violation of the religious order, as the failure to
comply with one's responsibilities in the narrowly religious sphere. On this
view a sinner is one whose participation in, or observance of, this sphere is
irregular. This is parallel to the view attributed to the Pharisees in the Gospels
who marginalize the religiously nonobservant as sinners, and contrasts with
Jesus' commitment to adopt the nonobservant as his companions.

But far more is at stake than a mere fetishizing of religiosity. For what
transpires here is that the injustice perpetrated against the neighbor, the
stranger, and the other, comes to be seen as a matter of less consequence
than, and as separate from, the question of one's appropriate attitude toward
God. Moreover the violation of the other person is then removed from the
sphere of one's relation to that person and becomes a transaction between
oneself and God, or between oneself and God's official representatives.
There is then no need to seek the forgiveness of the violated since it is
really God who has been violated and it is God's forgiveness that must be
sought, and this is dispensed by the official representatives of God in the
religious establishment.

The violation of the neighbor is then atoned for by virtue of one's relation to the religious establishment that is quite willing to dispense this forgiveness without requiring the inconvenience of dealing directly with those one
has wronged.[6]

In this way the verticalization of the doctrine of sin comes to serve the
interest of the maintenance of the current arrangements of power. For the violation of the vulnerable is ontologically less serious than one's relation to God.
And this relation is not dependent in any way on justice for the violated and
humiliated, nor is forgiveness to be sought from them but from God. And the
religious establishment is all too willing to administer this forgiveness either
through the sacraments or through a proclamation of cheap grace that assures
the relieved gratitude of the prosperous and powerful.

Any reconstruction of the doctrine of sin must pay attention to the "religious temptation" involved in supposing that there is such a thing as sin that is
not the violation of the other person or that the divine is in any way concerned
with sin that is not the violation of the fellow creature.

INDIVIDUALIZING OF SIN

One of the most remarkable transformations in the understanding of sin comes in the form of a transition from the prophetic view of sin as the deviation of society and its elites from the divine will for justice to an emphasis upon sin as the unrighteous act or attitude of individuals.[7] So self-evident does this move come to be that, in English, terms for justice are translated as righteousness (e.g., in Pauline literature) thereby entirely bracketing any social significance for the discussion.

Now the move toward an emphasis upon personal or individual responsibility and accountability may function in some circumstances to overcome the paralysis of apathy. Thus the emphasis upon personal responsibility may serve to clarify that the injustices characteristic of economic or political structures are not simply mechanical forces that operate inevitably and externally but rather solicit the complicity of persons, without which complicity such forces could not function or would be in Paul's phrase "weak and beggarly elemental spirits" (Gal. 4:9). The personalizing of sin makes it possible to imagine the withdrawal of compliance with systems of injustice and thus places in the hands of each person significant leverage for the general emancipation from such systems.

Thus the personalizing or individualizing of sin may serve an emancipatory impetus. It places value upon individual acts of noncompliance with social forces of domination and division. It does so by suggesting how my own cowardice may make me com plicitous in systems of violence or how my own anxiety about sustenance may make me complicitous in rapacious economic systems. The withdrawal of consent to, and complicity in, such systems may thus be seen as a significant blow to the viability of these systems and so may foster confidence in, and hope for, more radical and total transformation.

However, the individualizing of sin more often has the result of diverting attention away from social systems of injustice. In this case social, economic, and political spheres are abandoned in favor of individualistic perspectives both on sin and redemption. Social structures are thus immunized from the critique implicit in sin-talk or the insurgent hope implicit in redemption-talk. Thus the doctrine of sin is deployed in ways that insulate unjust social arrangements from critique and transformation.

While the reading of the prophets may continue to suggest the pertinence of faith for the critique and transformation of social reality, this dimension is ignored altogether in readings of Pauline literature. Thus righteousness substitutes for justice and the personal unrighteousness of the individual substitutes for Paul's critique of systems of legality. Only in certain approaches of liberation theology has the social dimension of Paul's talk of justice and of being made just (justification) been glimpsed against the background of a tradition that is virtually unanimous in ignoring this dimension.[8]

The challenge for a reconstruction of the doctrine of sin is the recovery of the essentially social significance of this category without surrendering moral agency (and thus participation in the redemptive process) to systems over which one has no power and for which one has no perceived responsibility.

CRIMINALIZING OF SIN

The individualizing of sin may be facilitated by way of an assimilation of sin-talk to the discourse of legality and criminality. Certainly the issue of legality and criminality does operate in significant sectors of biblical literature (legal texts) and was available as a prestigious discourse in the Roman Empire in terms of which to seek to render Christian talk of sin and redemption intelligible.

Such a move was fundamentally interdicted by the social location of Christianity as itself a "criminal" association in its early years and by its manifest noncompliance with the legal prescriptions of biblical law (e.g., Sabbath, purification, and dietary restrictions). That Jesus was recalled both as one who refused to comply with the notions of legality in normative Judaism and as one who was executed as a criminal by Roman authorities made this assimilation all the more difficult.

Moreover the argument in Romans concerning the inability of law as a system of legality to make for justice and the analysis of the way in which the law is subverted from its function as an indicator of the goal of justice and made instead into an instrument of injustice stands as a permanent critique of all legal systems in their pretension to embody the divine call for justice.

Once Christianity came to be perceived as the partner of legal power in society or empire and as the legitimation of such systems of law then the tendency to assimilate talk of sin to talk of crime became self-evident. On the one hand this helped to make Christianity intelligible by translating its categories into those familiar from social reality (justice as legality, sin as criminality, etc.). However this also served the further end of making compliance with the law the hallmark of righteousness, and so obedience to the social powers synonymous with righteousness as well. Correspondingly, the violation of the legal code becomes the violation of the divine will and so is rebellion not only against such social legal systems and authorities but rebellion against God as well.

But this means that righteousness comes to be compliance with the laws that articulate the existing social structure. And this means that talk of sin serves not to indicate the hope for, and anticipation of, radical transformation of the status quo but the preservation and perpetuation of the social order.

Once the association of sin with crime or the violation of laws, precepts or rules is made then it is simple enough to develop this analogy in ways that exceed the purview of the law strictly construed. Thus the way is open for the proliferation of petty rules of conduct which, though they lack the sanction of the law proper, are nonetheless understood as sins. The possibility of proliferation here makes possible, indeed inevitable, a preoccupation with the trivial that serves to deflect attention away from the serious matters of justice and mercy. This is the force of the critique of the Pharisees that Matthew places on the lips of Jesus (Mt 23:23).

To be sure the assimilation of sin with crime and thus the analogy of justice with law does retain an important social dimension for the category of sin.

It points to the public and historical sphere as an important domain for the actualization of justice. However the tendency to subordinate justice to legality makes it inevitable that the law will serve the interests of religious, economic, and political elites who manipulate the category of sin to reinforce compliance with the law of church and state.

INTERIORIZING OF SIN

While the individualizing of sin may be related to the appropriation of legal discourse in an atomizing of discrete acts of individuals it may also be expressed as a move into the interior of the will to focus upon desire and motive. When this happens sin is located primarily in an interior drama of conflicted desire. The texts that are summoned to give credence to this interiorization of sin are the seventh chapter of Romans where Paul allegedly confronts the impasse of a will that desires good but is incapable of performing it and Jesus' intensification of the commandments in Matthew chapter five where adultery is related to lust and murder to anger.

This interiorization of the drama of sin has no doubt been productive of much psychological insight both in monastic and in psychoanalytic contexts. But it also veers away from moral or ethical seriousness. For it encourages a preoccupation with one's own interior states rather than with a commitment to the welfare of the other as the test of life in harmony with the divine will.

Nor does this perspective have the secure textual basis often claimed for it. Jesus' words in the Sermon on the Mount concerning adultery certainly do extend the notion of adultery beyond the arena of sexual property rights of males but not in such a way as to make adultery solipsistic. Rather what is in view in the words of Jesus is the leering gaze that reduces the other to an object of virtual sexual possession. It is the degradation of women into objects of visible male aggrandizement that is in view. Similarly with respect to murder. The words of Jesus focus not upon invisible attitudes but upon the fury that breaks forth into degrading speech. In either case what is in view is the violation, humiliation, and degradation of the other person.

But by interiorization of the talk of sin the other becomes extraneous to the question of sin. The moral drama is reduced to a hall of mirrors and to the confrontation of me, myself, and I. Instead of exposing the continuity between attitudes and behavior that violates the other, this link is severed and we are led to concern ourselves with interior feelings alone, unconnected with the violation of the other person.

And this is no less true with respect to Pauline texts as well. For while it is no doubt true that Paul is concerned with the drama of the will and with basic attitudes or mind sets, that with which he is concerned is precisely the set of attitudes that produces enmity and strife within the community. What Paul fears and sees is that the community, instead of serving as a beachhead of a truly just and therefore harmonious society, becomes instead a mirror of the struggle for one's own advantage that favors the strong instead of the weak and results in the rule of elites over the disempowered. Thus, for Paul, it is of utmost importance to renounce the struggle for priority and prestige in favor of the "mind that was in Christ Jesus" (Phil 2:5).

To be sure the reflection on attitudes that lead to injustice may be a distinct gain for an understanding of how injustice is produced in human society. But when it is severed from the question of justice it becomes, for all its psychological profundity, morally bankrupt. It encourages a narcissistic self-preoccupation wholly cut off from the question of the violation of the other person.

And for the victims of violation it is turned into a critique of their righteous indignation (after all we should not be angry with one another) or into an alibi for "unintended" violations that should therefore not be held against the violator. (We are basically nice people, we don't intend for others to be damaged by our racism or consumerism, or what have you.)

The interiorizing of sin reinforces individualizing and verticalizing distortions of the doctrine of sin thereby rendering the doctrine a more useful tool for manipulation by religious elites and for the maintenance of the existing order. It prepares the ground for eroticizing strategies and conduces to analyses that purport to show how sin is ineradicable rather than the hallmark of a world that is already passing away.

REBELLION VERSUS ARROGANCE

Much of the Christian tradition has defined sin in terms of pride and this view does have strong biblical roots. But it is crucial to see how this identification is deployed, whether in emancipatory ways or as a mechanism of social control.

The identification of sin with pride in prophetic oracular utterance is typically directed against the behavior of domestic elites and the aspirations of imperial powers. That is, it has a fundamentally social location.

Even when the identification of sin as pride is adopted (most notably by Augustine) into the discourse of the post-Constantinian Church it retains something of this capacity for provoking a critique of the powerful. After all, it is the cultural elites represented by the clergy and the religious who are thereby enabled to recognize and struggle against pride in themselves.

Yet the critical force of this recognition is restricted and restrained by individualizing, horizontalizing, and interiorizing strategies. Thus pride comes to mean the interior attitude of the person before God rather than one's comportment vis-à-vis the poor and the powerless.

Thus restricted in scope and efficacy, the identification of sin as pride is available for redeployment against all who aspire to a transformation of the economic, social, and political order. Thus transformed, the aspiration of the poor for the redress of grievances is discounted as rebellion; the demand of women for equality is understood as egoism; the claim of the humiliated and the afflicted is pride. Pride exercised by those of lower station is, in this view rebellion, the surly rebellion of the slave against the natural or divinely ordained master.

In posttheological discourse this same tactic is deployed against those, like gays and lesbians, who demand equal rights. They are characterized as demanding "special rights" and so, implicitly, of self-centered pride.

The appropriate deployment of the prophetic identification of sin as the arrogance of elites who humiliate the vulnerable is essential to a reconstruction of the doctrine of sin. But the arrogance of elites is quite different from the aspiration of the marginalized. And when this distinction is lost sight of then the talk of sin as pride becomes a mechanism for social control rather than an index of the promised and hoped for reversal of the worldly order that issues in justice and thus in wholeness.

Feminist theology has been especially acute in its critique of the tradition from Augustine to Niebuhr that identifies sin as *superbia*. But it is also essential to critique the correlative notion in Niebuhr of sensuality. [9]

EROTICIZING OF SIN

One of the most efficacious strategies for the perversion of the doctrine of sin into a mechanism for social control—especially of the popular classes—has been the isolation and privileging of the sphere of the erotic as the special domain of sin.

To a degree the eroticizing of sin, the reduction of sin-talk to sex talk, corresponds to the quest for a substitute for martyrdom and thus for spiritual heroics as Christianity moved from a persecuted minority toward broad cultural acceptance and then to cultural and political domination. The turn to the desert and then to the monastery served to provide a sphere for the exertion of Christian heroics in the struggle against "sin."[10] The struggle with the desires of the body at first was generally understood in terms of all the appetites: for food, for drink, for sleep, for talk, and for sex . However, the general struggle with the body and its appetites comes to focus upon the domain of sex. Eventually Paul's reference to "the flesh" as well as to desire and so on will come to be understood in an almost exclusively sexual sense.

The turn to ascetic disciplines as a way of exerting the will against the dominion of sin served as well to connect Christian practice to prestigious practices of the Roman elites.[11] The subduing of the body was understood as the essential preparation for subduing or controlling the household and the empire. Thus the dominion over sexuality was ready made as a sign of dominion over women, children, slaves, and inferiors generally. It was not very far from this set of images to the association of the inferior classes with sexuality. Thus was prepared the ground for the association of women with sexuality and for the later attempt to link sexuality/sin with anyone who was to be subjected to rule. In the period of modernity with the invention of racism, the racial other was also sexualized. Hence the association under the hegemony of white supremacy of other races with sexuality and so with sin as well.

The codification of the regulation of sexuality as a primary locus for the struggle against sin is well underway with the Council of Elvira (Grenada, Spain) in the early fourth century.[12] From this point on, the rule of the church over people comes to be expressed as the control of other people's sexuality.

The association of sin with sexuality is a slow and complex process. But it manages to make itself seem to be self-evident. In consequence this eroticizing of sin is available to strengthen the tendency to interpret sin as both individual and inward. Desire itself rather than an act that violates another person comes to be seen as sin. Moreover the assimilation of sin with crime means the multiplication of sexual sins, at first for the purpose of clarifying to those who are in monastic life the subtlety of their enemy and then, as the monastic ethos in transferred with the Reformation into the sphere of popular piety, it is available as a means of social control.

This leads to the panic in the early modern period associated with masturbation and in the late modern period with homosexuality as loci of a rampant sexuality that could signify the domain of sin.

Of course the consequence of this association of crime, sex, individualism, and inwardness is that the social reality of sin is almost entirely lost sight of. Sin is available as a means of producing the need for forgiveness that the church can easily dispense. And it is a permanent reservoir of moral failure. Sintalk is utterly deflected from the social realm where it had been denounced by the prophets and it has instead inserted itself into the bedroom and indeed into the interiority of desire itself.

Even with secularization this association of sexuality with guilt and with the need for the deployment of professional help to assuage the guilt is not lost. It is recuperated in psychoanalysis that keeps the middle classes at least diverted from the recognition of the damaging (to other persons at least) results of the class exploitation and neocolonial exploitation on which the privilege of that class depends.

IRREMEDIABLE SIN

The category of original or universal sin has been deployed both in emancipatory and in destructive ways.

Its emancipatory potential consists in its ability to undercut the discrimination between sinners and the just when this discrimination has been based upon legalistic models of sin as crime. In this sense Karl Barth's dictum that it is when we know we are sinners we know that we are (sisters and) brothers has liberative potential. The doctrine is thus capable of being deployed in ways that undercut the privilege of those who imagine themselves to be righteous and their self-serving marginalizing of those who are not upright in the same way. Thus those who are characterized by a variety of social transgressions: the sexually marginalized, "criminals," or the religiously nonobservant may, by means of the idea of the universality of sin, be empowered to resist the rhetoric of religious and social elites that seek to marginalize them. The universality of sin or original sin has a somewhat democratizing tendency.

But this democratizing of the category of sin through the insistence upon the universality of sin may also be captured by tendencies to render the world impervious to radical or fundamental transformation.

Thus the universality of sin as the need and yearning for a total or universal transformation becomes an alibi for the perpetuation of an unjust social order. The assertion that "all have sinned and fallen short of the glory of God" becomes a way of saying that the aspiration for, and anticipatory actualization of, wholeness and thus of justice is itself not only unrealistic but also impious.

We may gain insight into this phenomenon by noticing the way in which perfectionist movements often constitute a protest against the world as it is and confidence that the world may be changed and is being changed.

Holiness movements in the early and midnineteenth century North America offered a powerful impetus for social and individual transformation. The hope for redemption not only from the guilt but also from the paralyzing power of sin provoked efforts of emancipation from self-destructive bondage to addiction and other-destructive habits of violence and self-loss. Thus stories of release from demon rum, from helpless miredness in underclass status, from patterns of spousal and child abuse became regular tropes of the testimony genre. This genre served to concretize the anticipatory reality of redemption as deliverance from bondage and brokenness. Precisely this reality of redemption could serve as the provocation to the aspiration for a wider, a more comprehensive, redemption. Thus the reality of redemption from bondage opened onto the prospect of emancipation from the social structures of division and domination. If a person could experience redemption from the intimate bondage to addiction, violence, and disempowerment, could not society itself be delivered from evil institutions of slavery, white racism, sexism, and the destructive forces of industrial dehumanization?

In consequence the rhetoric, experience, and practices of the holiness movement sparked movements for the abolition of slavery, the emancipation of women, and the empowerment of labor. However, the challenge to the social order implicit in the holiness project also sparked counterstrategies for the containment of the radical potential thereby unleashed.

Thus the doctrine of sin could be deployed either in frontal assault upon the aspirations of the holiness movement or in strategies of containment and canalization.

In the latter case the notion of sin susceptible to transformation could be limited or contained through individualizing, moralizing, and eroticizing strategies. Thus holiness movements that early on had unleashed liberative potentialities are regularly co-opted by limiting the aspirations for holiness to the individual and to the domain of illegality. Thus holiness movements became the site of petty moralizing with respect to smoking, drinking, dancing, sexual impropriety, or carelessness with respect to religious observance. In this way the impetus for transformation was domesticated into the acquisition of the habits of the work ethic and integration into industrial capitalism.

When containment strategies are broken through then recourse is had to a more fundamental strategy: that of using the universality of "original sin" as an alibi for the world as it is. Thus the doctrine of sin is deployed in such a way as to indicate the impossibility of real or (especially) radical change.

For the most part resort is had to this strategy when there is a question of social transformation. Normally it is only in popular psychological discourse that the impossibility of individual transformation is made into both an alibi for the perpetuation of individual habits, and for the permanent dependence of the client on the services of the psychological professional. This situation mirrors one that the church maintained for centuries with the confessional in which neither release from the power of sin nor from dependence on the religious professional was contemplated.

The doctrine of original sin is typically deployed in order to say why it is that fundamental social transformation is impossible. When, for example, Latin American liberation theology calls for the actualization of justice, establishment theologians regularly invoke the seriousness of original or universal sin to claim that proponents of radical transformation lack a certain "Christian realism." Indeed, establishment Protestant theologians invoke Niebuhr's "Christian realism" to precisely this effect. Thus the doctrine of sin is redeployed in order to deny that the world can be changed. It becomes a mechanism for social control. When this happens then the most basic "grammar" of the doctrine of sin is forgotten. No longer does talk of sin serve to indicate the scope and pertinence of redemptive transformation but the impossibility or unrealizability of transformation. It thus becomes a countergospel that substitutes for the good news of incipient redemption the insistence upon the intractability of the human predicament, its imperviousness to divine redemptive transformation, and the presumptuousness of human collaboration in that redemptive process.

Now this is not to say that the doctrine of original or universal sin is simply to be discarded. It brings to expression an important aspect of human experience and especially of the experience of those who are the unwilling victims of the injustice of other persons and of the societies in which they live. For sin as the deformation of human life is experienced as a power that has dominion both in the world and in our "members." But it makes a great deal of difference how this reality is brought to expression and made intelligible. For example, Paul had recourse to the metaphor of fundamental human solidarity in Adam and to the metaphor of dominant cosmic/historical powers (the Law, Sin, and Death). By means of these metaphors it was possible to bring to expression the reality that sin is something that seems always already to be there, a reality into which we seem to be initiated without consent, and against which we struggle (apart from Christ) without victory.

However the theological tradition has regularly sought to explain this reality in such a way as to make it (contrary to Paul) into an unalterable fate. Thus Augustine succeeded in using the biological metaphor of procreation to indicate how this reality is always already present in our experience but thereby also made it insuperable in experience. With Augustine's biologism we have already moved away from social and historical metaphors to the irreversibility of biological fact.

In the modern period the iron cage of sin has been constructed by ontologizing the inevitability of sin. Whether one follows Niebuhr in imagining a paradox of finite freedom or Tillich in imagining a fall from essence to existence, the human condition is represented as irremediably fallen at the most basic (ontological) level.

The result is a description of the powerlessness of the human vis-à-vis the most fundamental reality of sin. And this readily becomes an alibi for the perpetuation of sinful structures.

But this is completely contrary to the way in which Paul deployed his metaphors. For the assertion of social solidarity in Adam is counterpoised to the social solidarity of all humanity in Christ. And the historical cosmic powers are represented not as leaving humanity in an impasse but as already being overcome.

The sense of the overwhelmingness of sin, especially for those who are sinned against, does require something like a doctrine of the universality and overpoweringness of the reality of injustice. But this is but the shadow side of the hope for a radical transformation that is already overturning this dominion and launching the reign of justice and generosity and joy.

CONCLUSION

The reconstruction of Christian doctrine must begin with an awareness of the way in which the construction of doctrine has been in the hands of cultural elites who have often produced doctrinal formulations that serve the interests of a religious institution in alliance with the dominant social forces of the world. In respect to a doctrine of sin we must be aware of the way in which the formulation of this doctrine has all too often been placed in the service of social control and the preservation of basic social arrangements instead of serving to indicate that reality that is now in the process of being fundamentally transformed.

Thus in the reconstruction of doctrine it is not enough to ask about the coherence of new formulation with ancient texts and traditions nor to ask about the correspondence between doctrine and the prestigious discourses that theorize contemporary experience (psychology, sociology, etc.). Rather it is critical to ask in whose interest doctrinal formulations are deployed and whether formulations adequately represent the emancipatory intention of the gospel or become instead the legitimation of the perpetuation of the status quo of power.

What I have sought to illustrate relative to this doctrine is, I believe, true of others as well. In any theological labor we must ask how categories and subcategories of doctrine are deployed, whether the deployment is emancipatory or in service of the religious stabilization of existing arrangements of power. Thus an analysis of "doctrine and power" (to paraphrase Foucault) is essential to liberative theological labor. This is usually not a simple matter for, as we have seen, many of the strategies we have considered here are capable of both emancipatory and stabilizing deployment.

Perhaps the test that matters most in this process is whether our doctrinal discourse, like the interaction between Jesus and the paralytic, provokes an outburst of praise to God on the part of the vulnerable, humiliated, and violated masses who bear the brunt of the world's sin.

NOTES

1. For the view that Christian theology must concern itself with the construction and thus with the deconstruction and reconstruction of doctrine see my article, "Theology as the Construction of Doctrine," in *The Vocation of the Theologian* (Philadelphia: Fortress, 1985) 67–86.

2. For illustrations see my article, "Making Sense of God," in the *Companion Encyclopedia of Theology* (New York: Routledge, 1996) 895–916; and "Theological Anthropology," in *Theology and the Human Spirit* (Chicago: Exploration Press, 1994) 35–44.

3. For the use of these categories to replace the ideologically distorted category of sin see my book, *Liturgy of Liberation* (Nashville: Abingdon, 1988).

4. For development of this notion of a grammar of theological discourse see my book, *Beyond Theism: A Grammar of God-Talk* (New York: Oxford, 1985).

5. The term *son of man* has the meaning of human being. As the response of the masses indicates, this is not simply Jesus. See my article, "The Martyrdom of the Son of Man," in *Text and Logos*, ed. by T. W. Jennings Jr. (Atlanta: Scholars Press, 1990).

6. On this see Andrew Sung Park's *Wounded Heart of God* (Nashville: Abingdon, 1993) 87–98. A quite different approach to the same issue is made by Emmanuel Levinas in *Difficult Freedom: Essays on Judaism* (Baltimore: Johns Hopkins University Press, 1990).

7. To a certain extent this already occurs in some of the legal texts of the Hebrew Bible as the chapter in this book by Walter Brueggemann indicates.

8. See, for example, Jose Porfirio Miranda, *Marx and the Bible* (Maryknoll: Orbis, 1974); Elsa Tamez, *The Amnesty of Grace* (Nashville: Abingdon 1993); and Franz J. Hinkelammert, *Sacrificios humanos y sociedad occidental: Lucifer y la bestia* (San José, Costa Rica: DEI, 1991).

9. See Judith Plaskow, *Sex, Sin and Grace: Women's Experience and the Theologies of Reinhold Niebuhr and Paul Tillich* (Washington, D.C.: University Press of America, 1980).

10. See Peter Brown, *The Body and Society: Men, Women and Sexual Renunciation in Early Christianity* (New York: Columbia University Press, 1988).

11. See Aline Rousselle, *Porneia: On Desire and the Body in Antiquity* (New York: Basil Blackwell, 1988).

12. S. Laechli, *Power and Sexuality: The Emergence of Canon Law at the Synod of Elvira* (Philadelphia: Temple University Press, 1972).

CHAPTER SEVEN

THE CONUNDRUM OF
SIN, SEX, VIOLENCE, AND THEODICY

Marie M. Fortune

She was thirty-seven years old and had been battered weekly by her husband of ten years. Raised as an evangelical Christian to believe that *sin* and *sex* were synonymous terms, she accepted her husband's mistreatment of her as her punishment. When she was sixteen years old, she had been date raped by her twenty-year-old boyfriend, although she would not describe it as rape. She believed that she had "had sex outside of marriage" and that this was a sin for which God was now punishing her. The notion that she did not have to stay in a battering relationship but had the option to seek help, support, and protection from her abuser was beyond her comprehension.

Diagnosed three years ago as HIV positive and now experiencing the classic symptoms of AIDS, he believed what the televangelists were saying about him and thousands of other gay men. Being gay is a "sin" and God was punishing him for it. A year later, he was dead.

When her seven-year-old daughter was stricken with leukemia and died within the year, she longed for an explanation. Why her daughter? More to the point, why her? She finally confessed to her husband that she occasionally masturbated when he was out of town on business. She believed that this "sin" was the cause of God's punishment in taking their daughter from them. Her husband could not convince her otherwise.

She made the decision to leave her abusive husband the day he picked up their one-year-old child and threw him across the room. She had put up with his beating her in order to keep the family together but she refused to leave her child in danger. She left and went to a shelter and began divorce proceedings. Her husband went to her workplace, shot, and killed her with a semi-automatic weapon. Her priest refused to say a funeral mass for her because she

123

had sinned by leaving her husband and seeking a divorce. Her family was left bereft of pastoral support, believing that God had punished her for her "sin" of leaving her abuser.

In spite of the presumed sophistication of a postmodern world, so-called sexual sin and questions about theodicy are major subtexts in many pastoral situations. Clearly the two are intimately linked for many people. When faced with the suffering of abuse, illness, or death, humans predictably scan the horizon for an explanation, an answer to the "why?" of their experience. We may not like the answer but at least we want an answer. We are looking for some meaning because we earnestly believe that the only thing worse than suffering is meaningless suffering.

Unfortunately this healthy desire to comprehend our experiences of suffering and to address the issue of theodicy frequently runs head-on into a dominant moral framework which, for the marginalized (those who by virtue of race, gender, class, sexual orientation, age, ability, or other factors have less access to power and resources and are therefore less able to determine our own futures), does not offer adequate answers. Marginality often means increased vulnerability to abuse or violence. So according to this dominant framework, victimization or other suffering usually derives from the sin of the victim and the sin of the victim frequently derives from immoral sexual activity. As a result, the victim/survivor focuses on her/himself as the source of the suffering often ignoring the agent of harm who abused, assaulted, or violated her/him. Needless to say, this equation is useless to those of us at the margins.

Beginning with the reality of marginality and the accompanying vulnerability to violence, this chapter will examine the biblical and historical understanding of sin within the Western religious traditions with a focus on our understanding of sexual sin. In exploring the implications for ethics and pastoral care I will advocate reframing the theodicy issue and our understanding of sin within a moral framework that acknowledges the fact of victimization and the need for accountability for those who cause harm to others.

THE INADEQUACY OF THE DOMINANT MORAL FRAMEWORK

In all of these pastoral situations, those who are suffering answer the theodicy question with what they have labeled their "sexual sins." They recall their violation of a sexual rule or taboo probably taught to them in church youth groups and generally derived from the directive not to have any sexual activity outside of heterosexual marriage. So date-rape, being gay and sexually active, masturbating and, indirectly, leaving an abusive heterosexual marriage are all viewed by the victim/sufferer and/or surrounding community as "sins." What is interesting about these situations is how heavy the burden of guilt and self-blame is on the one who has been a victim of harm or on the one who suffers. This burden is created and sustained by the dominant moral framework that interprets the meaning of the situation and turns it back on the sufferer. At the same time, this framework relieves those who are agents of harm from any sense of responsibility. Rarely does the perpetrator of harm feel remorse for harm done to others; rarely is that person's behavior questioned or confronted.

Social location within our culture profoundly shapes one's theology of sin and suffering. The marginalized look to our own behavior for a theological understanding of our suffering. Since our conduct is the only thing over which we have any notion of control, we long to find the key to our suffering within the scope of our agency. Of course this practice does have its practical value: if she can just figure out what she did that "caused" her to be raped (e.g., had too much to drink, was hiking alone, or was asleep in her own bed) then she can be sure not to repeat that behavior and thus presume to be safe in the future. There is a distinctly simplistic quality about this reasoning, but for many victims/survivors, it is all that they have. The glaring absence of attention to the agent of harm, the one who actually caused her rape, is overlooked.

Our social reality within the dominant moral framework is constructed such that there is a relative inequality of resources that results in a relationship of power and vulnerability between most people, individually and collectively. Frequently these unequal relationships are unjust and predictably damaging to the marginalized groups such as the relationships created by racism (in the United States, the concentration of power and resources in the hands of Euramericans), and sexism (the concentration of power and resources in the hands of men).

Sometimes a relationship is necessarily one of inequality of resources and not unjust or harmful. For example, a teacher has power (i.e., greater resources such as knowledge, authority of role, often age, or perhaps physical size) and a student is vulnerable to the teacher due to fewer resources; a parent vis-à-vis a child; a doctor vis-à-vis a patient. Teachers, parents, doctors, and others, to do their jobs properly must bring their resources to the student, child, or patient in order to empower or, in some cases, protect that person. Consequently teachers, parents, and doctors can also *misuse* their resources to take advantage of or abuse the student, child, or patient. In these situations, vulnerability can create the circumstance for victimization.

An awareness of the necessary realities of power and vulnerability was the basis for the hospitality code in early Hebrew culture. The code recognized that there were vulnerable groups within the dominant society: widows, orphans, and sojourners. The dominant community was mandated to provide for persons in these groups (Ex 22.21–22). Altruism was not the reason for this mandate; rather it was a recognition that anyone (even the privileged) could experience vulnerability at any time and be in need of assistance (Deut 10:19).

Biblical texts also lift up the reality of unnecessary and inherently oppressive relationships of power and vulnerability. In these situations, race, gender, and class determined one's place in society and the narratives describe the damaging consequences of being so situated as well as the struggles to overcome the oppression.

Whether one has power or is vulnerable to the more powerful was and is a primary factor that shapes interactions with others and one's options within them. Whether one is a have or a have-not also shapes the ethical context within which choices are made and acted on. Therefore one's social location shapes one's experience of sin. In many situations, one is either the sinner or the sinned-against. An analysis of the dynamics of power and vulnerability is necessary to understand the experience of sin. An examination of the notion of sin provides a lens through which to consider the intersection of fundamental issues in both ethics and pastoral care as they relate to the experiences of the marginalized.

SIN DEFINED AND DEFINED AGAIN:
BIBLICAL AND HISTORICAL CONTEXT

HEBREW SCRIPTURE

Our Western conceptualizations of sin have been primarily shaped by Judaism and Christianity. There are three predominant themes that arise from the Hebrew experience. The first originates in the creation mythology surrounding Adam and Eve in the garden. Sin is understood as disobedience. Adam and Eve disobeyed God's order not to eat from the tree and as a result of their disobedience, we are left with the Fall that supposedly explains everything from pain in childbirth to profound alienation.[1] The second theme is that of "missing the mark."[2] Sin is then a matter of deficiency, not quite measuring up or specifically "the ethical failure of one person to perform a duty or common courtesy for another, as in the failure of a vassal to pay tribute to his overlord. . . ."[3] Like sin as disobedience, sin as missing the mark is ultimately viewed as a sin against God. One aspect of this theme is sin as violation of cultic practices or taboos, again directed at God. The third major theme is sin as crimes against persons—wickedness described as violence, treachery, oppression, etc.—which cause harm to others. The first narrative reference in Hebrew Scripture to sin as harm of another is Cain's murder of his brother Abel in Gen 4. The Prophets and Psalms carry the theme of harm done to others in rich detail.

Brueggemann places this third theme of sin-as-harm-done-to-others within the narrative of the Exodus.[4] It is here that the ethical notion of sin as harm done by one to another is described in the lived experience of the Jews enslaved by Pharaoh. Here we find the description of victim and victimizer, of oppressed and oppressor, and, as Brueggemann points out, the presence of a third party: God standing in solidarity with the victim and in judgment of the victimizer.

The notion that the unrighteous will suffer for their bad deeds, that "all of life is a series of interrelated components, each of which carries inescapable moral implications,"[5] does not apply to the Jews' experience. The Jews suffer here at the hands of Pharaoh undeservedly; they are victims of Pharaoh's sin, not of their own. This is the injustice that the Prophets rail against and that the Psalmist bemoans. In this case, the theodicy puzzle is appropriately resolved. The Jews enslaved by Pharaoh suffer because of Pharaoh's arrogance and cruelty, not because of God's will or their prior misdeeds.

The Prophets focused on the experience of bad deeds resulting in negative consequences but turn their attention to their own communities. Ezekiel explicates the consequences of wickedness for the sinner and the potential for repentance:

> Now you, mortal, say to the house of Israel, Thus you have said: "Our transgressions and our sins weigh upon us, and we waste away because of them; how then can we live?" Say to them, As I live, says the Lord God, I have no pleasure in the death of the wicked, but that the wicked turn from their ways and live; turn back, turn back from your evil ways; for why will you die, O house of Israel? And you, mortal, say to your people, The righteousness of the righteous shall not save them when they transgress; and as for the wickedness of the wicked, it shall not make them stumble when they turn from their wickedness; and the righteous shall not be able to live by their righteousness when they sin.
>
> Though I say to the righteous that they shall surely live, yet if they trust in their righteousness and commit iniquity, none of their righteous deeds shall be remembered; but in the iniquity that they have committed they shall die. Again though I say to the wicked, "You shall surely die," yet if they turn from their sin and do what is lawful and right—if the wicked restore the pledge, give back what they have taken by robbery, and walk in the statutes of life, committing no iniquity—they shall surely live, they shall not die. None of the sins that they have committed shall be remembered against them; they have done what is lawful and right, they shall surely live.
>
> Yet your people say, "The way of the Lord is not just," when it is their own way that is not just. When the righteous turn from their righteousness, and commit iniquity, they shall die for it. And when the wicked turn from their wickedness, and do what is lawful and right, they shall live by it. Yet you say, "The way of the Lord is not just." O house of Israel, I will judge all of you according to your ways! (Ezek 33:10–20)

Here the moral principal of accountability is set forth: those who do harm to others (sinners) will be called to account and will suffer the consequences. God's agenda is not arbitrary punishment but rather repentance by the sinner. The deeds—consequences equation is central to this moral order in addressing the agent of harm.

The problem arose when any individual attempted to use reverse logic to comprehend his/her experience of suffering in the absence of apparent bad acts. If bad acts result in negative consequences for the agent, then the one who is experiencing negative consequences is likely to look to his/her own acts as the source of these consequences (rather than to see one's experience of victimization, for example, as the result of another's actions). This theodicy problem (e.g., in Job's discourse) undercut the moral order and its reliability and could only serve to encourage a regression to superstition, that is: what rule did I break or ritual did I neglect in my past that now results in this suffering I'm experiencing?

Yet a different observation leads to the query, why do the wicked prosper? Jeremiah puts the question to God: I thought the wicked were supposed to suffer the consequences of their sins and this does not appear to be the case:

> You will be in the right, O Lord, when I lay charges against you; but let me put my case to you.

> Why does the way of the guilty prosper? Why do all who are treacherous thrive? You plant them, and they take root; they grow and bring forth fruit; you are near in their mouths yet far from their hearts.

> But you, O Lord, know me; you see me and test me—my heart is with you. (Jer 12:1–3)

God's reply acknowledges this apparent contradiction, offers the wicked one more chance to repent, and promises: "But if any nation will not listen, then I will completely uproot it and destroy it, says the Lord" (Jer 12:17). The moral order remains intact; deeds have consequences even when it appears otherwise. In other words, what goes around comes around—eventually. But no real explanation for the suffering of the innocent is offered.

CHRISTIAN SCRIPTURE

These three sin themes (disobedience, deficiency, and harm to others) are carried forward into Christian Scripture and tradition and are consistent with early Greek literature in which "'sin' can refer to almost any sort of error: missing the mark in throwing a javelin, committing a procedural mistake in sacrificing, or harming or disregarding others."[6] Sins (debts, trespasses, etc.) are a fact of life that Jesus addressed. He responded to the state of sinfulness and to sinful acts with a call to repentance that echoes the Prophets.

This emphasis in Jesus' teaching reflects what Brueggemann describes as the coherence and reliability of the moral order for the Hebrews as it was passed down through Torah and the wisdom tradition.[7] Based upon observation (partial though it might be), it became apparent that some conduct produced good results and other conduct produced bad results. The moral order rested on the connection between deeds and consequences that were generally reliable whether ascribed to God or to the natural order.[8] Correlative with this moral vision were the assumptions that human beings had choice and moral agency (Deut 30:15–18) and that they could change their ways (see Ezekiel in the preceding extract).

Jesus spent a great deal of time with those who were considered "sinners" by the dominant culture. E. P. Sanders suggests that the tax collectors who were included in this list were not sinners per se; the sin belonged to those who were dishonest and greedy.[9] Zacchaeus (Lk 19:1–10) repented of his sin and sought to make restitution to those he had harmed. Prostitutes were also part of Jesus' entourage and usually regarded by those around them as sinners. But it is not so clear that Jesus considered them sinners as those sinned-against. It is probable that Jesus understood the economic realities that shaped the prostitutes' lives and thus sought to offer them an alternative way of life. Jesus appears to have been very cognizant of the power dynamics at work in the situations he encountered and in the parables he used for teaching.[10] The breaking of rules and regulations was not Jesus' primary concern about sin. He was considered a sinner because he healed on the sabbath (Jn 9:16 and Lk 13:10–17). Jesus' primary concern was repentance from sin—individual transgressions, usually against other persons—which then resulted in a life of alienation and despair for the sinner. He called to account those who harmed others. The moral order that he taught paralleled that of the Prophets.

Paul worried much about the power of sin as a state of being that brings death and echoes the deeds-consequences equation: "For the wages of sin is death, but the free gift of God is eternal life in Christ Jesus our Lord" (Rom 6:23). Yet Paul also describes specific bad acts, a few of which are sexual but most of which are not, mostly deeds harmful to others that he describes as "foolish, faithless, heartless, ruthless" (Rom 1:31). In Rom. 2, Paul confronts hypocrisy and also builds on the prophets' deeds-consequences relationship and reasserts God's desire for human repentance: "Do you not realize that God's kindness is meant to lead you to repentance? . . . For [God] will repay according to each one's deeds: to those who by patiently doing good seek for glory and honor and immortality, [God] will give eternal life; while for those who are self-seeking and who obey not the truth but wickedness, there will be wrath and fury . . . the Jew first and also the Greek, but glory and honor and peace for everyone who does good, the Jew first and also the Greek" (Rom 2:4, 6–10).

Yet Paul most clearly lays out his concern for the moral order when he combines the teachings of Judaism and Christianity in summary: "Owe no one anything, except to love one another; for the one who loves another has fulfilled the law. The commandments, 'You shall not commit adultery; You shall not murder; You shall not steal; You shall not covet'; and any other commandment, are summed up in this word, 'love your neighbor as yourself.' Love does no wrong to a neighbor; therefore, love is the fulfilling of the law" (Rom 13:8–10). In this fundamental ethical mandate Paul asserts the priority for avoidance of sin as doing least harm to one's neighbor. The corollary is clear: sin is harm done to another in contradiction of the mandate to love.

THE EARLY AND LATER CHURCH

The early church appears to be more concerned with conversion through baptism into Christ and the accompanying salvation from sin than with repentance and restitution in response to sinful actions that were the primary themes in Judaism and reinforced by Jesus. Sanders asserts that the early church's eschatology overshadowed any serious concern for postbaptismal repentance. He further suggests that "The rite of penance was a major aspect of Christianity in the late antique and medieval periods, and one of the Luther's most important views was that the Christian is at the same time 'justified' in the sight of God and, in terms of actual performance, a sinner (*simul iustus et peccator*). The heirs of these traditions give the correction of sin, and repentance for it, a prominent place in life and worship."[11] This of course led to the discussion of the relationship of faith to works. Unfortunately the emphasis appears to have shifted to sin as the violation of new rules rather than as harm to others.

In the nineteenth and twentieth centuries, the preaching of sin as synonymous with sex has dominated the moral discourse;[12] the emphasis here is on violations of rules (no sexual activity outside of heterosexual marriage) rather than on harm to others (minimal attention to sexual violence as sin). Perhaps it is in reaction to the sin = sex equation that liberalism has succeeded in abstracting the notion of sin beyond recognition. The solution to the legitimate critique of the sin = sex equation was to eliminate "sin" from our vocabulary[13] and to psychologize antisocial behaviors (e.g., à la Freud). The vacuum that resulted has been filled now with clinical diagnoses of socially deviant behaviors (e.g., sociopathology and paranoid schizophrenia) such that we attempt to apply a medical model to many moral problems. While there is certainly value in the ability to diagnose and sometimes treat clinical problems, the absence of consensus as to a moral order to accompany it has created enormous confusion. For example, legally the fact that one can be found *not* guilty of murder by reason of insanity and with no definitive sanctions that would insure that this individual who has killed cannot do further harm to others is a moral contradiction that flies in the face of common sense.

THE PARTICULARITY OF SEXUAL SIN

An examination of "sexual sin" illustrates well the conflict between sin-as-disobedience and sin-as-harm-done-to-others. The effort by the powers that be in both church and society to maintain sexual sin as disobedience, and more specifically as violation of rules, rather than sin as harm-done-to-others, reflects the interests of the dominant, patriarchal culture and contradicts the interests of the marginalized.

For example, a convicted wife abuser used the First Amendment protection of one's religious beliefs to support his right to abuse his wife. Ramiro Espinosa believed that the teachings of the Roman Catholic Church (the rules) gave him the right to have sex with his wife whenever he chose because the marriage vows they exchanged signaled her consent to have sex with him and, that once given, this consent was ongoing.[14] Espinosa, fifty-four, equates breaking into his wife's locked room, slapping her, and ripping her clothes with legitimate foreplay. He believes that he is justified in using force because *she* has broken the rules by refusing to have sex with him. He, on the other hand, believes he is not breaking any rules (of the church) and cannot understand why his behavior is now considered illegal. Thankfully, the court was not swayed by his defense.

This is yet another tragic example of the appeal to church doctrine to justify wife abuse. While church leaders who were interviewed rejected Espinosa's argument saying that Roman Catholic doctrine teaches that sex should be part of a loving relationship, they had nothing else to say. There is virtually no recognition here of the harm done to the woman (which is the sin) and of the need to call the husband to account for his abusive behavior. Mr. Espinosa's understanding of his rights as a husband and of sin as violation of the rules combined with the church's passivity in response to this situation is evidence of the inadequacy of traditional Christian teaching on sexual ethics.[15]

TRADITIONAL ETHICS AND SEXUAL SIN

Traditional Christian sexual ethics as preached and practiced in Christian churches are patriarchal and seek primarily to prohibit sexual activity outside of heterosexual marriage. The purpose even today is twofold: to protect male property rights by controlling women's sexuality thereby assuring the paternity of offspring and to preserve heterosexual hegemony. The Christian notion of sexual sin has focused on heterosexual marriage and on a concern for the public form of the interaction (i.e., are a man and woman legally married before they engage in genital sexual activity?) more than on the private quality of the interaction (how do they treat each other in the relationship?). This means that whatever occurs sexually within heterosexual marriage is acceptable and whatever occurs sexually outside this context is not acceptable. For example, if a man forces a woman to whom he is not married to have sex, this is rape; if he engages in the exact same behavior two weeks after a marriage certificate is signed, this may not be legally (in some states) or morally considered rape. The absence of concern for women's bodily integrity and choice within marriage is startling. Many Christian churches do not hesitate to speak loudly against abortion and homosexuality and yet there is mostly silence in traditional Christian teaching regarding marital or date-rape, incestuous abuse, or the battering of women as sexual sins.

The reliance on patriarchal values (primarily male control of property) and sin-as-disobedience as the foundation of sexual ethics has clouded the Christian understanding of sexual sin. There remains a profound confusion about the nature of sexual sin that has distorted most efforts to provide useful guidance in sexual matters within our churches in recent years.

If sexual sin is understood as the violation of the rule that sexual activity should only take place within heterosexual marriage, then ethical questions about consent, bodily integrity, choice, power, and vulnerability are never asked. If, however, sexual sin is understood as the harm caused by violation of the bodily integrity of another person through sexual coercion, abuse, or assault, then questions about consent, bodily integrity, choice, power, and vulnerability take center stage. In the case of Mr. Espinosa, the law is clearer on this principle than is church teaching; the law was primarily concerned about the well-being of his wife.

The sin of sexual violence is a violation of the victim her/himself that causes physical and emotional harm. Why is it wrong to violate the sexual boundaries of another person? Because sexual violence is a violation of bodily integrity that denies a person the choice to determine her own boundaries and activities. Because sexual violence distorts and misuses sexuality. Because sexual violence destroys trust and violates relationship. Because sexual violence causes injury and harm.

HOMOSEXUALITY

The churches' obsession with homosexuality in recent years also illustrates the problem with sin-as-disobedience. Homosexuality and homosexual activity are considered sins by church and society because they represent disobedience to a heterosexual norm established by the dominant heterosexual culture. This norm has been incorporated in attitude and custom (heavily promoted by the church) and codified into law in, for instance, sodomy laws that are still on the books in some states and the denial of civil rights to gays and lesbians. It is ironic that one of the primary scriptural foundations of the church's position on homosexuality has been the Sodom and Gomorrah story in Gen 19. This narrative describes the attempted rape of the visiting angels (and in the Judg 19 version, that attempted rape of the visiting Levite and the actual rape and murder of his concubine). Yet the interpretation of these passages has focused on the "sin" of homosexuality rather than on the actual sin of sexual and physical violence, that is, on the violation of the rule against sexual contact between men rather than the overt harm done to persons.

The late-twentieth-century debate regarding state legislation to allow persons of the same sex to marry reflects the same problem once again. Marriage laws established by the heterosexual majority provide for legal privileges (taxes, inheritance, etc.) for married heterosexuals. Both church and state have asserted that homosexual activity is a sin because it takes place outside of heterosexual marriage (violation of rules). Since the argument that homosexuality is not a sin because it does not cause harm to anyone (anymore than does heterosexuality per se) has not prevailed, the current gay and lesbian strategy is to change the rules to allow persons of the same sex to marry and therefore not be "living in sin" (i.e., in violation of the rules). But more importantly this action would extend the privileges of legal marriage (inheritance, adoption, pension benefits to survivors, etc.) to nonheterosexuals. In the economy of power and vulnerability, this loss of privileges would not be acceptable from the perspective of those with power, hence the vociferous outcry and flurry of legislation to prohibit gays and lesbians to marry.

SIN-AS-HARM-DONE-TO-ANOTHER

If we are to find our way out of the confusion about the nature of sexual sin, we need to focus on sin-as-harm-done-to-another. Paul's ethical mandate in Rom 13:8 ff is instructive: after citing the commandments (rules), he asserts: "love does no wrong to a neighbor; therefore, love is the fulfilling of the law." Love of self precedes love of neighbor and *love does no harm to another*. If I am seeking to love another person, I can best begin by seeking not to do harm to that person or to myself. To do harm is to sin, to cause suffering, injury, and brokenness in relationship to another. This is the lesson that the church should be teaching to Mr. Espinosa. It might help him understand that he has no right by law or by church doctrine to have sex with his wife without her consent.

Our understanding of sexual sin should not be focused on the violation of arbitrary rules that only serve the interests of the privileged within a patriarchal structure. Sexual sin as harm done to others provides a moral framework that speaks to the marginalized (usually women, children, gays, and lesbians) as the possible sinned-against but also speaks to everyone's responsibility to do least harm sexually in relation to one another.[16]

TO CHOOSE A MORAL ORDER

At the beginning of the twenty-first century, our moral development as informed by the dominant moral framework and by its version of the teachings of Christianity leaves us adrift in churches where being a gay or lesbian person is more reprehensible than a pastor sexually abusing a congregant; where using contraception in marriage in order to plan one's family or using a condom to prevent the spread of life-threatening disease is a greater sin than raping one's wife. Too often liberals have responded to the complexity of these ethical issues with confusion and silence and little analysis of power leaving a vacuum readily filled with right-wing "family values" rhetoric and punitive social policy. In the face of these inadequacies, we must reexamine how we understand the nature of sin in our lives.

If one's social location shapes one's experience of sin and understanding of sin, then which of the primary themes that come from our Western religious traditions serve the interests of the privileged and powerful? Which serve the interests of the marginalized?

To view and promote "sin as disobedience" clearly serves the interests of the privileged: any challenge to the established order is sinful that then results in negative consequences (i.e., punishment) for the "sinner." Adam and Eve were cast out of the garden. Likewise the view of "sin as violation of rules" is a subset of "sin as disobedience." Again the interests of the powerful are served. It is they who establish the order and make the rules after all. The abusive parent demands obedience and cruelly punishes each and every infringement. The state arrests and imprisons those who protest using civil disobedience. The unjust employer sexually harasses employees and threatens to fire any who complain or resist.

To view "sin-as-harm-done-to-others" serves the interests of the marginalized and vulnerable and holds the powerful accountable. It provides a moral framework within which harm (i.e., injury, damage, exploitation, and abuse) can be named and judged as sin and as the result of the agency of one person against another. This framework then allows the possibility of accountability for harm done that may result in legitimate negative consequences for the sinner and justice and healing for the sinned-against. The roles of victimizer and victim are established and can be addressed. Here the deeds-consequences reality can be implemented for the agent of harm and is

not applicable to the one harmed. There is recognition of the injustice of violence as a violation of the moral order; this recognition provides a means to
rectify the injustice and restore moral order. Within Judaism and Christianity,
particularly in the story of the Exodus from slavery in Egypt, God is an active
advocate on behalf of the sinned-against and holds the sinner accountable.

RESISTANCE TO A VICTIM-FRIENDLY MORAL ORDER

There is predictably strong resistance to acceptance of a view of the moral
order in which sin is understood primarily as harm done to others particularly
when violence is involved. This resistance is evident in at least three areas. First,
the language used to describe violence done to persons viewed as marginalized
(women, children, people of color, gays, lesbians, etc.) is usually in a passive
voice and rarely identifies an agent. For example, "she was raped when she was
fifteen years old," "the two men who were beaten up outside of the bar were
thought to be gay," and "the predominantly African-American church was
burned to the ground." These events are stated as if there were no agent of
harm involved: "she was hit by lightening" or "he was buried in an avalanche."
Where is the agency? Someone raped the fifteen-year-old; someone beat up
the two men; someone burned down the church. In our common discourse,
we resist an accurate description of the incident in which there is a clear agent
of harm done to another.

The second indicator of resistance to viewing sin-as-harm-done-to-
another is the justification so readily offered in the face of the harm. This is
a common practice in response to men who batter an intimate partner.
"What did you do to provoke him?" is the first question put to the bruised
and bleeding woman. Or if the batterer *is* confronted, his first defense is her
supposedly provocative behavior: she burned the dinner, talked back at him,
or was running around on him. In other words, she sinned (was disobedient
or violated a rule) and so he had to punish her to keep her in line.[17] This was
his prerogative and responsibility because he sees himself as having power and
authority over her. Hence victim-blaming is the readily available mechanism
with which to distract any observer away from the perpetrator's actions and
responsibility for harm done to another person. Needless to say, this is all very
confusing for the victim.

A third indicator of resistance to viewing sin-as-harm-done-to-others is
the antivictim rhetoric that has emerged in backlash to the successes of the victims' rights movements in the United States in the 1980s. This rhetoric seems
to come from two sources. Some women have begun to refuse to self-identify
as "victims" saying that they "don't want to be victims anymore." They further
point out that women are strong and capable of taking care of ourselves, which
is true. But to suggest that if we don't *think* of ourselves as victims then we
won't be victimized is a rhetorical trick that does not work. We ultimately don't
have any choice about being a victim. That is what a victim is: someone who
is deprived of her/his resources (with which we might well have the strength

and capability to protect and care for ourselves) and as a result, suffers harm at the hands of the other. Fortunately the state of being a victim can be a temporary one. With support, advocacy, and protection from further harm (i.e., the restoration of resources), a victim becomes a survivor and hopefully experiences healing and restoration of some sense of well-being. But denial of the fact of being victimized by another does nothing to deal with the sin committed by one person against another.

The inadequacy of the "say it isn't so" strategy in responding to our potential to be victims becomes clear when a marginalized person who is victimized rallies her/his resources in self-defense. For example if a victim of rape or battering fights back and, using physical force or a weapon, injures or kills her/his attacker, a plea of self-defense in a criminal proceeding will be hard to prove, especially if there is any evidence of premeditation.[18] One of the reasons for this is that the moral question of "sin-as-harm-done-to-another" (i.e., the abuse of or attack on the woman) is superseded by "sin as disobedience or violation of rules." Again we see the question of whose interests take precedence, who gets to decide what the moral issue is? When a woman (or person of color) defends herself using physical force, she/he has stepped out of role and violated the rule against challenging (privileged) men's power. She/he will be punished accordingly.[19] While self-defense against men's violence is always a moral option for a woman, it does not necessarily result in a just moral resolution of her situation. The patriarchal power dynamics can quickly reconstitute the moral order from one that views sin-as-harm-done-to-another to one that views sin as disobedience and violation of established rules.

At stake in this discussion of the fact of victim and victimizer is the question of moral agency. Some women worry that if we allow ourselves to be called a "victim," we deny that we have moral agency. Again to possess moral agency (i.e., the ability to perceive real choices and act on them) presupposes some measure of resources (material and immaterial). This is at the heart of the persistent question posed to the battered woman, if it's so bad, why don't you just leave? She would if she could; she has probably tried to leave in the past; her abuser found her and brought her back. Her moral agency (her ability to choose to leave and implement that choice in order to protect her and her children) is compromised by her batterer's abuse. His actions have limited her access to money, information, friends, communication with others, and so forth and have established a context of fear within which she now tries to survive. She doesn't leave because *he won't let her*. Note where the balance of agency falls here. In fact, statistically she is in greatest danger of being seriously injured or killed if she tries to leave. This does not mean that she is totally powerless and passive in the face of his violence. Many women do leave; some fight back successfully, but not without great risk. The point is that it is not a failure of her moral character that keeps her trapped in a relationship with an abuser. She is a victim: her resources are diminished and her moral agency is compromised. The only moral framework that addresses her experience is to view sin as harm done by another. She is the sinned-against; he is the sinner. Yet this is the very framework she is unlikely to hear about from her church, family, or community.

IMPLICATIONS FOR ETHICS AND PASTORAL CARE

For victims of violence or harassment, there is a need for not only sensitive and compassionate support but also for an ethical and theological understanding of their experience in order to make some sense out of chaos and to clarify the ethical dynamics at work. In the absence of this clarity, "forgiveness" becomes a panacea that distracts the victim/survivor from finding justice and healing.

WHOSE INTERESTS?

Sin-as-disobedience to patriarchal rules clearly serves only the interests of the powerful and allows the powerful to avoid accountability for the harm they do to others (sin-as-harm-done-to-others). This does not mean that I am advocating an anarchistic rebellion against rules or laws per se. Clearly the value of the rule of law within society to provide for reasonable order is important. The ethical issue here is who makes the rules and for whose interests. For example, laws that enforced segregation in the United States or apartheid in South Africa were unjust and those who disobeyed these laws in order to bring about social change were punished for sin-as-disobedience. At the same time sins-as-harm-done-to-persons (racism, police brutality, lynching, etc.) were long overlooked and many of the powerful were never held accountable for these sins. However, it was finally civil disobedience and new legislation that overturned these unjust laws and practices and that provided a means for redress for past injustice. When the law (or rule) is used to protect the vulnerable, then sin-as-disobedience becomes consistent with sin-as-harm-done-to-others (e.g., rape as violation of sexual assault statutes) and all persons regardless of social location can be held to the same standard. The interests of the marginalized are served; and ironically, according to the Gospel, so are the real interests of the powerful. The powerful are confronted and offered the opportunity to repent and be reconciled in right relation with their sisters and brothers.

The problem with the utilization of sin-as-disobedience (of patriarchal rules) rather than of sin-as-harm-done-to-others is that the perpetrator of harm (usually violence) can frame the discussion and avoid accountability. Judith Herman describes the all-too-common scenario:

> To study psychological trauma is to come face-to-face both with human vulnerability in the natural world and with the capacity for evil in human nature. To study psychological trauma means bearing witness to horrible events. When the events are natural disasters or "acts of God," those who bear witness sympathize readily with the victim. But when the traumatic events are of human design, those who bear witness are caught in the conflict between victim and perpetrator. It is morally impossible to remain neutral in this conflict. The bystander is forced to

take sides. It is very tempting to take the side of the perpetrator. All the
perpetrator asks is that the bystander do nothing. He appeals to the universal desire to see, hear, and speak no evil. The victim, on the contrary,
asks the bystander to share the burden of pain. The victim demands
action, engagement, and remembering.

In order to escape accountability for his crimes, the perpetrator does
everything in his power to promote forgetting. Secrecy and silence are the
perpetrator's first line of defense. If secrecy fails, the perpetrator attacks the
credibility of his victim. If he cannot silence her absolutely, he tries to
make sure that no one listens. . . . After every atrocity one can expect to
hear the same predictable apologies: it never happened; the victim lies; the
victim exaggerates; the victim brought it upon herself; and in any case, it
is time to forget the past and move on. The more powerful the perpetrator, the greater is his prerogative to name and define reality, and the more
completely his arguments prevail. . . .

To hold traumatic reality in consciousness requires a social context that
affirms and protects the victim and that joins victim and witness in a common alliance.[20]

Power dynamics shape our response to the perpetrator. To clearly name the perpetrator as the agent of harm means that we must confront the perpetrator's
power (not the least of which is the power to name reality). This is especially
difficult when the victim and bystander have limited access to power and
resources. For this reason, Herman advocates collaboration between the victim
and the bystander in order to pool their power and resources to counter the
power of the perpetrator.

FORGIVENESS

The ethical and pastoral dilemmas that face many people come down to experiences of victimization in which there is a sinner and a sinned-against. Contemporary Christians most frequently have attempted to avoid the literal pain
of the victimization (not to mention the resulting rupture in relationship with
the perpetrator) by quickly encouraging the victim to "forgive and forget." Not
only is this response impossible to accomplish early in the healing process, it is
not helpful to any concerned. The "forgive and forget" panacea is attractive to
the bystanders because it has meant that we don't have to do anything in
response to this sin-as-harm-done-to-another. All we have to do is remind the
victims of their obligation to "forgive and forget." If the victim/survivor resists
this advice, then her/his lack of healing is her/his responsibility alone. This
panacea has also been attractive to victims/survivors because it conveys the illusion that they are now in control of their lives and that by their action alone
they can rectify their situation and find healing. Of course the perpetrator who
is looking for a way out of accountability is delighted by this response because
it virtually assures him/her that nothing is required of him/her and that there
will be no negative consequences for the harm he/she has done.

Quick "forgiveness" by the victim/survivor and cheap grace for the per-petrator are ineffective and serve no one's real interests. There is no healing for the victim/survivor, no call to repentance for the perpetrator, and no restora-tion of the moral order and social fabric. This fact was abundantly clear in a conversation with a group of incest offenders in a court-mandated treatment group. In this group of twenty-seven men, twenty-five identified themselves as active Christians and they had numerous religious concerns to discuss with me as a pastor. Finally at the end of the session, they summarized their situations and said to me, "Whenever you talk to clergy and church people, tell them for us not to forgive us so quickly." Everyone of them, when he was arrested for molesting his own children, went to his minister and every minister prayed over the perpetrators and sent them home "forgiven." They said that this was the worst thing anyone could have done for them because it meant that they still did not have to confront the sin they had committed against their children. The secular treatment program, not the church, was offering them a way to repent by holding them accountable.

Luke's gospel is equally clear on this issue:

> Jesus said to his disciples, "Occasions for stumbling are bound to come, but woe to anyone by whom they come! It would be better for you if a mill-stone were hung around your neck and you were thrown into the sea than for you to cause one of these little ones to stumble. Be on your guard! If another disciple sins, you must rebuke the offender, and if there is repen-tance, you must forgive. And if the same person sins against you seven times a day, and turns back to you seven times and says, 'I repent,' you must forgive." (Lk 17:1–4)

Rebuking (calling to account) the one who causes harm to the vulnerable is necessary in order for repentance to be possible. And repentance, meaning real change ("Repent and turn from all your transgressions; . . . get yourselves a new heart and a new spirit!" Ezek 18:30–31), is much more than the tears of remorse ("I'm really sorry, honey; I promise I'll never hit you again.").

Conversion also may or may not be real at this point. The perpetrator of violence who "finds Jesus" often then explains to the court that he need not be convicted of the crime he committed, nor go to any treatment program. A con-version that may be genuine is no replacement for the hard work he/she will need to do so that the repentance becomes real. It is up to the pastor to explain to the perpetrator that his/her conversion will be a tremendous resource of support and encouragement as she spends the next three years learning how not to repeat the abusive behavior that caused harm to another person.

Justice is needed in response to sin-as-harm-done-to-another. The vic-tim needs some experience of justice in order to find some measure of healing as a survivor. Justice requires that the victim have an opportunity to tell her/his story, to have that telling heard and acknowledged by people (or institutions) who matter to the victim, to receive compassion (a willingness to suffer with) from her/his community, to have protection of others from harm, to have the perpetrator held accountable by the community, to receive material restitution from the perpetrator (where there has been a material cost due to the victimization), and to be vindicated (set free from the memories) by the community.[21]

Tragically many victim/survivors deserve more justice than they receive. But healing seems to be possible even if one small fraction of this justice agenda is accomplished. It is finally up to the victim/survivor to determine what is adequate for her/his healing process. The process clearly is not dependent on the perpetrator's repentance although that is certainly a boon to the victim/survivor. But genuine repentance from a perpetrator is still an unusual response and the victim/survivor must be able to get on with her/his life whether or not it is forthcoming. Some degree of support from the victim/survivor's community seems to be critical to the healing process. Finally vindication (literally "to be set free") describes one's restoration to one's community without stigma and with support. This is the outcome described in Luke's gospel for the persistent widow who demands justice from the unjust judge and finally gets it because she wears him down (Lk 18:1–8). This was sufficient for the widow to be restored and to find healing.

The responsibility to make justice does not fall alone to the victim/survivor. In the final chapter of *The Fall to Violence*, Marjorie Hewitt Suchocki valiantly tackles the issues of suffering, sin, and forgiveness and provides a useful critique of traditional forgiveness as a sentimental pursuit of good feelings and acceptance of one's rapist, batterer, and so forth. She rightly refuses to accept that forgiveness means that a victim/survivor necessarily ever trusts or even relates to the perpetrator again. She is searching for a way to avoid the cycle of violence and vengeance and back to violence when she advocates forgiveness as "willing the well-being of the victim(s) and violator(s) in the context of the fullest possible knowledge of the nature of the violation."[22] But Suchocki's prescription falls short because it relies exclusively on the actions of the victim/survivor and requires nothing of the perpetrator or the community in which both live. Her well-meaning attempt at transformation of an often hopeless situation asks the victim/survivor to do all the work while we stand by and watch; the perpetrator need not confess, repent, or do penance. This effort can fall short of justice and healing, missing transformation of the situation for the future and can even make forgiveness impossible. Forgiveness, the letting go and moving on in spite of the scars, is a viable option when some degree of justice has been made.

An adult survivor of incest who was just beginning to remember the abuse by her uncle came to talk with me as a pastor. Her anger energized her and motivated her to confront her abuser. This only created a dilemma because her uncle was deceased and so she had nowhere to lay her complaint. So she decided to write to her father (whose brother had abused her) and tell him her story. We discussed her expectations about her father's response. She was uncertain of his response but decided that she needed to tell him regardless. She sent the letter; he received it and immediately got on a plane and came to his daughter. The first thing he said was, "I'm sorry I did not protect you from my brother." He said that he didn't know that his brother was sexually abusing her, but that he should have been there to protect her because he was her father. He told her that he knew she had been in therapy and that it cost money. How much had she spent? She told him. He said that a check would be in the mail the next day.

When she came back to see me two weeks later, she was a different person. She still had issues to work on with her therapist and would continue to go to her survivors' support group. But she had experienced some justice from her father and so forgiveness (letting go and moving on) had happened. She had been freed to forgive by the support of her father's response.

When a victim/survivor of abuse can see her/himself as the recipient of harm done by another person and can frame the experience in terms of being sinned against, then an appropriate moral framework can give shape to the pastoral response from her/his community. The community can call the perpetrator to account and protect the victim/survivor. We can create the possibility for justice (although there are no guarantees here) and be present during healing.

Wrapped up in a theodicy that reinforces our self-blame (what sin did I commit/what rule did I break that caused these disastrous consequences to befall me?) and denied a moral framework in which our victimization, harassment, and oppression could be clearly named as sin (in which someone sinned and caused harm to another), we have struggled to make sense of the dominant moral framework that was never meant to speak to our experiences at the margins. All of which has made it very difficult for the marginalized to exercise our moral agency and to find any moral coherency. For those of us who come out of the Christian tradition, we have a rich resource from both the Hebrew and Christian Scriptures that lifts up the notion of sin-as-harm-done-to-another (congruent with our experiences) and that posits God as an active participant on the side of the vulnerable in this drama. To subscribe to this moral framework is an act of faith that acknowledges that the innocent do suffer and that God is present in that suffering seeking to bring healing. This framework affirms that deeds do have consequences, that justice is God's will and God's way, that those who cause harm to others will be called to account regardless of our social location, and that forgiveness is God's gift to those who are harmed so that we may find healing and can get on with our lives.

It is an act of moral agency to choose a moral framework that makes sense in our lives, which serves our interests as marginalized people. This framework can then provide the means to comprehend experiences of violence and abuse and give direction to our responses to these experiences.

NOTES

1. As a reflection of patriarchal ideology and subsequent patriarchal ideology and subsequent patriarchal interpretations, the role of Eve is emphasized as the ultimate source of the disobedience; hence all women bear the burden of her sin and are viewed as the source of all sin.

2. See Robin C. Cover, "Sin, Sinners. Old Testament," in *The Anchor Bible Dictionary*, Vol. 6, 32, ed. by David Noel Freedman (New York: Doubleday, 1992).

3. Ibid. See 2 Kings 18:14; Gen 31:36, 43:9, and 44:32; Ex 5:16; and Judg 11:27.

4. See Walter Brueggemann, "The Shrill Voice of the Wounded Party," in this book.

5. Ibid.

6. E. P. Sanders, "Sin, Sinners. New Testament," in *Anchor Bible Dictionary*, Vol. 6, 41.

7. Brueggemann, "Shrill Voice of the Wounded Party."

8. Ibid.

9. Sanders, "Sin, Sinners. Old Testament," 43.

10. Frederick Keene analyzes Jesus' teaching on forgiveness in light of the power realities that the people faced. He argues persuasively that those who had less power in a relationship were never in a position to forgive (to let go) until the power imbalance was rectified. The powerful could forgive a debt of the less powerful or peers could forgive the debts of each other. See Keene, "Structures of Forgiveness in the New Testament," in *Violence Against Women and Children: A Theological Sourcebook in the Christian Tradition*, ed. by Carol Adams and Marie Fortune (New York: Continuum Publishing Co., 1995).

11. Sanders, "Sin, Sinners. Old Testament," 42.

12. See, for example, Marjorie Hewitt Suchocki, *The Fall to Violence* (New York: Continuum, 1994) 28, where she notes but argues against this equation.

13. Hence Karl Menninger's book in 1973 titled, *What Ever Became of Sin?* (New York: Hawthorn Books, 1973).

14. "Defendant Says He Has Right to Sex with Wife," Alan Abrahamson, *Los Angeles Times*, 29 January 1996.

15. The real issue here is authentic consent, a concept that appears to be outside of the awareness of Mr. Espinosa. Both sexual partners must have information, awareness, equal power, and the option to say "no" to sexual activity without being punished as well as the option to say "yes." Consent should never be confused with submitting, going along, or acquiescing in the face of force or coercion. Consent is an alien concept to persons (mostly women) whose life experience has been that sex is something someone does to them; in other words, they feel that they have never had any say in the matter, in marriage or outside of it. In sexual interaction, authentic consent requires communication and agreement that "no" means no, "yes" means yes, and "maybe" means maybe—even in marriage. "No" will not be punished by withdrawing or by more coercive tactics. "Maybe" requires waiting for "yes," not cajoling, and pushing.

16. For further discussion, see Marie M. Fortune, *Love Does No Harm: Sexual Ethics for the Rest of Us* (New York: Continuum Publishing Co., 1995).

17. A local news story reported that a man hanged himself in his jail cell where he was being held for the murder of his girlfriend. His suicide note said he was sorry. The sheriff commented: "He thought she was going out with someone else. Whether she was or not, I don't know." ("Inmate Hangs Self in Buncombe Jail," Glenn O'Neal, *Asheville Citizen-Times*, 13 June 1996) This comment is an attempt to justify the man's murder of his partner. If the man *thought* she was going out with someone else, then that explains his violence toward her.

18. This legal conundrum began to be addressed in the 1990s with statutory changes and judicial decisions that take account of gender as a factor in a self-defense plea and now may apply the Reasonable Woman standard when adjudicating a case where a woman defended herself against abuse or attack.

19. The average prison sentence for men who kill their woman partners is two to six years; the average sentence for women who kill their partners is fifteen years despite the fact that most women who kill do so in self-defense.

20. Judith Herman, *Trauma and Recovery* (New York: Basic Books-Harper Collins) 7–9.

21. See Fortune, *Is Nothing Sacred?* (San Francisco: Harper and Row, 1989) and Fortune, Woolley et al., *Clergy Misconduct* (Seattle: Center for the Prevention of Sexual and Domestic Violence, 1992) for further discussion of justice-making.

22. Suchocki, *Fall to Violence*, 144.

CHAPTER EIGHT

TEACHING JUSTICE AND RECONCILIATION
IN A WOUNDING WORLD

Mary Elizabeth Mullino Moore

In the summer of 1999, our family moved from California to Georgia, travel-
ing by car through beautiful countryside, uplifted by mountains and stretched
by plains. This countryside was once the home of Native tribes and nations,
most of whom have been forced to move into smaller spaces with limited job
options for supporting their families. On that journey we also stopped in Oklahoma City where, four years earlier, a bomb had exploded in a federal building filled with women, men, and children. We drove into the center of the city
where two hundred people, like us, were crowding around the bombing site to
remember that fateful day in 1995. The fence around the site was dotted with
stories and pictures of the victims, as well as letters written to them by families, friends, and pilgrims; the fence postings provided a folk memorial that
would stand in place until a larger, more permanent memorial could be completed. Why are people so touched by this event and so moved to commemo-
rate it? One could give obvious answers to this question, but I invite readers to
live with the unanswered question as a way to empathize with the alienation
and woundedness in our world.

    Alienation is embodied in the lives of Native people whose lands have
been overtaken by migrant outsiders; it is embodied in the hundreds of people
who were killed, maimed, and filled with fear after the terrorist bombing in
Oklahoma City. It is embodied in white supremacy groups who perpetuate acts
of hate on people of color, and in youth who beat other youths—gay and lesbian—to their deaths. It is embodied in fragile peace agreements in Kosovo,
Northern Ireland, Israel, and Palestine that unravel before the ink is dry. It is
embodied in families who beat their children or batter one another with
words. It is embodied by the poor who struggle to survive and are told they are

worthless. It is embodied by well-intentioned religious folk who feel over-whelmed and do nothing. This is indeed a wounding and wounded world.

The purpose of this chapter is to reflect on aches in this world, under-scoring the radical need to change.[1] The purpose, specifically, is to reflect on the need to teach justice and reconciliation in a wounding world. The exploration involves (1) analyzing the fear of knowing—a fear that underlies much of the world's alienation; (2) reflecting on the yearning to know—a yearning that has within it seeds of hope; (3) making proposals for educational searching; and (4) offering visions for teaching justice and reconciliation. The first two sections are analytic, describing and reflecting on realities of alienation; the last two sections are visionary, proposing directions for education and life practice.

THE FEAR OF KNOWING

The experience of alienation is permeated with fear, and the particular fear that is the subject for this chapter is the fear of knowing. Many of the fears that are identified throughout this book actually erupt in the process of education because, according to the thesis of this chapter, people live with an underlying fear of knowing, or a fear of being in relationship. Some fears of knowing have been discussed elsewhere,[2] but the particular focus of this chapter is to reflect upon the fear of knowing violence, the fear of not finding answers, and the fear of facing the abyss (knowing what we do not know).

The Fear of Knowing Violence

Many years ago a young woman, a college student, was very much involved in her local church's ministry.[3] Because she was so regular, she carried much responsibility and she was a mentor for younger students and youths within her church. Soon this young woman began to sense a special calling—a calling to some kind of Christian service. This decided, she began to purify her heart with frequent prayer, worship, and pastoral coun-seling. The journey was a rich one, and the young woman felt herself growing deeper and more compassionate. Her life seemed to be opening to greater joy as the days passed . . . until one day, the pastor with whom she met regularly seduced her.

Many years ago, this young woman lost her youth and her sense of hope with the touch of a man who used her. She was torn apart from a relationship of trust with this pastor and his church. She was torn apart from her family, who hurt with her but did not know how to be with her. She was torn apart from her religious vocation because she now thought herself unworthy. She was torn apart from her sense of self, and she felt unclean, unwhole, and unwholesome. The young woman went into a depression that lasted many years. Her depression blotted out many memories of sexual acts with this once-trusted pastor, but her depression did not dissolve the pain.

Over a period of years, this young woman sought counseling; she herself became a teacher and youth leader. In counseling, she learned to live quietly and to moderate her depression. She found a new vocation, and she did it well. But depression returned again and again until, finally, she followed it deep inside herself where she discovered her mem-ories. Months of difficult work followed—recovering memory after memory and anger upon anger. When finally the young woman felt purged of her past, she was not young anymore. All of her young adulthood was lost, and much of her middle adulthood as well. But she was again clean and whole and wholesome. Now this woman tells her story, and has invited others to tell her story. This is her way of teaching others in pain.

In this case, much is revealed about the fear of knowing violence. First is revealed the reality that people are wounded everywhere we go, and we do not know it. Violence is often hidden, as it was for the family and friends of the woman in this case. The young woman was seen by the people around her as a model of calm compassion, as a strong person without pain. The case also reveals that abuse in one relationship affects all other relationships, including the relationships within oneself. Reconciliation is needed, but not first with the offender. Reconciliation is needed with the Spirit of Life and with oneself, then with family and friends and colleagues.

THE FEAR OF NOT FINDING ANSWERS

I recently visited a large bookstore in search of a book recommended to me by a student. Having been told by the clerk where I could find the book, I was searching the childcare shelves. Sitting on a stool in front of the shelf where I was searching was a young woman who was deeply engrossed in reading a book. In order to look for my book, I had to stand beside her. Even with my embarrassing closeness, she seemed oblivious to me, never turning her head from her book and never acknowledging my presence in any way.

After a few minutes, a young child came up to the woman and said, "Mommy, time to go." The woman responded, "Just a minute, son; I am almost finished." "Mommy, time to go," came the reply. The little boy walked away and came back shortly with a young man, who appeared to be his father. The woman showed her husband the two books she had been reading. She said, "These books just skirt around the issues; they are no help at all." He glanced at the books as she continued, "This book looks like it is just what we are looking for, but it does not give any answers at all." The man responded with a chagrined look, and the two of them walked away with their son.

After the family had walked away, I could not resist looking at the titles of the books that had caused such consternation. They were Children at Risk: What You Need to Know to Protect Your Family *and* The Challenging Child: A Guide for Parents of Exceptionally Strong-Willed Children.[4] *The second of these books was the one the mother had expected to be "just what she was looking for." As I perused this book, I thought that the index and chapters revealed the authors' attempts to give practical guidance; regardless of their intent, the mother did not find what she was hoping to find.*

As I reflect on this case, I am struck with the deep concern of these parents for their child. I know nothing more than the case scenario that I have shared, but the case calls into question my own glib judgments of self-help books. These parents seemed to be searching for answers to their immediate needs, and to those of their son. They had apparently come to this bookstore with considerable hope that they could find practical guidance in child-rearing.

The case raises another aspect of the fear of knowing, that is, the fear of knowledge that raises new questions and does not provide the answers we need to deal with urgent matters of daily living. How are we to build justice and reconciliation if we are walking through a fog without clear guidance? In this case, the mother was looking for very particular advice, apparently to build a reconciling relationship with her son. Two books explicitly written to give such advice fell short of responding to her particular questions. In short, she not only wanted answers, but she wanted particular answers to particular questions. What she found was advice that was related to slightly different questions, and this was not helpful. The case scenario was intensified for me when I realized that the first book was written by James Dobson and Gary L. Bauer. Dobson is reputed for giving very practical advice of a particular kind. The other book, likewise, was filled with suggestions, both general and specific. Yet both fell short of meeting the needs of this woman who sat in rapt attention on her stool.

The parents of this simple story are joined by many other people who are afraid of not finding answers to their most pressing concerns. They are joined by people who are afraid to admit, even to themselves, that they are overwhelmed with chronic depression or unresolved anger. These people might also look for easy answers, whether in self-help books, special diets, or alcohol and drugs; all the while, they dread the horror of exploring parts of themselves where no simple answers can be found. The parents in the case study are also joined by people who are afraid to work against war or poverty or racism for fear that no easy answers will be found. These socially aroused people might also look for easy answers, tempted to accept destructive social conditions as inevitable, beyond repair, or to seek surface solutions based in platitudes, stereotypes, or projections of blame onto others. In all of these cases, people might look for answers, but never dare to dive beneath the surface, fearing they they will simply find more questions. This leads naturally to a third fear—the fear of facing the abyss, or knowing what we do not know.

THE FEAR OF FACING THE ABYSS

Recently, I moved back to the Southern United States, home of my childhood and youth and home of my ancestors. In doing so, I knew that the pull was deeper than I understood on the surface; I could say no more. In the months of packing, before leaving California, I heard a lecture on public television about one of my more famous Southern ancestors, a general in the Civil War. I knew that some of my ancestors had owned slaves but, on this day, I learned something more. This particular ancestor had not only been a wealthy slaveholder, but he had also taken much land from the Creek people, displacing them in order to expand his own holdings. I did not want to know this!

This personal experience placed me on the edge of an abyss, aware that I was about to learn horrors about myself and my people, but also aware that there are no clear guides or guarantees on the road to justice and reconciliation of race, culture, and class. My homeland is surely no better or worse than others, but it is mine. By returning, I face an abyss where I will have to stand, trembling, without much comfort. In this experience I face a moment of new honesty and a sense of worthlessness. I also become emboldened with a wisdom reminiscent of Ecclesiastes, in which the author examines his own knowledge, acknowledging what he does not know and the worthlessness of what he does know. I know very little of my ancestors, or the anguishing history of the antebellum South. What I do know is frightening, for it makes me responsible to those who have been sinned-against and those who have been victims of the oppressive slave history of our nation, whether as slaves or as oppressors of slaves. As I face this reality, I am afraid of learning more of what I do not know; I am also afraid of learning that I will never really know. Teetering on the edge of the abyss, I will have to live with the ambiguity of knowing and not knowing.

To confirm my sense of how uncomfortable this abyss can be, I recall studying Ecclesiastes with three groups of passionate women. On the first meeting of each class, the responses were energetic. Frequently, the women asked: "Why are we studying this book? It is so depressing!" "Why was this book even included in the Bible?" "I would prefer something that is inspirational." In short, they were asking why we needed to spend our time at the abyss, dwelling so much on what we do not know.

Certainly, Qohelet (the name ascribed to the author of Ecclesiastes) anguished about the passing nature of wisdom and the failure of his own wisdom; this *is* depressing. In fact, he bequeaths to his reader complex patterns of thought that run counter to many dominant assumptions in his world and ours.[5] Out of Qohelet's thought come several controversial ideas: that everything is vanity (*hebel*, translated also as a "puff of wind" or "breath" or "worthlessness"); that time is repetitive and cyclic ("nothing new under the sun," Eccl 1:9b); that wisdom is limited in its rewards; that consolation and profit are not dependable and lasting; and that relationships are suspect, especially with women and children.

These messages evoke a sense of alienation that runs in many directions at once—alienation from the tradition, from the values of modern society, and even from family. The first of the controversial ideas is the most obvious, for the word *hebel* appears twenty-eight times in Ecclesiastes, and it undercuts the expectations of accomplishment or progress that are dear to modern society and to Protestants who value a work ethic. The second idea that time is cyclic stands in tension with commonly held Jewish and Christian worldviews grounded in linear time. The recognition of the limits of wisdom contrasts with other wisdom literature (e.g., Proverbs) in which wisdom is held in higher esteem. Furthermore, Qohelet's accent on the limits of consolation and profit resonates with the Book of Job, but does not fit with modern accents on happiness and material gain. Finally, Qohelet's questioning of relationships is starkly judgmental of women and children; in his patriarchal context, he fears that women will lead to peril and children will squander men's accomplishments. We are left in the end with some of the most telling questions in the Bible, but thus they remain—as questions that hauntingly remind the readers of what we do not know, leaving us with questions of interpretation and decision. Alienation is real, but so is the yearning to know, to which we now turn.

THE YEARNING TO KNOW

Even in the midst of such fear of knowing, people still yearn to know. They ask questions; they wonder. They cling to hope that new knowledge will open possibilities of justice and reconciliation. The purpose of this section is to explore the yearning for *wisdom—questing to know God and the world in a deep and responsive way*. This is the stuff out of which justice and reconciliation are made. Wisdom is *questing after good relationship, searching for vision, knowledge, and direction*. This search is filled with vulnerability; we become accountable for what we envision and know. Perhaps the issues of fear and alienation are not surprising after all.

As I consider the case studies just analyzed, I am aware that the cases themselves, and the fears they arouse, are evidence that questing is taking place. They are probably evidence also that people are trying to avoid the demands of questing, for wisdom has to do both with knowing deeply and with responding to that which is known. What yearnings emerge in the midst of such fearful questing?

Yearning to Find Life Beyond Violence

If knowing is grounded in experience and relationships, then it cannot always be happy and satisfying. On the other hand, the yearning to know is more than yearning to know harsh realities. I taught a course this past fall entitled Issues of Women and Theology in Christian Tradition. In that course, the African-American women, without exception, wanted to focus their papers on subjects of hope. One woman said that, in her black community, reflecting on suffering is not enough; women need to see a world beyond suffering. From these women and untold others, I learn that wisdom is *facing the hard realities that life forces upon people and, also, questing for the life and hope that lies beyond violence*.

The earlier case study of the young woman who was seduced further reveals that the yearning for life beyond violence is a long and difficult path. One has to travel through memories and hurts. The path is filled with rage, and sometimes the only hope one experiences is the rage itself, which, if nothing else, is a cry for justice and an impetus for healing and new life. The yearning for life beyond violence is not naive hope. Victims of violence know that healing and reconciliation do not remove wounds or restore lost years. People hope for the deeper joy of finding self and God—a joy that the young woman of the case study came to know in her inner life and in relationship to those people closest to her. This was a joy that she also wanted to spread to others so they could share in it.

One other learning from the case of the young woman is that yearning for life beyond violence requires truth-telling—telling stories that tell truth.

The woman came to recognize that her work in teaching and counseling with young people is grounded in her own story. She finds now that she sometimes needs to share that story explicitly with others, especially when they are facing violence on their journeys. Her story has become a source of strength and wisdom and a pathway to life beyond violence.

YEARNING TO FACE QUESTIONS WITHOUT ANSWERS

If knowing is understood as a relationship, then, answers are not so important as exploring and acting on relationships. Wisdom has to do with *engaging the questions that emerge in the midst of living life, and engaging them without the certainty of finding answers.* The burden of wisdom is that it sometimes involves questing without resolution. The questing itself is the act of wisdom, but questing may surface new questions rather than clear and useful answers.

Here we see the accent on questing itself—a natural human activity, but one that has often been used as a tool of control or an activity limited to the intellectual elite. Consider scientific questing as a case in point. The social structures of science reveal how the most adventurous forms of questing are limited to a small, elite group. Consider how women have been foreclosed from scientific quests throughout much of Western history, especially since the sixth century.[6] Margaret Wertheim demonstrates that women are still "chronically underrepresented in physics," a situation with parallels in religion:

> The struggle women have faced to gain entry into science parallels the struggle they have faced to gain entry into the clergy. On the one hand, women have had to fight for the right to interpret the books of Scripture, and on the other hand, for the right to interpret what was traditionally regarded as God's "other book"—Nature.[7]

Wertheim describes how these limitations on women in science were influenced by clerical reforms that limited higher education to men preparing for the church, and by separate education for women and men, tightened episcopal control of women's religious communities, the shift to Latin for clerical learning (only accessible to clerics), and the shift to celibacy for clergy and academics.[8]

Whatever the causes, Sandra Harding notes, "Women have been more systematically excluded from doing serious science than from performing any other social activity except, perhaps, front-line warfare."[9] If one thinks of the sciences as centers of questing, then, one wonders why women have been excluded and what have been the consequences. Wertheim argues that the lack of women's participation has fostered a willingness among some in the recent physics community to seek a "theory of everything," with minimal interest in applications to ordinary human life.[10]

In relation to wisdom as questing without finding answers, this approach to physics not only excludes women from questing after knowledge of the natural world, but it excludes women from the worldview-building and value-framing role that physics has played in the modern world. Pushed farther, the exclusion of many ethnic communities from this visionary enterprise has shaped popular values, accentuating theories of everything over contributions to the well-being of the world. It is exemplified in Pythagoras' equation of numbers with gods and with timelessness, immutability, and incorruptability.[11] It is further exemplified in Newtonian science and in *social* Newtonianism in which society is understood as "a 'natural' order ordained by God."[12] This view has too often been used to preserve the status quo, to protect the elitism of the elite, and to prevent the incursion of women and others into the formal halls of science.

The problematic in all of this is the exclusion of women and all other people outside the intellectual elite from participation in constructing the ideas, systems, and actions that govern society. More fundamentally, the possibility of wisdom is diminished and people are denied the value of questing without finding answers. The search for definitive explanations of the universe, rigid social structures, and elitist views of knowledge go hand in hand. Perhaps this is why questions without answers are so alarming; such questions threaten to deconstruct existing explanations, social structures, and the understanding of knowledge and wisdom. Perhaps what is needed is a disruption of explanations, structures, elitism, and exclusion. What is needed is an understanding of wisdom in which the very act of questing is more valued than the momentary answers that are found along the way, and all people are invited to join the quest.

YEARNING TO FACE THE ABYSS

In the earlier case studies of my encounter with racist roots and Qohelet's writing in Ecclesiastes, major issues of fear were identified: the fear of learning hard lessons, the fear of discouragement without comfort, the fear of knowing what we do not know, and the fear of knowing that our knowledge is fleeting and inconsequential in the movements of the world. In the case of Ecclesiastes, we see the courage of a writer who raised questions he could not answer, and faced reality as he saw it without smoothing his despair with trivial responses. We also see the courage of the women who studied Ecclesiastes, wrestling with the text unrelentingly, opening their own questions and exploring their vulnerability. These are acts of wisdom—facing the abyss.

In other wisdom literature, as in Ecclesiastes, we are confronted by the *quest to live with the tension between the human desire to know and the awareness of not knowing.* Thus, the wisdom literature in general can open possibilities as well as questions. Consider, for the sake of focus, the wisdom that emanates from the Book of Job. What is communicated in Job regarding the act of knowing what we do not know?

Reflect on the story told in the first two chapters of Job—a story of cosmic horror as God and Satan play with Job's life. The opening scene points the reader to a long-ago and faraway land of Uz, and to a blameless and upright man named Job—a man who feared God and turned away from evil. This begins as a hero journey, but the stakes in the tale are very high. In the following verses, the readers listen to a committee meeting of heavenly beings in which Satan challenges God, who has boasted of Job's righteousness—a righteousness that Satan claims is only possible because of Job's comfortable life. And then, the cosmic horror *really* begins; God gives Satan permission to take power over everything that Job has, as long as he leaves Job alone. Job is soon faced with the loss of his flock, his servants, and then his sons and daughters. His response to the incredible sweep of violence might be described as long-suffering, or as sick: "Naked I came from my mother's womb, and naked shall I return there; the Lord gave and the Lord has taken away; blessed be the name of the Lord" (Job 1:21).

In the very next scene, another committee meeting takes place among the heavenly beings. This time, Satan insists that Job is only faithful to God because his own body has been spared, so God gives permission to Satan to prove his point and Satan inflicts Job with loathsome sores (Job 1:4–8).

As Job and his family stumble along in this story, readers will find no clear answers, just a lot of urgent questions. But in the story, Job accuses his wife of being foolish when she starts to raise questions. As Job sits on the ash heap scraping his sores, she says, "Do you still persist in your integrity? Curse God and die" (Job 2:9). Or, perhaps you could read her as saying, "So you still persist in your integrity. Bless God and die." However you translate the words of this unnamed woman, she is asking questions and naming realities; she is not giving answers, or even expecting anyone else to give them.

In fact, traditional interpretations have equated Job's wife with Eve, Delilah, and Jezebel, who tempted good men into self-destruction.[15] As late as 1985, one commentator described Job's wife as "the earthly mouthpiece for the hidden Satan."[16] He did not even stop there: "She is clearly not a patient comforter who, like the friends, waits seven days before presenting her ideas. Her function, as Augustine said, is to play the role of *diaboli adjutrix*, the Satan's unwitting ally."[17] But I ask this commentator, why are you so quick to read clarity where there is none, and so quick to read impatience in a woman whose children are dead, whose servants and animals are dead; whose whole way of life is dead, and whose husband is afflicted? Thus far, Job's wife is the one in the story who is uniquely able to face what she does not know.

The many answers that are offered in the Book of Job are just that— many answers. Among other things, the Book offers no less than five names for God—no singular, clear image here![18] Edwin M. Good, one of the most prolific interpreters of Job, confesses that he has changed his mind many times about this perplexing book,[19] and now he sees Job as an "open text"—one that has no "lidded container of meaning."[20] In fact, he adds, "I find the Book of Job immensely more fascinating, more moving, more humanly true than ever I did when I thought my job was to jam a single truth down upon it."[21] How hard that must sound to people looking for certainty of knowledge and answers to every question; how reassuring it is to those who have encountered disasters in life and discovered that surety and answers are short-lived; the most we can hope for is the continuing presence of God.

Wisdom has little to do with completed knowledge or clear answers to painful questions. Wisdom has to do with struggling and hoping; it has to do with walking and talking with God, sometimes limping as we walk, sometimes sitting and waiting, sometimes pushing or being pushed by others, sometimes praising God, sometimes venting our fury at the injustice and pain of this earth. In times of crisis, we know best of all that wisdom is *simply being real with God*. No wonder that Jews around the world so often read Job together in times of crisis!

The idea of being real with God is thoroughly distasteful, even threatening, in a world where individuals and nations put so much effort into making good impressions on others, where certainty is valued, and where the admission of not knowing is tantamount to defeat. Furthermore, this is a world where people *are* fooled by appearances, and where the desire to impress others is often stronger than the desire to do justice and walk in integrity.

What possible hope comes from the wisdom literature and the Book of Job? Perhaps, the only hope is the presence of God—the God who was present before Job was born, who converses with heavenly beings and with Job, whose ways are not easy to explain or to justify. But this is the same God who received Job's confusion and anger and who cared enough to debate with Job. In the end, neither Job nor his wife received simple answers to their questions. And although the Book of Job offers much to feed theological debates about the relation of God to evil, it does not answer the questions of contemporary readers anymore than it answered Job's. Job's integrity, which seemed at the beginning to be his blamelessness and faithfulness, is shown in the end to be his persistence in the face of pain. Job's wisdom finally mirrors his wife's wisdom; he is *simply real with God and with those around him*. The reward for this wisdom, according to the story of Job, is not answers to questions, but the continuing presence of God.

Thus is the journey of knowing what we do not know! The journey of wisdom—questing to know God and the world in a deep and responsive way will lead us time and again to moments of not knowing. And in those moments, being real in the presence of God is perhaps the most important act of wisdom that is available to us.

EDUCATION AND SEARCHING

What is the role of education in such a world where wisdom is controversial and filled with alienation and fear? What is the role when central symbols are being questioned in the name of emancipatory transformation, but alternative symbols are being scorned and the fear of these alternatives is near panic? This is a particularly pressing question in light of Rollo May's long-ago essay when he made the point that a society, when its central symbols are in tact, can carry on its therapeutic functions through education, religion, and family life, but a society faced with the disintegration of its central symbols turns to psychoanalysis.[22] *If education is to support and enhance knowing, then teachers will need to engage people in experiencing, exploring, deconstructing, and reconstructing symbols.* And if knowing is relational, then the starting point for engaging symbols will be those symbols that emerge as people relate with God, and with their intimate communities of family and friends, their religious communities, and the whole of creation.

THE PRACTICE OF TRUTH-TELLING

One clear direction for education that fosters searching is *truth-telling*. Both from the case of the woman who was seduced and from the case of Job who was devastated, truth-telling is identified as a basic and urgent response to alienation. Truth-telling is *talking straight with God and oneself and others*; such talking straight is a prelude to any genuine justice and reconciliation. When people attempt to repair relationships without honesty, the results are shallow, and even destructive. Urging victims of rape to forgive rapists, for example, is forcing victims to take responsibility for acts done against them.

To speak of genuine reconciliation, or genuine ethical action, is to respect "the power of anger in the work of love."[23] According to Beverly Harrison, who introduced that oft-quoted phrase, the way for persons to act morally is to begin, not by running away, but by joining together with collective power. She speaks explicitly of the collective power of women. She says, "My basic thesis is that a Christian moral theology must be answerable to what women have learned by struggling to lay hold of the gift of life, to receive it, to live deeply into it, to pass it on."[24] For Harrison, men can, and hopefully will, be in this struggle with women. What is important is the struggle.

For the purposes of this chapter, we need to focus on the collective power of *all* who are alienated, oppressed, or hurting. Harrison herself emphasizes throughout her writing that the cry for justice must not only be a concern for gender-justice, but fundamentally a concern for justice for people of all races, social classes, and sexual orientations. The struggle is critical, and those who know oppression need to lead the struggle with their collective power. These are the very people who need to speak truth and to guide the human community toward wisdom. These are the teachers.

THE PRACTICE OF LIVING WITH QUESTIONS

We said earlier that wisdom has to do with questing without always find answers. Education, thus, has to do with *living with questions*. This idea will be developed briefly here, but it has to do with *educating in the messiness of life*— educating on the hospital ward, in the soup kitchen, on the streets, in an explosive argument, in a counseling session, at a political rally, and in committee meetings of religious communities.

This kind of education is planned, to be sure, but it is not predictable. It is *purposeful* in that the aim of education is to engage in significant action in the world, and to reflect on the meaning and value of that action in relation to the past, present, and future of the world. It is *experimental* in that educators engage with people in action that none have ever tried before, at least not in this way. It is *reverent* in that the community is encouraged to revere God and God's creation in all they do. And it is *open-ended*; people are encouraged to engage the questions that are most pressing for them, their community, their religious tradition, or the larger world.

We said earlier that wisdom has to do with engaging the questions that emerge in the midst of living life, and engaging them without the certainty of finding answers. The four qualities of education that have just been named—purpose, experimentation, reverence, and openness—are essential to living with questions. Purpose assures that the questions are not just empty exercises. Experimentation assures that people probe the edges of their knowing and questioning. Reverence evokes a sense of transcendent mystery, and it inspires awe and appreciation for the sacred reality that is far larger than human questions. Openness invites people to hope for answers, for new questions, for guidance, and, most important of all, for a deep engagement with God and the world.

THE PRACTICE OF SEARCHING AND DARING

The earlier discussion of wisdom ended with an admonition to know what we do not know, or in simple terms, to be real with God and with others. Educationally, this suggests that *the environment we create needs to be safe, an environment where trust is nurtured so that searching and daring can be encouraged.* A safe environment is built, in part, by all that has been said above about seeking to know and respond to God, living with questions, and seeking to know ourselves and the world. All of these acts can contribute to sensitivity, trust, and trustworthiness. But a safe environment is also created by hope. I walked out of my class recently and realized that the sensational sharing, analyzing, and listening was not my creation; it was a gift of grace. I had given my best to discern and prepare, but beyond that, I could simply hope and pray. The rest was a gift.

But what about those educational meetings (like my class the very next week) when nothing seems to click into place, when people arrive with tired faces, and the carefully prepared process is unsuccessful in energizing the community? *The educational process also needs to be responsive to shifting movements within the learning community*—to the issues, intellectual debates, inspirations, moods, confusions, frustrations, eagerness, and tiredness. This is not to say that the perfect educational process will anticipate all of these movements and respond appropriately to maintain a high level of eagerness and robust study. It is to say, rather, that the movements *will* come; the educational challenge is to discern what is taking place, how the community dynamics are related to dynamics within the subject matter, and how future learning can be enhanced by responding to the shifting movements. If people are to know what they do not know, they will need opportunities to relate to the dynamics of community life, the intense study of texts and realities of the larger world, and their own deepest impulses.

To this end, *education also needs to explore below the surface, going ever deeper into questions, and it needs to instill playfulness with ideas and narratives and images.* The depth exploration is not always serious, and the playfulness is not always fun, but both are important to enhance the human yearning to know and the need to know what we do not know. The postmodern move toward deconstruction is one way of exploring deeply and playfully. The gift of postmodern reformulations of the learning process is that people are encouraged to look at a taken-for-granted reality from a new angle and to dismantle it, only to recon-struct it again at a later time. Edwin M. Good makes a helpful distinction between deconstruction and destruction:

> I find that deconstruction has to do far less with smashing things with sledgehammers than with slipping playfully out from under the walls and fences that the search for Truth has erected around us. The deconstruc-tionist searches for the text's multiple possibilities, its fascinating and liber-ating inconsistencies, its simultaneous contraries—the ways the mind and the text play their mutual games.[25]

The purpose of such deconstruction is to open people's eyes to what they do not know without filling them prematurely with reassurance and answers. The very act of not knowing is rich with "multiple possibilities."

A lifelong scholar of biblical wisdom literature, J. Gerald Janzen, expresses a similar sensitivity. He is concerned not just with multiple possibil-ities, but most especially with the *being* of that which is studied. He says of the Book of Job, for example, "The aim should not be to find out from the com-mentator what the Book of Job means, but rather to attend sensitively and with sympathetic imagination to the concreteness of the text, to what Archibald MacLeish . . . calls the *being* of a poem rather than its *meaning*."[26] With these words from Janzen, we have circled back to the idea of wisdom as questing to know God and the world in a deep and responsive way. This view of knowing is relational, having to do with sensitivity and a sympathetic imag-ination. The accumulation of facts and mastery of skills are only important if they nourish relationships.

In a relational view of knowing and a relational approach to education, one inevitably meets that which one does not know. A person or community is laid bare to discover yet again what is not known, to be disrupted (sometimes uncomfortably), and to be inspired once again to continue the quest. And the quest itself is wisdom!

EDUCATION FOR JUSTICE AND RECONCILIATION

The questing that has been described in the preceding section is the ground in which justice and reconciliation are planted. *Justice is the restoration of full life potential for every person and community, fostered through equitable social structures and conditions that foster well-being and flourishing. Reconciliation is the restoration of good relations between God and humanity, and among people*; it is a coming together in right relationship. Both are a gift from God—a holy trust that cannot be forced, but one that *can* be planted and nourished. To say this is to draw insights from modern psychology, which warns against superficial justice and forced recon-ciliation. We can also draw insights regarding reconciliation from Paul's letter to the contentious early Christian community at Corinth:

> All this is from God, who reconciled us to himself through Christ, and has given us the ministry of reconciliation; that is, in Christ God was reconciling the world to himself, not counting their trespasses against them, and entrusting the message of reconciliation to us. (2 Cor 5:18–19)

This text lifts a theme that is found predominantly in the Pauline literature (Rom 5:10–11, 11:15; Eph 2:16; Col 1:19–22, in addition to 2 Cor 5:16–20). In that literature, Paul ascribes the work of reconciliation to the acts of God in Christ.

This raises a major educational question. If justice and reconciliation are gifts from God, then how might a community educate for a just and reconciled world? Certainly, the 2 Cor. text suggests that God gives people the ministry of reconciliation; likewise, we see in Scripture that the call for people to practice justice is God-given. This chapter closes with five proposals for teaching justice and reconciliation in a wounding world. All of the proposals draw impetus from the Jewish and Christian traditions, and all build upon the search for wisdom that has been described in the previous section.

THE PRACTICE OF BUILDING JUSTICE AND
RECONCILIATION ONE STEP AT A TIME

Several years ago, I was responsible for cochairing a conference on Ecology and Native American Traditions. My partner was a Choctaw man with whom I enjoyed working very much. During the conference, however, major problems erupted and the Native American participants became suspicious and vocal in decrying the audacious, oppressive leadership of white women (me) in this conference. I was devastated because I had bent over backward throughout the planning and leadership process to be a helper and colleague. I took the critique to heart, to process it over the next several months. One final comment in the conference was particularly helpful to me in that ongoing process. A Native American elder said to the non-Native people in the meeting, "If you want to join with us, you have to commit yourself to walk with us on the long journey; we do not want or need you if you are here one weekend, then gone again." This was a powerful reminder that building justice and reconciliation requires *taking one step at a time.*

This long journey requires a willingness to walk through a fog, facing questions without answers. It also requires a willingness to walk to the edge of an abyss, where guarantees fade in the deep canyons below. This kind of walking really does require daring; and yet, daring sometimes works better than caution. Consider, for example, the work of Dorothy Day, establishing Houses of Hospitality for poor people across the United States and founding the *Catholic Worker* to stir conscience among people who care. Robert Ellsberg describes the step-by-step daring of the *Catholic Worker:*

> Objectively speaking, the *Catholic Worker* has aspired to a kind of "holy folly." After fifty years, it has amassed no board of directors, no foundation, no computerized mailing list. The newspaper, which is mailed by hand, has

never advertised. None of the staff has ever received a salary. The sole fund-raising strategy, if one can call it that, has entailed the occasional printing of an appeal in the paper, which sells today, as it always has, for a penny a copy. It is likely that any responsible management consultant, invited to survey the organization of the movement, would issue a grim forecast on its future. And yet it has continued these many years, while so many other better-organized efforts have failed.[27]

Such "holy folly" work is possible, one step at a time. From where does the vision come for such daring work? One important source is in envisioning alternatives.

THE PRACTICE OF POSING ALTERNATIVES

In the early 1950s, Howard Thurman was serving the Church of the Fellowship of All Peoples. Thurman was an African-American minister, and his congregation was made up of people of many races, cultures, and nationalities. One day he received a call about a member of his congregation, Miss L., who was ill in Stanford University Hospital. He journeyed to the hospital and to the nurse's station on Miss L.'s floor. Arriving in this all-white hospital, with its all-white patients and medical staff, Thurman was greeted by a desk nurse who did not seem at all eager to see him. He explained his purpose, and she questioned him about being a minister. "Are you sure?" He responded with these words: "Before I answer your question, I must explain to you why you are reacting to my presence as you are. There is nothing in the total experience of your young years that would prepare you for such an occasion as this. Miss L. is a member of the Church for the Fellowship of All Peoples—an integrated church in the San Francisco community. I am her minister and have the minister's privilege of visiting her."[28] The nurse seemed unconvinced, but at that moment, Miss L.'s private nurse appeared on the floor and invited Thurman to follow her to the room where Miss L. was waiting for him. He vis-ited Miss L. every day after that, and the hospital had "a totally new experience."[29]

*   Some time later Thurman was again visiting a parishioner in another hospital, and he was again met by a resistant nurse. She appeared panicked and reached for the telephone when she saw him. This time, he explained that he had been called to spend some time with Mrs. Brown. Suspiciously, the nurse escorted Howard Thurman to the room of his parishioner, but she stood in the doorway as he read Scripture with Mrs. Brown. In time, Mrs. Brown fell asleep, and he left the room, greeting the nurse as he departed. She asked about Thurman's unusual church, and he explained. On many Sundays thereafter, this white nurse was in worship at the Church of the Fellowship of All Peoples.[30]*

These are stories of teaching justice and reconciliation in a wounding world. For Thurman and his congregation, teaching justice and reconciliation had to do with *posing alternatives*. In a world that was torn by racial warfare and injus-tice, they sought to witness to another way simply by *being a just and reconciling community*. Thurman and his congregation self-consciously sought to be what Paul described in the same Corinthians letter that was just quoted: "If anyone is in Christ, that person is a new creation; old things have passed away; behold, all things have become new" (2 Cor 5:17).

Reflecting on the Pauline corpus, Paul does seem to assume that the dissolution of human enmities is intimately connected to reconciliation with God. This is particularly evident in Ephesians where Paul's concern for unity between Jewish and Gentile Christians is expressed with direct connection to the reconciling work of God in Christ (Eph 2:14–16). Paul says of Christ, "For he is our peace; in his flesh he has made both groups into one and has broken down the dividing wall, that is, the hostility between us." This text is far more complex than can be discussed here, but it does point to Paul's practice of posing alternative ways of living in community. Like Thurman's practice, Paul's approach to teaching had the potential to stir one's imagination regarding how people might live together as one—with difference, yes, but with hostility, no.

This act of posing alternatives is not passive; it is active, proactive, and longlasting. Thurman's responses to the two nurses came from his own long practice of envisioning alternatives; he was thus prepared in a crisis moment to pose them for others. This kind of work requires bold vision, careful elaboration, and courageous implementation. Nowhere is this more evident than in the global nonviolence movement, which has been visionary, insistent, and radically nonviolent. Rajmohan Gandhi, grandson and biographer of Mahatma Gandhi, describes the movement as "direct non-violent resistance"; Andrew Young, civil rights leader and United States ambassador to the United Nations, calls it "aggressive, organized, disciplined goodwill."[31] Posing alternatives is active and difficult. It is also not safe. Both Mahatma Gandhi and Martin Luther King Jr., lost their lives to assassin's bullets. On the other hand, such boldness in posing alternatives can topple alienation and woundedness; it can change the world.

THE PRACTICE OF REPENTENCE

To engage in justice and reconciliation is not easy, but it has a great deal to do with the *practice of repentance*. People yearn to be reconciled—to cease worrying about trivial things, to make a difference in things that matter, to be loving in all things, and to contribute to a more just society—but the practice of reconciliation is virtually impossible. The difficulties, even in relating with God and with those we love the most, are vividly revealed in the gospel of Luke, particularly in the familiar story found in Lk 15:1–32.

The scene opens with Jesus in the midst of a big controversy. In Luke's gospel, Jesus was often targeted for controversy because he received tax collectors and other assorted sinners; he even ate with them. Luke tells his readers that while the folks were complaining about these matters, Jesus told them three stories. One of these stories—the most familiar—is about a certain man who had two sons. The younger son asked his father to give him his inheritance early. The father agreed to do as his son requested, and the son took his bounty and departed to live a lively and wasteful life. The young man did in time use up all of his money, and when faced with a famine in the land, he resorted to the only work he could find, feeding pigs. This was dirty work— even unholy work—and the pigs were eating better than he was. The young man began to think of home and wished that he could return to live as one of his father's servants. He decided that he would return and confess to his father his sin; he would request to be hired as a servant. As the young man approached his father, however, his father saw him a long way off and had compassion. He ran to greet his son; he embraced and kissed him. The father, then, gave his son his best robe, the ring of sonship, and a grand party, much to the disappointment of his older brother.

The story is familiar, but it jolts common sensibilities. The story communicates dramatic reconciliation for the young son, but in the story, the young man does little or nothing for such a reconciliation; he simply turns around and returns home. He never even speaks the "I'm sorry" speech that he has prepared. He has done the most central act of repentance, however; he has acknowledged his shame and turned himself around to return home. His father overwhelms him with a lavish welcome, including a restoration of the sonship that he had flaunted and thrown away—a sonship that he had really taken away from his older brother in the first place. His older brother had the right to receive the major part of the inheritance, and he also had the major responsibility for his parents. He had lost a substantial part of the inheritance, but was left with the full responsibility. If we draw the association between the father of this story and God, as the story in Luke would suggest, we are left with a very unfair story—a story in which one person gets the goods, and the other gets the responsibility. Is the welcoming of the younger brother really a just act of reconciliation?

Certainly, we live today in a world that is filled with conflict, and even the best efforts to effect justice and reconciliation in Bosnia-Hertsogovina, Northern Ireland, Haiti, Rwanda, or Israel and Palestine, slip and slide. We live in a culture of war—a worldwide culture in which seventy thousand more dollars are spent each year on the average soldier than on the average student. In this culture of war, religions have contributed more to peace than any other social force, but they have also contributed more to war (to the Crusades, the Inquisition, and the perpetuation of slavery and apartheid). In such a context, can any act be regarded as an unqualified act of justice and reconciliation?

If we take seriously Luke's story, the response of God is not conditioned by words of repentance. The father in Luke's story acted before the prodigal spoke; on the other hand, the prodigal's turning around placed him before his father. If one message of the prodigal son is God's giving and if another is repentance, perhaps those messages are critical for the present Christian community. God has given peace, and people have made war. God has given relationships, and people have hurt one another. God has given the creation, and people have abused it. Perhaps, Luke's passion is one that contemporary communities might share, which is the passion to trust God and simply to turn around.

This kind of repentance is actually beginning to take place in many places of the world, and not only by Christians, but also by people in other religions who realize their part in war and destruction and their yearning for reconciliation. The importance of reconciliation was recognized by the Parliament of the World's Religions that met in Chicago in 1993. They produced this Declaration:

> The world is in agony. The agony is so pervasive and urgent that we are compelled to name its manifestations so that the depth of this pain may be made clear.
>
> Peace eludes us . . . the planet is being destroyed . . . neighbours live in fear . . . women and men are estranged from each other . . . children die!
>
> This is abhorrent!
>
> We condemn the abuses of Earth's ecosystems.
>
> We condemn the poverty that stifles life's potential; the hunger that weakens the human body; the economic disparities that threaten so many families with ruin.
>
> But this agony need not be. (Emphasis in text)[32]

As recognized in this declaration, conflicts around the world are not only found in wars among nations, but also in our homes and neighborhoods and workplaces. Declaring our abhorrence for life-destroying practices is a critical step in the process of repentance; then, comes the honest and difficult confession of our wrongs and turning around to find another way. Archbishop Desmond Tutu, drawing from the struggles of South Africa and the riches of Christianity, argues that repentance is central to human action for reconciliation. Rajmohan Gandhi, drawing from the struggles of India and the riches of Hinduism, argues the same.[33] Perhaps no time is more urgent than now for the practice of repentance.

THE PRACTICE OF REMEMBERING AND CELEBRATING COVENANT

Not unlike the Lukan story, the Hebrew Bible text that is often paired with Luke 15 in lectionaries is Josh 5:9–12. The message of this text is an overwhelming announcement that God has *already* reconciled the people: "The Lord said to Joshua, 'Today I have rolled away from you the disgrace of Egypt'" (Josh 5:9a). Shortly after this pronouncement, the people kept Passover; they ate the covenant meal. And on the day after Passover, they ate the produce of the land, signaling that they no longer needed manna, but could eat from the crops of Canaan. Again this text is too complex to engage in depth here, but the relevance of food to the relationship of God with the people, and the people with one another, is unmistakable. Again, God is the initiator and giver, but the response of *remembering and celebrating with a covenant meal* is the role of the people.

This is a theme that carries strongly through the Christian tradition as well. Rather than rehearse the tradition here, I will share a personal story that reveals something of how the tradition functions. I once attended an international Christian gathering that began with a joyful service of worship, resplendent with rich music and colorful flags from all of the countries represented. In this service, the sermon was harsh, especially critical of people whose views were different from the preacher's and condemnatory toward churches in certain parts of the world. I was so angered by the sermon that I came close to walking out. I was only restrained by knowing that the people around me had gathered from all over the world to seek understanding and solidarity. When the sermon ended, the service of Eucharist began. Slowly, thousands of Christian people walked to various stations around the great hall to receive the bread and the cup. Slowly I made my way, and when I received the bread and wine, I *knew* the reconciliation of Eucharist.

The table of Eucharist is a table that binds people together in a covenant relationship even when they strongly disagree and even when they do not like one another or find a way of working together in the work of God. People are reconciled with God and the world as they eat together—as they remember God's acts and celebrate the covenant meal. Thus, teaching reconciliation has to do with remembering and celebrating as a community.

THE PRACTICE OF MEETING IN ORDINARINESS

Thus far, the practices of teaching justice and reconciliation have been acts that are highly visible in the Christian communities. But the covenant relationship is also mediated in many common and crazy ways, often *through ordinary interchanges with ordinary people*. In 2 Cor, those ordinary people are Paul and Timothy, who claimed to be ambassadors for Christ, entreating the people to be reconciled with God. In the stories of Thurman, the ordinary people were Thurman and his congregation, who witnessed to a new way of being church.

The power of ordinariness struck me vividly in an event that took place a few years after the maddening service of worship that I just described. Time had passed, and I was in another international meeting with the same person who had preached in the earlier worship. By this time, he and I had been together in a long series of meetings, and we had locked horns more than once. We almost never agreed on anything, and while we could be cordial, we did not work together with enthusiasm; we were both deeply committed to our opposing perspectives. One early morning in this international theological seminar, however, a funny thing happened. We were all staying in college dormitories, and the dorms had shower rooms in the middle of each floor. One morning, I awoke quite early to take my turn in the shower. As I walked to the women's shower room, carrying soap and towel, I almost walked into my "friend," who was headed to the men's shower room. He was wearing only a towel wrapped around his waist, and with his chest and face turning red, he shouted a loud "Good morning" as we passed. Although he was quite well covered, he somehow seemed very human in that moment. We were, after all, just two ordinary human beings who needed a shower. The experience of reconciliation was given in a humorous moment—a moment when all pretensions faded and two ordinary human beings were standing face-to-face. In this moment, our relationship changed, and even though we still did not agree on most issues, we had a new respect for one another as real people. The respect was born of a moment filled with embarrassment and humor—a moment without pretension. Thereafter, we continued to work for justice, each in our own way, but we had a new ability to listen to one another and to seek common ground when it could be found.

Sometimes such moments happen serendipitously and we have only to recognize them. Consider one last story from Jerusalem on a snowy day near Jaffa Gate:

> The *shabaab* (Palestinian male youth) were taking great joy throwing snowballs at whoever walked through the gate. . . . At one point, an old *Haredi* Jewish man passed through Jaffa Gate. He was slightly bent over and shuffling along. As he came through, the youth let loose with the snowballs. Unbeknownst to them, the old man had a snowball tucked in his cloak. All of a sudden, he stood up, broke out in a huge grin and threw his snowball. It was a direct hit! The Palestinian youth were overjoyed! Here, in this corner of the Old City, an old Orthodox Jewish man and a few Palestinian young boys found a moment of sheer joy together. As the man walked on his way, all were laughing, smiling and waving to one another.[34]

This kind of meeting, spontaneous and human, can transform life.

This chapter closes with a sober reminder of the fears that fill a wounding world. In such a world, reconciliation is indeed a gift, but it is not a gift to take for granted. It is a gift for which people yearn and search. It is a gift known in acts of questing: truth-telling, facing questions without answers, and walking up to the abyss. Furthermore, it is a gift that invites people into action: the actions of building justice and reconciliation one step at a time, posing alternatives, repenting (turning around), remembering and celebrating covenant, and engaging in ordinary interchanges with ordinary people.

Will all of this make the world sweet and eliminate the alienation, fear and abuse that abound? Not likely! But, in the Christian tradition, the recurring affirmation is that reconciliation is possible because God has loved us and reconciled with us before we do anything ourselves; God has run out to embrace us. In such a context, we can do no less than to teach justice and reconciliation!

NOTES

1. I have wrestled with this subject for several years. Another version of this article is found in: Mary Elizabeth Mullino Moore, "Teaching for Justice and Reconciliation in a Conflicted World," in *Globalisation and Difference: Practical Theology in a World Context*, ed. by Paul Ballard and Pam Couture (Cardiff, Wales: Cardiff Academic Press, 1999). Although the two articles overlap in content, the earlier, shorter article focuses more specifically on the dynamics of conflict—contradictions, paradox, and struggle.

2. Moore, "Wisdom, Sophia, and the Fear of Knowing," *Religious Education* vol. 92, no. 2 (Spring 1997) 227–243. This article is an analysis of the fear of knowing (par-

ticularly the fear of knowing God and the fear of knowing ourselves and the world); attention is also given to the nature of wisdom and education. The ideas of the article are complementary to those developed in this chapter.

3. This story is developed as a composite of three different stories for the sake of protecting the identities of the people involved.

4. James Dobson and Gary L. Bauer, *Children at Risk: What You Need to Know to Protect Your Family* (Dallas: Word, 1990); and Mitch Golant and Donna G. Corwin, *The Challenging Child: A Guide for Parents of Exceptionally Strong-Willed Children* (New York: Berkley Books, 1995).

5. R. B. Y. Scott, *The Anchor Bible: Proverbs and Ecclesiastes* (Garden City, N.Y.: Doubleday, 1965) 191–207; R. N. Whybray, *The New Century Bible Commentary: Ecclesiastes* (Grand Rapids, Mich.: Eerdmans, 1989) 22–30; Michael V. Fox, *Qohelet and His Contradictions* (Sheffield, England: Almond, Sheffield Academic Press, 1989); Roland E. Murphy, *The Anchor Bible Reference Library: The Tree of Life—An Exploration of Biblical Wisdom Literature* (New York: Doubleday, 1990); Kathleen A. Farmer, "Psalms," and Carole R. Fontaine, "Ecclesiastes," in *The Women's Bible Commentary*, ed. by Carol A. Newsom and Sharon H. Ringe (Louisville: Westminster/John Knox, 1992) 137–144, 153–155.

6. Margaret Wertheim, *Pythagoras' Trousers: God, Physics and the Gender Wars* (New York: Times Books, Random House, 1995) 9–10 and 17–18.

7. Ibid., 9.

8. Ibid., 10–11 and 38–46.

9. Sandra Harding, *The Science Question in Feminism* (Ithaca, N.Y.: Cornell University, 1986).

10. Wertheim, *Pythagoras' Trousers*, 12–15.

11. Ibid., 29. Wertheim argues that this stirred an escape from nature that "also implied transcending the 'feminine.'" The psyche (identified as male) was thus elevated above the body (identified as female).

12. Ibid., 132.

13. Ibid., 132–133.

14. Edwin M. Good, *In Turns of Tempest: A Reading of Job* (Stanford: Stanford University Press, 1990) 199–200; Daniel J. Simundson, *The Message of Job: A Theological Commentary* (Minneapolis: Augsburg, 1986) 38–39.

15. Simundson, *Message of Job*, 38.

16. Norman C. Habel, *The Book of Job: A Commentary* (Philadelphia: Westminster, 1985) 96.

17. Ibid.

18. William D. Reyburn, *A Handbook on the Book of Job* (New York: United Bible Societies, 1992) 21–24.

19. Good, *In Turns of Tempest*, vii–viii.

20. Ibid., 180.

21. Ibid., viii.

22. Rollo May, "The Significance of Symbols," in *Symbolism in Religion and Literature*, ed. by May (New York: Braziller, 1960) 33.

23. Beverly Harrison, "The Power of Anger in the Work of Love," in *Making the Connections*, ed. by Carol S. Robb (Boston: Beacon, 1985) 3–21.

24. Ibid., 8.

25. Good, *In Turns of Tempest*, 181.

26. J. Gerald Janzen, *Job: Interpretation* (Atlanta: John Knox, 1985) 16.

27. Dorothy Day, *By Little and By Little: The Selected Writings of Dorothy Day*, ed. by Robert Ellsberg (New York: Knopf, 1983) xvi–xvii.

28. Howard Thurman, *With Head and Heart: The Autobiography of Howard Thurman* (New York: Harcourt, 1979) 154.

29. Ibid.

30. Ibid., 154–154.

31. "Dialogue with Rajmohan Gandhi and Andrew Young," Emory University, Atlanta, Georgia, 7 February 2000.

32. Hans Kung and Karl-Josef Kuschel, *A Global Ethic: The Declaration of the Parliament of World Religions* (London: SCM, 1993) 13. The quote is from the abridged version of "The Principles of a Global Ethic"; the summary was written to be read aloud in the closing plenary of the Parliament and, also, for publicity purposes.

33. "Dialogue with Rajmohan Gandhi and Desmond Tutu," Emory University, Atlanta, Georgia, 1 February 2000.

34. Letter from Jerusalem, Sandra Olewine, 1 February 2000.

CHAPTER NINE

HOSPITALITY TO VICTIMS:
A CHALLENGE FOR CHRISTIAN WORSHIP

Ruth C. Duck

What would it mean for liturgies to be more hospitable to those who have been violated and sinned-against? Liturgy is not always hospitable to sinners; some congregations literally exclude from worship those whom they have identified as sinful. In many congregations, Christians hide their struggles and flaws, presenting only successes and virtues. Furthermore, as feminist theologians have shown, the way in which congregations confess often focuses on the sins of the privileged and powerful.[1] Yet, however inadequately, liturgies usually address the experience of sinners, whether in rituals of confession and forgiveness or in prayers, sermons, and hymns. By contrast, Christian worship does not consistently address the experience of being violated. When worshiping congregations say they welcome everyone, yet remain silent about the human experience of violation, they are less than hospitable to persons in the fullness of their lives.

This chapter explores how liturgy could be more hospitable to the experience of those victimized by others' sins. The word *hospitality* in the sense of welcoming and giving space seems best to describe how the church could better respond to violated persons. Just as all have sinned, all have been violated in some sense; but the church has rarely treated experiences of violation as appropriate subject matter for Christian worship. Christian worship does not welcome the full range of persons and human experiences when it fails to address experiences of victimization through acts of naming, lament, healing, and justice. This chapter suggests ways of fuller hospitality.

In contrast to Christian liturgy's frequent inhospitality to the violated, the Psalms, the prayer book of the Bible, give voice to the "shrill cry of the victim."[2] They move to trust and praise in God only after passing through the depths of lament. If worship addresses the experience of victimization at all, it is often in sermons demanding that victims forgive before they even have time to name and lament their pain. When this happens, worship serves the interest of the victimizer by trying to pacify the victim; this is the liturgical equivalent of sending someone home to forgive a battering spouse whether or not the violence ceases. I hope through this chapter to present approaches to worship that serve the needs of victims.

UNDERSTANDINGS OF SIN AND VICTIMIZATION

The purpose of this chapter is not to present an original theology of sin and reconciliation, but to apply emerging theological insights to the practice of Christian worship. Articulating my own theological assumptions may, however, clarify the analysis and proposals that follow.

Marjorie-Hewitt Suchocki provides a good working definition of sin in her book *The Fall into Violence.*[3] She says that "sin is a rebellion against creation in the unnecessary violation of the well-being of any aspect of existence."[4] Violence and abuse are prime expressions of violation, which is also expressed through racism and sexism and other ways in which one negates truth, love, and beauty in forms other than one's own.[5] As Suchocki redefines original sin, it points to the impossibility of escaping participation in sin either as violator or victim, given the way all creation is relationally intertwined.[6] Obviously, however, the realities of unjust social structures mean that "the degree of guilt is variable depending upon one's freedom and one's possibilities."[7]

In her definition of sin, Suchocki challenges understandings of sin emphasizing human rebellion against God expressed by theologians from Augustine of Hippo to Reinhold Niebuhr. This challenge has important implications for liturgy and ethics, for it points to the relational and historical nature of sin and salvation. It would hardly be a caricature to say that liturgy has pictured sin as a substance to be washed away in baptism and addressed through the medicine of holy Communion. Nor would it be an exaggeration to say that Christians could assume from liturgy that to confess and receive forgiveness every Sunday would suffice to deal with sin—without reference to Christians' daily relationships with other people and creation. For if sin is defined in terms of rebellion against God, then presumably the remedy for sin involves only or primarily God. Picturing sin as a generalized condition that all humanity shares trivializes specific acts of love, violation, or reconciliation. The common idea that Sin (with a capital S) and not sins (with two small s's) is the human problem removes sin from relational and historical reality; the cure is to admit one's condition to God and accept forgiveness, rather than to cease from harmful acts. Of course this runs counter to the teaching of Jesus found in the Gospels, for example, the instruction to be reconciled before offering one's gifts to God (Mt 5:23–24). When it deals with sin exclusively in terms of the divine-human relationship, liturgy serves the violator, not the victim of sin—for it does not invite changed human relationships.

If, on the other hand, sin refers to rebellion against the well-being of creation, and original sin is participation in violation through one's relation to a violent world, then specific actions of good or of violence make a difference in the interconnected reality of life. It follows that liturgy should deal with sin by rehearsing a new reality to be lived out in daily life, rather than dealing with sin as a substantial transaction or as a private spiritual matter.

As Suchocki affirms, violation of the well-being of creation is also sin against God, who shares in all experiences as a coparticipant, and who suffers with any part of reality that suffers.[8] One could quibble with Suchocki when she says that sin is rebellion more against creation than God,[9] for the life of God is intertwined with the life of all reality. The point is, however, that Western theology and liturgy have erred by understanding sin primarily in terms of the relationship between humans and God, for this understanding renders the victims of sin invisible.[10]

Andrew Sung Park, in his groundbreaking book, *The Wounded Heart of God*, notes that Christian theology has concentrated mainly on the experience of the sinner-violator and not on the experience, or han, of the one who is violated: "Traditional Christian understandings of sin have all but unilaterally focused on the sinner."[11] This concentration actually reverses the priorities demonstrated in the ministry of Jesus, who focused his attention on the violated and oppressed of society.[12] *Han* is a Korean word that describes the experience of being violated or oppressed, with its attendant feelings of anger, resentment, powerlessness, and desire for revenge; Park uses "wounded heart" as a metaphor for this complex of experience and feeling. Victims of racism, sexism, economic exploitation, and other forms of injustice may know han as a defining experience of life; for, as Kang Nam-Soon writes, han "is not a one-time psychological response to an unjust situation or treatment but an accumulation of such feelings in response to numerous unjust, oppressive experiences."[13] Theology and liturgy that address only sinners who need forgiveness, and not victims who need justice and an end to violence, perpetuate the privilege of violators. Instead, as Park argues, the way Christians theologize and worship should foster a reorientation of relationships in which violators repent and change, violated persons compassionately confront injustice, and all work together in relationship with God to bring justice and peace to all creation.[14]

All people have the potential both for being violated and violating others. Worshiping congregations include both victims and violators; in fact, the same person may be victimized in one context and violated in another. Worship that is hospitable to the whole of human reality will address experiences of violating and being violated, without giving priority (as Western liturgy has done) to the sinner-violator.

Due to the influence of Augustine and others, Christian worship since the fifth century has given inordinate attention to the problem of sin. All of the sacraments and rites of the church, as well as preaching and other aspects of worship, have tended to focus on sin, excluding other themes. Recently a friend told me that in the German church she attends, few go forward to receive

Communion on the rare occasions when it is offered. She says that people wonder what terrible things those few have done, that they feel they must receive Communion. The idea that the main purpose of receiving Communion is to deal with sin addresses only the needs of violators (not victims) and then only in the context of their relationship with God. It is a woefully narrow understanding of the Eucharist, which may embody reconciliation with God and neighbor, but also embodies thanksgiving to God, welcome of all, life in community, and the hope of God's reign.

Given the pervasive emphasis of Christian liturgy on sin from the perspective of the violator, sweeping changes have been needed not only to honor the perspective of the victim, but also to bring forward other neglected parts of Scripture, tradition, and Christian experience. Fortunately, the ecumenical liturgical renewal movement has promoted broader understandings of the Eucharist, but old traditions are tenacious. Exploring alternatives reveals that many traditions are in need of change. For example, New Testament scholar Robert Jewett has pointed out that, by quoting Matthew's version in which Jesus says the cup is "my blood of the covenant, which is poured out for many *for the forgiveness of sins*" (Mt 26:27–28), traditional liturgies encourage "an introspective, guilt-ridden spirituality."[15] Using Paul's account of the Last Supper (1 Cor 11:23–26), which has no mention of sin, would be more in keeping with the ministry of Jesus, who welcomed those who had been shamed and violated. Jewett writes that this explains why "traditional communion services often tend to be avoided by persons whose problems are deeper than sin, who feel that their life is without promise or hope, that nobody respects them."[16] Marjorie Procter-Smith provides a more sweeping critique of tradition. She observes that "this is my body . . . this is my blood" are part of a sacrificial symbolism through which the death of Jesus promotes the self-sacrifice of victims of abuse. Thus, she urges that communion prayers draw on scriptural passages such as Jesus' table communion, the miraculous feeding stories, and the messianic feast, since "the communion food need not be identified with suffering, sacrifice and death, but with life, joy, abundance, and community."[17] These issues regarding Holy Communion show how many dimensions of worship might bear reconsideration so that worship would be more hospitable to victims. We will explore just a few of the many dimensions of welcoming the violated: liturgies of lament, liturgies of healing, sensitivity concerning forgiveness, and liturgy as it relates to actions of love and justice.

THE VOICE OF LAMENT

If confession is the cry of the sinner, then lament is the cry of the victim. As many as fifty-nine of the one hundred fifty Psalms are psalms of lament.[18] These psalms speak openly of suffering violence, lies, persecution, abandonment, and exile. They respond with terror, rage, tears, and bitter pleas for help from a God who may seem to be absent or to tolerate injustice. These psalms honestly express feelings of doubt or trust, anger or thanksgiving, as people pursue relief from violation. The psalms of lament give us clues for designing liturgies which are hospitable to those who have been victimized.

Naming is central to the psalms of lament; in fact, the psalms can be graphic in describing experiences of violation in a way that would be difficult to imagine in most twentieth-century liturgy. Consider Psalm 22, with its image of people shaking their heads in ridicule (v.7) and encircling the victim like strong bulls who "open wide their mouths at me like a ravening and roaring lion" (v.12–13). In comparison, much modern liturgy does not name but avoids mention of victimizing life experiences.

Psalms of lament vividly express emotion. Again, Psalm 22 is graphic: "I am poured out like water . . . my heart is like wax" (v.14). To be sure, because liturgy is a public event, it may express feeling through poetry or silence more than through an intimate description of raw individual feeling. But why, if congregations "weep with those who weep" when facing death or life-threatening illnesses, can they not be hospitable to the experience of those who have suffered violence and abuse? If the size or formality of regular weekly worship makes such expression inappropriate, smaller gatherings that welcome expression of feelings may serve a great need.

The psalms of lament also point to the importance of our imagery about God. Admittedly, the psalms show a God who is in control of human events, who in Psalm 22 lays the victim in the "dust of death." Such a view of God's influence ultimately puts God on the side of violators. But the psalmists base their appeal on the assumption that God is affected by human suffering and acts to relieve it. Such a God is not the unmoved mover of the philosophers or the God of culture religion who sides with whoever happens to be in power. The Psalms also make their plea based on God's connection to the covenant people: "In you our ancestors trusted; they trusted and you delivered them" (Ps 22:4). Here is a God who is fundamentally affected by relation to the faith community, and who ultimately can be trusted to provide deliverance. Liturgies of lament, then, name the story of violation honestly, they express profound feelings, and they picture God as one who is affected by suffering and who is involved in historical process to alleviate suffering.

In one of the few recent books that focuses on lament in worship, J. Frank Henderson offers helpful guidelines for designing liturgies of lament appropriate to various contexts.[19] He suggests that lament may occur in a number of worship settings. In the weekly liturgical assembly or in evening prayer, lament may occur through the reading and response to Scriptures that depict violence and the resulting suffering; the assembly's prayers of intercession can also remember victims of violation. Quarterly services can involve prayer and fasting focused on particular areas of need, for example, violation of the environment or violence toward women. Ecumenical or interfaith services could lament the Holocaust in hope and commitment that such devastation will never happen again. People from varied faith communities could gather to lament violent community experiences, as churches in Oklahoma City did following the bombing of the federal building there. Groups who share a particular experience of violation could gather to tell their stories, name their feelings, and seek healing together.

Take and Make Holy: Honoring the Sacred in the Healing Journey of Abuse Survivors focuses on a particular group: adult survivors of childhood sexual abuse.[20] The author Mari West Zimmerman describes a healing process that includes group worship providing ample opportunities for lament, while also expressing hope for healing and deep trust in God. In one service that addresses the "Shame of Lost Innocence," survivors are given the opportunity to tell their stories and to name their feelings, including their honest feelings toward God.[21] Another service, directed at "Mourning the Loss of a Survivor's Childhood," includes the option of ritually burying some symbol of the "survivor's destroyed childhood," such as a photograph or stuffed toy.[22] The services, which recognize that healing may take an extended time, use psalms of lament, silence, and ritual acts to focus and honor emotion and experience. They invite individual storytelling, while speaking in gracious liturgical language that does not manipulate feeling but leaves room for people to participate or not participate as they feel comfortable.

Feminist liturgies often include elements of naming and lament. For example, Rosemary Radford Ruether has designed a "Rite of Healing for Wife Battering" that interplays the lament of Psalm 22 with descriptions of the pain and alienation of victims of battering.[23] The service ends with the commitment to end the terror and the silence. Miriam Therese Winter has developed a liturgy named "Why Do You Weep?" that tells the stories of biblical women such as Hannah who lament, and invites participating women to consider why they, too, weep.[24] The worship service ends with a song of commitment to build a new world of justice.[25]

Liturgies of lament and deliverance are hospitable to the experience of those who have experienced violation, providing ritual channels for deep feelings, naming violation for what it is, and affirming that God suffers with victims and seeks their deliverance. Songs of lament in a plaintive mode are needed to complement the church's many joyful hymns of praise. A church that can sing its lament and weep with those who weep will be able to offer a fuller, deeper, more honest song of praise to the One who suffers with us and labors with us to build a new creation.

WORSHIP AND THE ENEMY

Considering the need for liturgies of lament raises the question of how Christian worship conceives of the violator, the "enemy," to use the language of the Gospels.

One approach is to name and condemn the actions of violators in the name of love and justice, for the sake of their victims. Jesus provides a model by naming the actions of those who place heavy burdens on others that they themselves are unwilling to carry (Mt 23:1–4) and condemning those who cause little ones to stumble (Mk 9:42). Some recent liturgies also name the actions of violators. An earth day celebration by Ruether names companies that destroy the environment and asks deliverance from them.[26] "Litany for Divine Intervention," a ritual for gay/lesbian communities written by James Lancaster, asks for deliverance from enemies who oppress and victimize gay and lesbian people, and asks that their evil words and actions come to naught.[27] Lancaster warns that such liturgies should be planned with care, for such a "ritual is not a judgment on the souls of persons" but a channel for "justifiable anger and outrage."[28] The danger of such liturgical naming is that it may seem to demonize persons and institutions who may, in fact, do both good and evil. For example, when Ruether's earth day celebration liturgy was used in a seminary worship service, a prayer asking for deliverance from General Motors distressed a student from Michigan, where GM contributes to the well-being of residents as a major employer. On the other hand, to avoid naming violators may make the church complicit in acts of violation.

Another approach, which also finds grounding in the Gospels, is to pray for the enemy and to ask for God's transforming grace for the violator. According to Mt 5:43–44, Jesus said, "You have heard that it was said, "You shall love your neighbor and hate your enemy." But I say to you, love your enemies and pray for those who persecute you." This teaching should not lead churches to demand that persons instantly forgive their violators even before violation ceases or without a process of facing and resolving feelings of violation. Nevertheless, prayer for the enemy is possible long before forgiveness is. I have discovered in personal prayer that regular prayer for someone who has hurt or angered me can release me from the burden of my hurt and anger, thus empowering me to relate to the person more assertively and effectively. At times such prayer has helped me perceive other people with something of God's compassion, realizing that their hurtful behavior stems from their own woundedness. Such compassion can empower us to relate to people on the basis of a shared humanity, without ceasing to press for justice. Prayer for enemies in public worship might also be empowering. At times, the church's tradition of praying for political or church leaders can only be continued in the sense of praying for violators—for example, those who abandon the needs of poor children for political gain.

A touch of humor or satire may provide another liturgical avenue related to the enemy. Martha Scott, a United Methodist pastor and district superintendent, served a church that was taking an active stand against racism in Chicago. The Sunday before the Ku Klux Klan had planned a march in the neighborhood, the passage in Eph 6 that speaks of putting on the "whole armor of God that you may be able to stand against the wiles of the devil" appeared in the lectionary. In a creative liturgical response, members were supplied with pans from the kitchen that they carried to symbolize the full armor of God; they beat on the pans in a cacophony of defiance to racism. This liturgy used symbol and humor to laugh at the "spiritual forces of evil" (Eph 6:12) and thus to gain confidence in taking their faithful stand. This ritual exemplifies another approach toward naming enemies in worship.[29]

Some may feel that naming enemies and their actions in liturgy does not adequately express Christian love. Nevertheless, injustice and violence reap a deadly harvest in the world, and it is difficult to change anything that is not named. Exploring appropriate approaches to naming enemies and their acts of violation might help liturgy contribute to the well-being of creation.

HEALING LITURGIES

One significant liturgical development in the twentieth century related to the experience of victimization is the recovery of anointing and healing in services of common worship. While individuals such as Hildegard of Bingen carried on ministries of healing throughout Christian history,[30] in recent decades worship services focused on healing have become more common. Typically, these services invite people to ask for healing prayer and ritual in response to any part of their lives where they feel wounded. The services have supported the process of healing the wounds that come from violation, and not only physical ailments.

In the late medieval Roman Catholic Church, anointing of the sick, like many other aspects of Christian liturgy, became focused on issues of human sin and divine forgiveness. As Walter H. Cuenin writes, with the Scholastic period, anointing of the sick came to be seen as "a spiritual cleansing of sins before death rather than as a ritual involved with the healing of the body."[31] Thus, "extreme unction" (as it was now called) was administered at death by anointing the eyes, ears, nostrils, mouth, hands, feet, and loins to symbolize forgiveness of sin associated with different parts of the body.[32] Since Vatican II, the Roman Catholic Church has recovered the anointing of the sick as a sacrament of healing to address serious illness, and not only impending death.[33]

Protestant churches have practiced pastoral care of the sick, but until recently, anointing or healing has not often been part of their common worship. The first edition of the Book of Common Prayer allowed for anointing of the sick as part of pastoral care, but anointing disappeared in 1552.[34] The Church of the Brethren of the early eighteenth century was the first Protestant church to recover anointing of the sick.[35] Pentecostal churches recovered ministries of healing of the sick (by laying on of hands, but not anointing) as a part of worship in the early twentieth century. Among liberal Protestants, the Episcopal Church in the United States was the pioneer, with Agnes Sanford, author of The Healing Light, in the lead.[36] In the 1950s, Episcopal churches began to have corporate services of anointing and healing; the 1979 Book of Common Prayer includes an order of worship for ministration to the sick.[37] Promoting liturgical ministries of healing is a central goal of the Order of St. Luke in the United Methodist Church; the order published a liturgy for healing that was adapted and published both in the Book of Worship: United Church of Christ (1986) and The United Methodist Book of Worship (1992).[38] A number of other liberal Protestant denominations in the United States and Canada also have published healing liturgies recently.

These healing liturgies usually include the following elements:

Prayer of confession and assurance of forgiveness

Reading of Scriptures such as James 5:13–16, which present healing as a part of the church's ministry; and reading of gospel stories showing Jesus healing the sick

Some form of preaching or witness expressing confidence in God's healing power

Prayer over oil as a symbol of God's healing power

Invitation to come forward for the healing of body or spirit

At healing stations an opportunity to name one's particular need, prayer with laying on of hands, and/or anointing by carefully prepared teams

Prayer of thanksgiving for healing

Intercessory prayer is also often a part of healing services. Orders often stress the importance of providing an inviting, accessible environment and choosing gentle music that will support prayer and trust in God. Theologically, the services emphasize trust in God, without exaggerated claims about particular outcomes, such as healing of a disability. They do not emphasize the charismata of particular "faith healers," but the working of the Spirit for good in every aspect of human life.

At times the services focus on particular needs, such as living with AIDS or healing from sexual abuse. When general services of anointing provide people with an opportunity to name their needs, people often name experiences of abuse, battering, wounded relationships, and other hurts. It is hard to say why the movement toward liturgical healing has grown in our day, but one reason may be that it provides a needed ministry to the victims of violation.

The important role healing services can play in ministering to those who have been violated suggests some guidelines in developing such services.

Healing services often provide the opportunity to name particular wounds, including experiences of violation. At times, in the interest of time, the teams administer laying on of hands and anointing with set prayers, without taking time to hear and honor specific prayer requests. Generally speaking, it would be better to provide more healing stations and to find ways to keep prayers brief than to miss this opportunity for naming. Naming the violation out loud to one caring person can be an important step toward the healing of wounds.

Such naming is a sacred trust and must be treated with utmost care and confidentiality. There should be enough space between healing stations so that people will not overhear others' requests and prayers. It is also good to recognize that this is a ritual naming and not an invitation toward further conversation. Members of healing teams should not probe for further information outside the liturgy, but allow persons to reveal information according to their own comfort level.[39]

The awareness that numerous church members carry the wounds of abuse and violation means that other ritual elements should be treated with care. Some abuse survivors are uncomfortable with touch; because of memories or allergies, others may be disturbed by any scent in the oil. Therefore the invitation to come forward should include (1) a clear description of the usual procedure at the healing stations, with information as to whether and how the oil is scented; and (2) permission to tell the team exactly how one wishes to participate. For example, one person might want to ask for prayer, but not desire laying on of hands and anointing. Another might want to be anointed, but not to reveal any particular need. The fact that some will not be comfortable with particular aspects of the service should not necessarily lead churches to dispense with ritual such as laying on of hands and anointing. These nonverbal expressions of care may, for some, be a way of addressing wounds in a symbolic manner in a way that words alone cannot do.

A final element of healing services that requires attention as one considers the experience of victims and survivors is their theology of sin. One danger comes from the tendency to think of healing mainly in terms of forgiveness of sin. The texts of some liturgies of "healing" emphasize sin and forgiveness almost to the exclusion of other themes. Another danger is the theology that assumes that suffering results from sin, a theme that unfortunately is not absent from healing liturgies. In services with victims of abuse and violence, it may be better to omit the prayer of confession than to reinforce the undeserved shame that may accompany violation. At times, acknowledging the way one has violated others may remove barriers to healing; thus, a brief act of confession at the beginning of the service (not immediately before the healing ritual) can be appropriate.

At times dramatic and instantaneous transformations related to physical illnesses occur through healing services. Healing emotional wounds is, I would venture to say, always a process that happens over time, but healing services support this process by orienting the victim toward the resources of the faith community and the constant love of God.[40] The emergence of liturgies of healing is a hopeful sign in regard to the ministry with victims. Such services, when designed with care, can help the church be more hospitable to the victims of violence.

RECONCILIATION AND FORGIVENESS

Addressing victimization adequately in preaching and in other aspects of worship calls for a sensitive and nuanced theology of forgiveness. Forgiveness and reconciliation were at the heart of Jesus' ministry, as he welcomed marginalized "sinners" such as prostitutes and tax collectors to table communion and told parables such as the forgiving father (Lk 15:11–32) and the unforgiving servant (Mt 19:23–35). Jesus' words, "forgive us our sins, for we ourselves forgive everyone indebted to us" (Lk 11:4a), need not be interpreted to make God's forgiveness conditional on the forgiveness we show one another. Still, it seems clear that for Jesus, human relationships with one another, including forgiveness and reconciliation, are intertwined with human relationships with God.

Jesus' message of forgiveness is distorted when used to silence victims and reinforce their victimization. It is one thing to encourage church members to reconcile following a conflict over whether a particular poem should be read at a church dinner, as I once did as a local church pastor. It is another thing to address abusive situations by instructing victims to forgive or by offering forgiveness to abusers without taking appropriate action to end the abuse. Sensitive pastoral care and preaching about forgiveness must be accompanied by a commitment to end situations of violation. It calls for the awareness that people may need a long time to integrate experiences of violation to the extent that they can genuinely forgive.

Survivors of violent crime or war atrocities (and those who mourn them), as well as survivors of childhood sexual abuse, have suffered violations that may continue to traumatize them long after the violation has ceased. Every worshiping congregation includes persons who have these and similar experiences, in numbers greater than most church members would like to think. Neither liturgy nor short-term pastoral care by clergy suffices to resolve this depth of traumatization, which ordinarily may call for extended therapy with a professional counselor. Such a therapeutic process may in time enable forgiveness of the violator(s), but first the survivor must tell the story honestly, acknowledging whatever feelings may surface, whether they be outrage, despair, or even desire for revenge. A blanket call to instant forgiveness may cause people to distance themselves from feelings they must experience or actions they must undertake, if they are to experience true forgiveness. Such a call may evoke needless guilt in someone who is attempting to live according to Christian values while healing from wounds of abuse.

Church members may also suffer victimization due to racism, sexism, heterosexism, handicappism, or other forms of social injustice, all of which are so widespread that they affect many people daily. Affirming life and finding peace in the midst of injustice is the spiritual task of a lifetime, often accomplished with the help of God only as one gains freedom to voice anger and work for change. In this case also the church cannot demand forgiveness. The church can best respond by welcoming the voices of the victims of injustice, removing injustice from its own life, and working for justice in society.

Considering the experience of victims of traumatic violation and systemic injustice highlights key issues concerning forgiveness. The call to forgive must never encourage passive acceptance of victimization, lest the church throw its support behind victimizers. Also, it is important to recognize that honest naming of the hurtful or unjust experience and the feelings it evokes is part of the process of forgiveness. Thus, the call to forgive must acknowledge that coming to terms with experiences of victimization takes time in proportion to the degree of violation. It must give permission for people to be as honest before God with their feelings as those whose cries the psalms record.

Hospitality toward the violated calls for sensitivity concerning prayers of confession and words of forgiveness in Christian liturgy. The content of prayers of confession bears consideration, do we ask people to confess their affirmation or protection of self—the very qualities needed to end abusive situations and heal from memories of abuse?[41] The words of forgiveness also require reflection: Do we imply that words of confession are enough, without true remorse or commitment to change? Do we promote the idea that sin is primarily between the sinner and God, without any movement toward restitution or reconciliation with violated persons? While God's grace is infinite, and reconciliation with God and neighbor are central to Christian liturgy, it is possible that corporate confession and general absolution are not the best ways to embody these realities. Certainly, churches should reflect carefully about the best way to support people who seek to acknowledge their acts of sin, to change their lives, and if appropriate make amends or reconciliation with anyone they have harmed.

Marie Fortune reports, in an article entitled "Forgiveness: The Last Step":

> A group of incest offenders in a treatment program sent a powerful plea: "Don't forgive so easily." All were Christians and had gone to their pastors as soon as they were arrested, asking to be forgiven. Each had been prayed over, forgiven, and sent home. They said that this pastoral response had been the least helpful to them because it enabled them to continue to avoid accountability for their offenses.[42]

She recommends delaying words of absolution until certain conditions are met; interestingly enough, in this she echoes the earliest practices of private confession, which delayed absolution until an act of penance had been performed.[43] Marjorie Procter-Smith has suggested that churches devise new rituals to hold abusers accountable through acts of confession and restitution toward those who have been harmed, before forgiveness is proclaimed to them in liturgy.[44] This points to a larger need for liturgy to serve the process of conversion to lives of love and justice. Unless liturgy supports empowerment of victims and survivors and accountability for violators, acts of confession will be empty.

Forgiveness heals and reconciliation brings the estranged together; yet these outcomes cannot be manufactured by liturgical fiat. Liturgy that is hospitable to victims must be spacious enough to accommodate the breadth of their feelings in the presence of God and patient enough to let the Spirit work slowly to bring the healing that makes genuine forgiveness possible.

WORSHIP THAT EMBODIES JUSTICE

This discussion of forgiveness highlights one final way in which worship should be hospitable to victims: by embodying and rehearsing justice, calling people to live in love and justice in the world, and praying for victims and for justice. The scope of this chapter permits only brief exploration of a few dimensions of the relation of worship and justice. At the same time, these reflections would be incomplete without such exploration, since providing liturgies of lament and healing, as well as exercising care in our talk about forgiveness, are not enough without acts of justice.

Worship *embodies* justice to the extent that its ritual and symbol, and words and leadership lift up the value and dignity of humanity in all its diversity, based on the one baptism all Christians share. Given great human diversity, this affects many dimensions of worship. It means that leadership is shared and members of the different groups within a congregation are represented in various leadership ministries. It means that metaphors for God will honor both female and male, and that symbols will be drawn from varied cultures and classes, reflecting the groups represented within a congregation. It means that space, action, and leadership will be accessible to people of differing abilities. Worship that favors one sex over another, demeans persons on the basis of their preference for same-sex relationships, devalues children and older people, or reflects unjust social values in any other way, does not embody justice but reinforces victimization and thus is not hospitable to victims.

Christian worship should *rehearse* life lived according to God's will of love and justice on earth. This means that in worship Christians would practice an ethical way of life, learning the words and actions that lead to loving and just lives in the world. The act of worshiping together can transform lives and provide a foretaste of what it would be like to live in justice, love, and peace in the world.[45] Worship that rehearses justice gives hope to victims so that they can imagine loving and just ways of relationship in contrast to the violation they have experienced. In a more practical sense, Christian worship rehearses justice by preparing people for just and compassionate action in the world. This could be as concrete as inviting people in worship to volunteer at a shelter for battered women or to express their views on legislation coming up in their country that would affect the lives of victims.

Worship also *invites* people to live according to God's will of love and justice through the preaching event. The embodiment and rehearsal of love and justice in worship provides a context in which preaching for justice is credible; preaching provides the opportunity to address concrete contexts of violence and victimization directly. In her discussion of forgiveness from the perspective of the victims of domestic violence, Fortune suggests that the church can be hospitable to victims by hearing and believing their stories, by taking family violence seriously, by acting to protect people who are at risk, and by calling violators to account.[46] Preaching can contribute to this by naming specific kinds of violation and the damage they inflict, and by calling Christians to turn from acts of injustice, violation, and oppression. It can also tell the stories of victims, their suffering and acts of freedom, from sources such as newspaper accounts, fiction, and published autobiographies. In the words of Christine Smith, preaching can weep with victims of injustice, confess the truth of oppression, and evoke resistance to the evil of injustice and violation.[47] Preaching that is hospitable to victims also portrays God as one who weeps with victims, affirms their worth, and empowers them to speak and act on their own behalf—not as one who creates and promotes the status quo of injustice and violation. Thus preaching invites Christians to live in relationship with God and one another in a communities of resistance to violence and injustice.

Christian worship *intercedes* for justice. Indeed, when teaching people how to pray, Jesus told a parable about a widow, a member of a powerless and victimized group in his society, who sought justice from an unjust judge. While scholars interpret this passage in various ways, it is clear that it assumes that one of the main reason why people pray is to ask for justice: "Will not God grant justice to [the] chosen ones who cry to [God] night and day?" (Lk 18:7a). Rather than blessing the world as it is and lifting up those with privilege, Christian worship shows hospitality to victims by naming their particular sufferings before God and by asking for justice in confidence that God identifies with the violated and takes their part.

This brief discussion lifts up possibilities for worship that would be hospitable to victims, by embodying justice in word, symbol, and leadership; by rehearsing and inviting people to just and loving existence; and by interceding on the behalf of victims. Worship, then, would be intertwined with justice, by realistically naming violation in the world and by presenting alternative possibilities for human life.

CONCLUSION

The necessary revolution in Christian theology that persons such as Marjorie Hewitt Suchocki and Andrew Sung Park propose has profound implications for Christian liturgy. Considering the perspective of victims means offering liturgical options such as lament, healing, and prayer that names violations and violators. It means rethinking the way Christians speak of forgiveness, confession, and absolution in preaching and liturgy. Fundamentally, it means reorienting liturgy so that it is a foretaste and rehearsal of justice and reconciliation on earth. Without doubt, this is a large agenda for Christian leaders, but it is an essential task. Only in showing hospitality to those who have been violated can the church rightly honor and praise the God of Jesus Christ, who weeps at violation and rejoices when humans turn toward justice and right relationship with one another and with God.

NOTES

1. Refer to Valerie Saiving, "The Human Situation: A Feminine View," in *Womanspirit Rising*, ed. by Carol P. Christ and Judith Plaskow (San Francisco: Harper and Row, 1979) 25–42; Plaskow, *Sex, Sin and Grace: Women's Experience and the Theologies of Reinhold Niebuhr and Paul Tillich* (Lanham, Md.: University Press of America, 1980); and Ruth Duck, "Sin, Grace, and Gender in Free-Church Protestant Worship," in *Women at Worship*, ed. by Marjorie Procter-Smith and Janet Walton (Louisville: Westminster John Knox, 1993) 55–69.

2. Refer to Walter Brueggemann's chapter, "The Shrill Voice of the Wounded Party," in this book.

3. Marjorie Hewitt Suchocki, *The Fall to Violence* (New York: Continuum, 1994).

4. Ibid., 66.

5. Ibid., 80.

6. Ibid., 82–99.

7. Ibid., 149.

8. Ibid., 48–64.

9. Ibid., 16.

10. Ibid., 18.

11. Andrew Sung Park, *The Wounded Heart of God* (Nashville: Abingdon, 1993) 69.

12. Park, "The Bible and Han," in this book.

13. Kang Nam-Soon, "Han," in *Dictionary of Feminist Theologies* (Louisville: Westminster John Knox, 1996) 134–135.

14. Park, *Wounded Heart of God*, 137–176.

15. Robert Jewett, *Saint Paul Returns to the Movies* (Grand Rapids, Mich.: Eerdmans, 1999) 43.

16. Ibid., 43–44.

17. Marjorie Procter-Smith, "The Whole Loaf: Holy Communion and Survival," in *Violence Against Women and Children*, ed. by Carol J. Adams and Marie M. Fortune (New York: Continuum, 1995) 477.

18. J. Frank Henderson, *Liturgies of Lament* (Chicago: Liturgy Training Publications, 1994) 54–56.

19. Ibid., 13–21.

20. Mari West Zimmerman, *Take and Make Holy: Honoring the Sacred in the Healing Journey of Abuse Survivors* (Chicago: Liturgy Training Publications, 1995).

21. Ibid., 48–72.

22. Ibid., 108–120.

23. Rosemary Radford Ruether, *Women-Church: Theology and Practice* (San Francisco: Harper and Row 1985) 153–158.

24. Miriam Therese Winter, *Woman Prayer, Woman Song* (Oak Park, Ill.: Meyer-Stone Books, 1987) 91–98.

25. Ibid., 229.

26. Ruether, *Women-Church*, 267–273.

27. Kittredge Cherry and Zalmon Sherwood, eds. *Equal Rites: Lesbian and Gay Worship, Ceremonies, and Celebrations* (Louisville: Westminster John Knox, 1995) 140–144.

28. Ibid., 140.

29. Martha Scott, conversation with the author, 4 September 1996.

30. Refer to Barbara Newman, *Sister of Wisdom: St. Hildegard's Theology of the Feminine* (Berkeley/Los Angeles: University of California Press, 1987) 142–148.

31. Walter H. Cuenin, "History of Anointing and Healing in the Church," in *Alternative Futures for Worship: Anointing of the Sick*, ed. by Peter E. Fink, S.J. (Collegeville, Minn.: Liturgical Press, 1987) 69–70.

32. James F. White, *Introduction to Christian Worship* (Nashville: Abingdon, 1990) 263.

33. Cuenin, "History of Anointing and Healing in the Church," 70.

34. White, *Introduction to Christian Worship*, 264.

35. Ibid., 264.

36. Agnes Sanford, *The Healing Light* (New York: Ballantine Books, 1983).

37. "Ministration to the Sick," in *The Book of Common Prayer* (New York: Church Hymnal Corporation, 1979) 453–461.

38. Timothy Crouch, lecture in a class on Healing and Reconciliation, Garrett-Evangelical Theological Seminary, 23 April 1996; *Book of Worship: United Church of Christ* (New York: Office for Church Life and Leadership, 1986) 306–320; and *The United Methodist Book of Worship* (Nashville: United Methodist Publishing House, 1992) 613–629.

39. Participants in the continuing education event at St. Stephen's College in Calgary, Alberta, in May 1996, J. Frank Henderson, Don Saliers, and I provided many of these suggestions in regard to considering the needs of abuse victims and others in healing services.

40. Reading a draft of Susan L. Nelson's chapter in this book, and discussing it with Lallene Rector, my colleague in Religion and Psychology, made me realize how important it is for theologians and liturgists to be in dialogue with their colleagues who study depth human psychology. For example, theories and clinical data about the sources of how human behavior develops and changes should be considered in developing a doctrine of sin or a methodology of healing ministry.

41. Refer to Duck, "Sin, Grace, and Gender in Free-Church Protestant Worship," for further exploration of this concern.

42. Marie M. Fortune, "Forgiveness: The Last Step," in *Violence Against Women and Children*, ed. by Adams and Fortune, 205.

43. Ibid., 206; Peter E. Fink, "History of the Sacrament," in *Alternative Futures for Worship: Reconciliation*, Vol. 4 (Collegeville, Minn.: Liturgical Press, 1987) 81–82.

44. Procter-Smith, "Whole Loaf," 474 f.

44. I was introduced to the idea of worship as rehearsal by the book *Worship: A Searching Examination of the Liturgical Experience* by John E. Burkhart (Philadelphia: Westminster Press, 1982), refer to pp. 31–32 for further explanation of this term, and pp. 92–93 for an important discussion of Eucharist as rehearsal.

46. Fortune, "Forgiveness," 202–203.

47. Christine Smith, *Preaching as Weeping, Confession, and Resistance: Radical Responses to Radical Evil* (Louisville: Westminster John Knox Press, 1992) title and pp. 1–14.

BIBLIOGRAPHY

Ahn, Byung-mu. "Jesus and the Minjung." In *Minjung Theology: People as the Subjects of History*. Edited by CTC-CCC. Maryknoll: Orbis, 1981.

Alvez, Rubem. *Tomorrow's Child*. New York: Harper and Row, 1972.

Augustine. *City of God*. An abridged version. Translated by Gerald G. Walsh et al. New York: Doubleday, 1958.

Babcock, Marguerite and Christine McKay. *Challenging Codependency: Feminist Critiques*. Toronto: University of Toronto Press, 1995.

Barbe, Dominique. *Grace and Power: Base Communities and Nonviolence in Brazil*. Translated by J. P. Brown. Maryknoll: Orbis, 1987.

Barth, Karl. "God and Nothingness." In *Church Dogmatics III*. Edinburgh, Scotland: T. and T. Clark, 1960.

Batstone, David. "What's Your Price: Ten Principles for Saving a Corporate Soul." In *Sojourners*. January–February 2000.

Beauvoir, Simone de. *The Second Sex*. Translated by H. M. Parshley. London: Jonathan Cape, 1953; New York: Alfred A. Knopf, 1953.

Bello, Walden. "Global Economic Counterrevolution: In the North-South Confrontation, Its Apocalypse or Solidarity." In *Christianity and Crisis*. 17 February 1992.

Benjamin, Jessica. *The Bonds of Love*. New York: Pantheon, 1988.

Berry, Wendell. "The Futility of Global Thinking." In *Harper's*. September 1989.

Boal, Augusto. *Games for Actors and Non-Actors*. Translated by A. Jackson. New York: Routledge, 1992.

Bohlin, Torgny. *Die Theologie des Pelagius und ihre Genesis*. Uppsala, Sweden: Lundequist, 1957.

Bradshaw, John. *Healing the Shame that Binds You*. Deerfield Beach, Fla.: Health Communications, 1988.

Brandt, Barbara. *Whole Life Economics: Revaluing Daily Life*. Philadelphia: New Society Publishers, 1995.

181

Brecher Jeremy and Tim Costello. *Global Village or Global Pillage: Economic Reconstruction from the Bottom Up.* Boston: South End Press, 1994.

Breton, Denise and Christopher Largent. *The Paradigm Conspiracy.* Center City, Minn.: Hazelden, 1996.

Bringle, Mary Louise. *Despair: Sickness or Sin?* Nashville: Abingdon Press, 1990.

Brock, Rita Nakashima. *Journeys by Heart: A Christology of Erotic Power.* New York: Crossroads, 1988.

Brown, Bruce. *Marx, Freud, and the Critique of Everyday Life: Toward a Permanent Cultural Revolution.* New York: Monthly Review Press, 2000.

Brown, Peter. *The Body and Society: Men, Women and Sexual Renunciation in Early Christianity.* New York: Columbia University Press, 1988.

Brown, Robert McAfee. *Kairos: Three Prophetic Challenges to the Church.* Grand Rapids: Eerdmans, 1990.

Brueggemann, Walter. *Old Testament Theology: Essays on Structure, Theme, and Text.* Edited by Patrick D. Miller. Minneapolis: Fortress, 1992.

————. *Interpretation and Obedience: From Faithful Reading to Faithful Living.* Minneapolis: Fortress, 1991.

————. *Finally Comes the Poet: Daring Speech for Proclamation.* Minneapolis: Fortress, 1989.

————. "The Exodus Narrative as Israel's Articulation of Faith Development." In *Hope Within History.* Atlanta: John Knox Press, 1987.

————. "Psalms 9–10: A Counter to Conventional Social Reality." In *The Bible and the Politics of Exegesis.*

Burkhart, John E. *Worship: A Searching Examination of the Liturgical Experience.* Philadelphia: Westminster Press, 1982.

Burton, Laurel Arthur. "Original Sin or Original Shame." In *Quarterly Review.* Winter 1988–1989.

Calvin, Jean. *Corpus Reformatorum.* Edited by Guilielmus Baum, Eduardus Cunitz, and Eduardus Reuss. Brunsvigae: C. A. Schwetschke, 1869.

Calvin, John. *Institutes of the Christian Religion.* Translated by Henry Beveridge. Grand Rapids: Eerdmans, 1957.

Capps, Donald. "The Scourge of Shame and the Silencing of Adeodatus." And "Augustine as Narcissist: Of Grandiosity and Shame." In *The Hunger of the Heart: Reflections on the Confessions of Augustine.* Edited by Capps and James E. Dittes. West Lafayette, Ind.: Society for the Scientific Study of Religion, 1990.

Cherry, Kittredge and Zalmon Sherwood, eds. *Equal Rites: Lesbian and Gay Worship, Ceremonies, and Celebrations.* Louisville: Westminster John Knox, 1995.

Clark, David. *Basic Communities: Towards an Alternative Society.* London: SPCK, 1977.

Clark, Elizabeth. "From Originism to Pelagianism: Elusive Issues in an Ancient Debate." In *Princeton Seminga Bulletin* 12, no. 3, 1991.

Collins, Chuck, Betsy Leondar-Wright, and Holly Sklar. *Shifting Fortunes: The Perils of the Growing American Wealth Gap.* Boston: United for a Fair Economy, 1999.

Cone, James Cone. *A Black Theology of Liberation.* Maryknoll: Orbis, 1990.

Cover, Robin C. "Sin, Sinners. Old Testament." In *The Anchor Bible Dictionary.* Vol. 6, 32. Edited by David Noel Freedman. New York: Doubleday, 1992.

Croft, Stephen. *The Identity of the Individual in the Psalms.* JSOT Supp. 44; Sheffield, England: Sheffield Academic Press, 1987.

Crosman, Robert. *Reading Paradise Lost.* Bloomington: Indiana University Press, 1980.

Cuenin, Walter H. "History of Anointing and Healing in the Church." In *Alternative Futures for Worship: Anointing of the Sick.* Edited by Peter E. Fink, S.J. Collegeville, Minn.: Liturgical Press, 1987.

Day, Dorothy. *By Little and By Little: The Selected Writings of Dorothy Day.* Edited by Robert Ellsberg. New York: Knopf, 1983.

Duck, Ruth. "Sin, Grace, and Gender in Free-Church Protestant Worship." In *Women at Worship.* Edited by Marjorie Procter-Smith and Janet Walton. Louisville: Westminster John Knox, 1993.

Durland, William. *People Pay for Peace: A Military Tax Refusal Guide for Radical Religious Pacifists and People of Conscience.* Colorado Springs: Center Peace Publishers, 1982.

Emeth, Elaine. "Recovery and the Christian: A Bibliographic Essay on Addiction." In *Sojourners.* December 1990.

Engel, Mary Potter. "Evil, Sin, and Violation of the Vulnerable." In *Lift Every Voice: Constructing Christian Theologies from the Underside.* Edited by Susan Books Thistlethwaite and Mary Potter Engel. San Francisco: HarperCollins, 1990.

Farley, Edward. *Good and Evil: Interpreting a Human Condition.* Minneapolis: Fortress, 1990.

Farley, Wendy. *Tragic Vision and Divine Compassion.* Louisville: Westminster John Knox, 1990.

Farmer, Kathleen A. "Psalms." In *The Women's Bible Commentary.* Edited by Carol A. Newsom and Sharon H. Ringe. Louisville: Westminster John Knox, 1992.

Fink, Peter E. "History of the Sacrament." In *Alternative Futures for Worship: Reconciliation.* Vol. 4. Collegeville, Minn.: Liturgical Press, 1987.

Finnerty, Adam Daniel. *No More Plastic Jesus: Global Justice and Christian Lifestyle.* New York: Dutton, 1977.

Foerster, W. "*Epiousios.*" In Kittel, *Theological Dictionary of the New Testament.* Vol. II. Translated and edited by Geoffrey W. Bromiley. Grand Rapids: Eerdmans, 1964.

Fontaine, Carole R. "Ecclesiastes." In *The Women's Bible Commentary.* Edited by Carol A. Newsom and Sharon H. Ringe. Louisville: Westmister John Knox, 1992.

Fortune, Marie M. *Love Does No Harm: Sexual Ethics for the Rest of Us.* New York: Continuum Publishing Co., 1995.

———. *Is Nothing Sacred?* San Francisco: Harper and Row, 1989.

——— and Woolley et al. *Clergy Misconduct.* Seattle: Center for the Prevention of Sexual and Domestic Violence, 1992.

Fossum. Merle A. and Marilyn J. Mason. *Facing Shame: Families in Recovery.* New York: Norton, 1986.

Fox, Michael V. *Qohelet and His Contradictions*. Sheffield, England: Almond, Sheffield Academic Press, 1989.

Freehof, Solomon B. *Book of Job: A Commentary*. New York: Union of American Hebrew Congregations, 1958.

Freire, Paulo. *Pedagogy of the Oppressed*. Translated by M. Ramos, reprint. New York: Continuum, 1992.

Fretheim, Terence E. "The Plagues as Ecological Signs of Historical Disaster." In *Journal of Biblical Literature*. Vol. 110 (1991) 285–296.

Gerstenberger, Erhard. *Der bittende Mensch: Bittritual und Klagelied des Einzelnen im Alten Testament*. WMANT 51; Neukirchen-Vluyn: Neukirchener Verlag, 1980.

———. *Wesen und Herkunft des 'apodiktischen Rechts'*. WMANT 20; Neukirchen-Vluyn: Neukirchener Verlag, 1965.

Gibbons, Kaye. *Sights Unseen*. New York: Putnam, 1995.

González, L. Justo. *Mañana: Christian Theology from a Hispanic Perspective*. Nashville: Abingdon, 1990.

———. *Christian Thought Revisited: Three Types of Theology*. Nashville: Abingdon, 1989.

Good, Edwin M. *In Turns of Tempest: A Reading of Job*. Stanford: Stanford University Press, 1990.

Gutiérrez, Gustavo. *On Job: God-Talk and the Suffering of the Innocent*. Translated by Matthew J. O'Connell. Maryknoll: Orbis, 1987.

———. *A Theology of Liberation: History, Politics, and Salvation*. Translated by Sister Caridad Inda and John Eagleson. Maryknoll: Orbis, 1973.

Habel, Norman C. *The Book of Job: A Commentary*. Philadelphia: Westminster, 1985.

Hall, Douglas John. "The Political Consequences of Misconceiving Sin." In *The Witness*. March 1995.

Harding, Sandra. *The Science Question in Feminism*. Ithaca, N.Y.: Cornell University, 1986.

Harris, Marvin. *America Now: The Anthropology of a Changing Culture*. New York: Simon and Schuster, 1981.

Harrison, Beverly. "The Power of Anger in the Work of Love." In *Making the Connections*. Edited by Carol S. Robb. Boston: Beacon, 1985.

Hegel, Georg Wilhelm Friedrich. *Lectures on the Philosophy of Religion: Together With a Work on the Proofs of the Existence of God*. Translated by E. B. Speirs and J. Burdon Sanderson, and edited by E. B. Speirs. London: Routledge and K. Paul, 1895.

Henderson, J. Frank. *Liturgies of Lament*. Chicago: Liturgy Training Publications, 1994.

Herman, Judith. *Trauma and Recovery*. New York: Basic Books–Harper Collins.

Hinkelammert, Franz J. *Sacrificios humanos y sociedad occidental: Lucifer y la bestia*. San José, Costa Rica: DEI, 1991.

Hunter, J. "Subjectivization and the New Evangelical Theodicy." In *Journal for the Scientific Study of Religion*. Vol. 21, no. 2.

Jaimes, M. Annette. *The State of Native America: Genocide, Colonization and Resistance*. Boston: South End Press, 1992.

Jameson, Frederic. *Postmodernism, or the Cultural Logic of Late Capitalism*. Durham, N.C.: Duke University Press, 1991.

Janzen, J. Gerald. *Job: Interpretation*. Atlanta: John Knox, 1985.

Jennings, Theodore W. Jr. "Making Sense of God." In *Companion Encyclopedia of Theology*. New York: Routledge, 1996.

———. "Theological Anthropology." In *Theology and the Human Spirit*. Chicago: Exploration Press, 1994.

———. *The Liturgy of Liberation: The Confession and Forgiveness of Sin*. Nashville: Abingdon, 1988.

———. *Beyond Theism: A Grammar of God-Talk*. New York: Oxford, 1985.

———. "Theology as the Construction of Doctrine." In *The Vocation of the Theologian*. Philadelphia: Fortress, 1985.

Jeremias, Joachim. *New Testament Theology*. New York: Scribner, 1971.

———. *Jerusalem at Jesus Time*. Philadelphia: Fortress, 1969.

———. *The Lord's Prayer*. Translated by John Reumann. Philadelphia: Fortress, 1964.

Jewett, Robert. *Saint Paul Returns to the Movies*. Grand Rapids, Mich.: Eerdmans, 1999.

Kaminer, Wendy. *I'm Dysfunctional, You're Dysfunctional: The Recovery Movement and Other Self-Help Fashions*. New York: Addison-Wesley, 1992.

Kant, Immanuel. *Religion within the Limits of Reason Alone*. Translated by Theodore M. Greene and Hoyt H. Hudson. New York: Harper and Row, 1960.

Kasl, Charlotte Davis. *Women, Sex and Addiction: A Search for Love and Power*. San Francisco: Harper and Row, 1990.

Kaufman, Gershen. *Shame: The Power of Caring*. Rochester, Vt.: Schenkman Books, 1992.

Kavanaugh, John. *Following Christ in a Consumer Society: The Spirituality of Cultural Resistance*. 2d ed. Maryknoll: Orbis, 1992.

Keene, Frederick. "Structures of Forgiveness in the New Testament." In *Violence Against Women and Children: A Theological Sourcebook in the Christian Tradition*. Edited by Carol Adams and Marie Fortune. New York: Continuum Publishing Co., 1995.

Kierkegaard, Søren. *The Concept of Anxiety*. Translated by R. Thome and A. B. Anderson. Princeton: Princeton University Press, 1980.

———. *The Sickness Unto Death*. Translated by Walter Lowrie. Princeton: Princeton University Press, 1951.

Kilbourne, Jane. *Deadly Persuasion: Why Women and Girls Must Fight the Addictive Power of Advertising*. New York: Free Press, 1999.

King, Paul, Kent Maynard, and David Woodyard. *Risking Liberation: Middle Class Powerlessness and Social Heroism*. Philadelphia: John Knox Press, 1988.

Koch, Klaus. "Is There a Doctrine of Retribution in the Old Testament?" In *Theodicy in the Old Testament*. Edited by James L. Crenshaw. Philadelphia: Fortress, 1983.

Kraus, Hans-Joachim. *Die prophetische Verkündigung des Rechts in Israel*. TS 51; Zollikon: Evangelischer Verlag, 1957.

Kung, Hans and Karl-Josef Kuschel. *A Global Ethic: The Declaration of the Parliament of World Religions.* London: SCM, 1993.

Kurtz, Ernest. *A. A.: The Story.* San Francisco: Harper and Row, 1988.

Laechli, S. *Power and Sexuality: The Emergence of Canon Law at the Synod of Elvira.* Philadelphia: Temple University Press, 1972.

Lasch, Christopher. *The Minimal Self: Psychic Survival in Troubled Times.* New York: Norton, 1984.

Lasn, Kalle. *Culture Jam: The Uncooling of America.* New York: Eagle Brook, 1999.

Lee, Sun-ai and Don Luce, eds. *The Wish: Poems of Contemporary Korea.* Translated by Sun-ai Lee. New York: Friendship Press, 1983.

Lerner, Michael. *Surplus Powerlessness: The Psychodynamics of Everyday Life . . . and the Psychology of Individual and Social Transformation.* Atlantic Highlands, N.J.: Humanities Press International, 1991.

Levenson, Jon D. *Creation and the Persistence of Evil.* San Francisco: Harper and Row, 1988.

Levinas, Emmanuel. *Difficult Freedom: Essays on Judaism.* Baltimore: Johns Hopkins University Press, 1990.

Lindström, Fredrik. *Suffering and Sin: Interpretation of Illness in the Individual Complaint Psalms.* Coniectanea Biblica Old Testament 37; Stockholm: Almquist and Wiksell, 1994.

————. *God and the Origin of Evil: A Contextual Analysis of Alleged Monistic Evidence in the Old Testament.* Coniectanea Biblica 21. Lund, Sweden: Gleerup, 1983.

Marcuse, Herbert. *An Essay on Liberation.* Boston: Beacon, 1969.

————. *One Dimensional Man: Studies in the Ideology of Advanced Industrial Society.* Boston: Beacon, 1964.

Marx, Karl. *Marx's Economic and Philosophical Manuscripts.* Translated by T. B. Bottomore. In Marx's *Concept of Man*, by Erik Fromm. New York: Ungar, 1961.

May, Gerald. *Addiction and Grace.* San Francisco: Harper and Row, 1998.

May, Rollo. "The Significance of Symbols." In *Symbolism in Religion and Literature.* Edited by May. New York: Braziller, 1960.

McCormick, Patrick. *Sin as Addiction.* New York: Paulist Press, 1989.

McGuire, Ellen. "A Place Called Hope." In *The Nation,* 28 December 1992.

Meadows, Donella, Dennis Meadows, and Jorgen Randers. *Beyond the Limits.* Post Hills, Vt.: Chelsea Green, 1992.

Menninger, Karl. *What Ever Became of Sin?* New York: Hawthorn Books, 1973.

Miles, Jack. *God: A Biography.* New York: Knopf, 1995.

Miller, G. Tyler. *Living in the Environment: Principles, Connections, and Solutions,* 8th ed. Belmont, Calif.: Wadsworth Publishing Co., 1994.

Miranda, Jose Porfirio. *Marx and the Bible.* Maryknoll: Orbis, 1974.

Moore, Mary Elizabeth Mullino. "Teaching for Justice and Reconciliation in a Conflicted World." In *Globalisation and Difference: Practical Theology in a World Context.* Edited by Paul Ballard and Pam Couture. Cardiff, Wales: Cardiff Academic Press, 1999.

————. "Wisdom, Sophia, and the Fear of Knowing." In *Religious Education.* vol. 92, no. 2 (Spring 1997).

Muilenburg, James. "The Office of the Prophet in Ancient Israel." In *The Bible in Modern Scholarship.* Edited by J. Philip Hyatt. Nashville: Abingdon Press, 1965.

Muller, Wayne. *Sabbath, Restoring the Sacred Rhythm of Rest.* New York: Bantam Books, 1999.

Murphy, Roland E. *The Anchor Bible Reference Library: The Tree of Life—An Exploration of Biblical Wisdom Literature.* New York: Doubleday, 1990.

Myers, Ched. *Who Will Roll Away the Stone? Discipleship Queries for the First World Christians.* Maryknoll: Orbis, 1994.

————. "God Speed the Year of Jubilee: The Biblical Vision of Sabbath Economics." In *Sojourners.* May–June 1990.

Neal, Mary A. *A Socio-theology of Letting Go: The Role of a First World Church Facing Third World Peoples.* New York: Paulist Press, 1977.

Nelson, Susan. *Beyond Servanthood.* Lanham, Md.: University Press of America, 1985.

Nelson, Susan L. (Dunfee). *Healing the Broken Heart: A Conversation about Sin, Healing, and the Broken Heart.* St. Louis: Chalice, 1998.

————. "The Sin of Hiding: A Feminist Critique of Reinhold Niebuhr's Sin of Pride." In *Soundings.* Fall 1982.

Newman, Barbara. *Sister of Wisdom: St. Hildegard's Theology of the Feminine.* Berkeley/Los Angeles: University of California Press, 1987.

Orgel, Stephen and Jonathan Goldberg, eds. *John Milton.* New York: Oxford University Press, 1991.

Pagel, Elaine. *Adam, Eve, and the Serpent.* New York: Random House, 1988.

Park, Andrew Sung. *The Wounded Heart of God: The Asian Concept of Han and the Christian Concept of Sin.* Nashville: Abingdon Press, 1993.

Pedersen, Johannes. *Israel: Its Life and Culture III–IV.* Copenhagen: Branner, 1940.

Perdue, Leo G. and John G. Gammie, eds. *The Sage in Israel and the Ancient Near East.* Winona Lake, Ind.: Eisenbrauns, 1990.

Peters, Ted. *Sin: Radical Evil in Soul and Society.* Grand Rapids: Eerdmans, 1994.

Piercy, Marge. *Circles on the Water: Selected Poems of Marge Piercy.* New York: Knopf, 1982.

Pixley, George V. "Micah—A Revolutionary." In *The Bible and the Politics of Exegesis: Essays in Honor of Norman K. Gottwald on His Sixty-Fifth Birthday.* Edited by David Jobling et al. Cleveland: Pilgrim Press, 1991.

Plantinga, Cornelius Jr. *Not the Way It's Supposed to Be: A Breviary of Sin.* Grand Rapids: Eerdmans, 1995.

————. "Locked in Sin: The Theology of Corruption." In *Christian Century.* 21–28 December 1994.

Plaskow, Judith. *Sex, Sin and Grace: Women's Experience and the Theologies of Reinhold Niebuhr and Paul Tillich.* Washington, D.C.: University Press of America, 1980.

Procter-Smith, Marjorie. "The Whole Loaf: Holy Communion and Survival." In *Violence Against Women and Children.* Edited by Carol J. Adams and Marie M. Fortune. New York: Continuum, 1995.

Rausch, Thomas. *Radical Christian Communities.* Collegeville, Minn.: Liturgical Press, 1990.

Rauschenbusch, Walter. *Christianizing the Social Order.* New York: Macmillan, 1916.

————. *Theology for Social Gospel.* Nashville: Abingdon Press, 1945.

Reyburn, William D. *A Handbook on the Book of Job.* New York: United Bible Societies, 1992.

Ricoeur, Paul. *The Symbolism of Evil.* Boston: Beacon, 1967.

————. *The Conflict of Interpretations: Essays in Hermeneutics.* Edited by Don Ihde. Evanston: Northwestern University Press, 1974.

————. *Fallible Man.* Translated by Charles A. Kelbley. New York: Fordham University Press, 1986.

Rousselle, Aline. *Porneia: On Desire and the Body in Antiquity.* New York: Basil Blackwell, 1988.

Rubenstein, Richard. *The Cunning of History.* New York: Harper Colophon Books, 1978.

Ruether, Rosemary Radford. *Women-Church: Theology and Practice.* San Francisco: Harper and Row, 1985.

Russell, James C. *The Germanization of Early Medieval Christianity: A Sociohistorical Approach to Religious Transformation.* New York: Oxford University Press, 1994.

Saiving, Valerie. "The Human Situation: A Feminine View." In *Womanspirit Rising.* Edited by Carol P. Christ and Judith Plaskow. San Francisco: Harper and Row, 1979.

Sanders, E. P. "Sin, Sinners. New Testament." In *The Anchor Bible Dictionary.* Vol. 6, 41. Edited by David Noel Freedman. New York: Doubleday, 1992.

Sands, Kathleen M. *Escape from Paradise.* Minneapolis: Fortress, 1994.

Sanford, Agnes. *The Healing Light.* New York: Ballantine Books, 1983.

Schaef, Anne Wilson. *When Society Becomes an Addict.* San Francisco: Harper and Row, 1987.

———— and Diane Fassel. *The Addictive Organization.* San Francisco: Harper and Row, 1988.

Schleiermacher, Friedrich *Christian Faith.* Edited by H. R. Mackintosh and J. S. Stewart. 2 vols. New York: Harper and Row, 1963.

Schmid, Hans Heinrich. *Gerechtigkeit als Weltordnung: Hintergrund und Geschichte des Alttes-tamentlichen Gerechtigkeitsbegriffes* (Beiträge zur Historischen Theologie 40; Tübingen, Germany: J.C.B. Mohr (Paul Siebeck), 1968).

Schweizer, Eduard. *The Good News According to Matthew.* Translated by David Green. Atlanta: John Knox Press, 1975.

Scott, R. B. Y. *The Anchor Bible: Proverbs and Ecclesiastes.* Garden City, N.Y.: Doubleday, 1965.

Sewell, Arthur. *A Study of Milton's Christian Doctrine.* London: Oxford University Press, 1939.

Simundson, Daniel J. *The Message of Job: A Theological Commentary.* Minneapolis: Augsburg, 1986.

Slater, Philip. *Wealth Addiction.* New York: Dutton, 1983.

Smith, Christine. *Preaching as Weeping, Confession, and Resistance: Radical Responses to Radical Evil.* Louisville: Westminster John Knox Press, 1992.

Steinbeck, John. *Five Novels.* New York: Octopus Books, 1988.

Stendahl, Krister. "Paul and the Introspective Conscience of the West." In *Paul Among Christians and Jews and Other Essays.* Philadelphia: Fortress Press, 1977.

Suchocki, Marjorie Hewitt. *The Fall to Violence.* New York: Continuum, 1994.

Tamez, Elsa. *The Amnesty of Grace.* Nashville: Abingdon 1993.

Thomas, Aquinas. *The Summa Theologica.* Translated by Fathers of the English Dominican Province. 3 vols. New York, Benziger, 1947–1948.

Thurman, Howard. *With Head and Heart: The Autobiography of Howard Thurman.* New York: Harcourt, 1979.

Tillich, Paul. *A History of Christian Thought.* Edited by Carl Braaten. New York: Simon and Schuster, 1967.

Trible, Phyllis. *Rhetorical Criticism: Context, Method, and the Book of Jonah.* Minneapolis: Fortress, 1994.

———. *Texts of Terror: Literary-Feminist Reading of Biblical Narratives.* Philadelphia: Fortress Press, 1984.

Wachtel, Paul. *The Poverty of Affluence: A Psychological Portrait of the American Way of Life.* Philadelphia: New Society Publishers, 1989.

Westermann, Claus. "Struktur und Geschichte der Klage im Alten Testament." *Forschung am alten Testament.* ThB 24; München, Germany: Chr. Kaiser Verlag, 1964.

White, James F. *Introduction to Christian Worship.* Nashville: Abingdon, 1990.

Whybray, R. N. *The New Century Bible Commentary: Ecclesiastes.* Grand Rapids: Eerdmans, 1989.

Wiesel, Elie. *Messengers of God.* Translated by Marion Wiesel. New York: Random, 1976.

Williams, P. L. *The Moral Theology of Abelard.* Lanham, Md.: University Press of America, 1980.

Williams, William Appleman. *Empire as a Way of Life.* New York: Oxford University Press, 1980.

Wilson, Robert R. *Prophecy and Society in Ancient Israel.* Philadelphia: Fortress Press, 1980.

Winter, Miriam Therese. *Woman Prayer, Woman Song.* Oak Park, Ill.: Meyer-Stone Books, 1987.

Wolff, Hans Walter. "Micah the Moreshite—The Prophet and His Background." In *Israelite Wisdom: Theological and Literary Essays in Honor of Samuel Terrien.* Edited by John G. Gammie et al. Missoula: Scholars Press, 1978

Wurmser, L. *The Masks of Shame.* Baltimore: Johns Hopkins University Press, 1981.

Zimmerli, Walther. "The Place and Limit of Wisdom in the Framework of the Old Testament Theology." In *Scottish Journal of Theology.* vol. 17 (1964).

Zimmerman, Mari West. *Take and Make Holy: Honoring the Sacred in the Healing Journey of Abuse Survivors.* Chicago: Liturgy Training Publications, 1995.

CONTRIBUTORS

WALTER BRUEGGEMANN is William Marcellus McPheeters Professor of Old Testament at Columbia Theological Seminary. He is interested in interpretive issues that lie behind efforts at Old Testament theology. This includes the relation of the Old Testament to the Christian canon, the Christian history of doctrine, Jewish-Christian interactions, and the cultural reality of pluralism. He has published numerous books and articles. Some of his most recent books are: *Theology of the Old Testament: Testimony, Dispute, Advocacy, Cadences of Home: Preaching among Exiles, Isaiah 1–39*, and *Isaiah 40–66*.

RUTH C. DUCK is Associate Professor of Worship at Garrett-Evangelical Theological Seminary in Evanston, Illinois. She is coauthor of *Praising God: The Trinity in Christian Worship* and author of *Finding Words for Worship*, as well as many hymn texts and worship resources. She is a member of Church of the Three Crosses (UCC/United Methodist) in Chicago.

MARIE M. FORTUNE is the Founder and Senior Analyst at the Center for Prevention of Sexual and Domestic Violence in Seattle, Washington. She is a pastor, author, educator, and practicing ethicist and theologian. Ordained in 1976 in the United Church of Christ, she has written numerous books including *Sexual Violence: The Unmentionable Sin, Keeping the Faith: Guidance for Christian Women Facing Abuse*, and *Is Nothing Sacred? A Christian Theological Sourcebook* with Carol Adams. She is editor of *The Journal of Religion and Abuse* and serves on the National Advisory Council on Violence Against Women for the U.S. Department of Justice.

JUSTO L. GONZÁLEZ is the Director of the Hispanic Summer Program. He has taught at several seminaries, including Evangelical Seminary in Puerto Rico and the Candler School of Theology of Emory University. A native Cuban, he is an ordained United Methodist minister and has published a number of books and articles both in Spanish and English. His recent publications include *Alaba-*

191

dle!: Hispanic Christian Worship, Christian Thought Revisited: Three Types of Theology, and *For the Healing of the Nations: The Book of Revelation in an Age of Cultural Conflict.*

THEODORE W. JENNINGS JR. is Professor of Biblical and Constructive Theology at the Chicago Theological Seminary. He has also taught at the Candler School of Theology at Emory University and at the Seminario Metodista de Mexico. He has lectured widely in the United States and England as well as in Asia, Africa, and Latin America. He has served as consultant to the United Methodist bishops for the Episcopal Initiative on Children and the Poor. He is the author of nine books including *The Liturgy of Liberation: The Confession and Forgiveness of Sins, Good News to the Poor: John Wesley's Evangelical Economics,* and *Loyalty to God: The Apostles Creed in Life and Liturgy.*

MARY ELIZABETH MULLINO MOORE is Director of the Program for Women in Theology and Ministry, and Professor of Religion and Education at Candler School of Theology, Emory University. She is the author of *Teaching from the Heart: Theology and Educational Method, Ministering with the Earth,* and other books and articles focused on theology, education and repair of the world.

CHED MYERS is a writer, teacher, and activist living in Los Angeles. He holds a degree in New Testament from the Graduate Theological Union, and is the author of several books, most recently *"Say to This Mountain": Mark's Story of Discipleship.* He writes regularly for *Sojourners, The Other Side,* and *The Witness* magazines, and travels nationally and internationally working with faith-based social justice groups.

SUSAN L. NELSON is Professor of Theology at Pittsburgh Theological Seminary. She is the author of *Healing the Broken Heart: Sin, Alienation and the Gift of Grace* and *Beyond Servanthood: Christianity and the Liberation of Women* and numerous articles on sin and its other side.

ANDREW SUNG PARK is Professor of Theology at United Theological Seminary, Dayton, Ohio. He is an ordained minister in the United Methodist Church and taught at Claremont School of Theology, California. His publications include *The Wounded Heart of God: The Asian Concept of Han and the Christian Concept of Sin* and *Racial Conflict and Healing: An Asian-American Theological Perspective.*

INDEX